THE
LAST STAND
OF
PAYNE STEWART

THE LAST STAND OF PAYNE STEWART

THE YEAR GOLF CHANGED FOREVER

KEVIN ROBBINS

New York Boston

Hachette Books
Hachette Book Group
1290 Avenue of the Americas
New York, NY 10104
hachettebookgroup.com
twitter.com/hachettebooks

First Edition: October 2019

Hachette Books is a division of Hachette Book Group, Inc.
The Hachette Books name and logo are trademarks of Hachette Book Group, Inc.

The publisher is not responsible for websites (or their content) that are not owned by the publisher.

The Hachette Speakers Bureau provides a wide range of authors for speaking events. To find out more, go to www.hachettespeakersbureau.com or call (866) 376-6591.

Print book interior design by Six Red Marbles, Inc.

Photo credits: p. xi: Photo courtesy of the *American News*. p. 1: AP Photo/Kevork Djansezian. p. 43: John M. Burgess/*Sports Illustrated*/Getty Images. p. 101: Tom Able-Green/Allsport/Getty Images. p. 153: Craig Jones/Allsport/Getty Images. p. 207: Craig Jones/Getty Images Sport. p. 253: Tony Bullard/AFP/Getty Images. p. 255: Darren Carroll/*Sports Illustrated*/Getty Images. p. 264: ©Kevin Robbins.

Library of Congress Control Number: 2019946921

ISBNs: 978-0-316-48530-2 (hardcover), 978-0-316-48529-6 (ebook)

Printed in the United States of America

LSC-C

10 9 8 7 6 5 4 3 2 1

For Henry and Lila

and in the memory of Mary Frances Robbins

CONTENTS

All I kept thinking about, over and over, was "You can't live forever, you can't live forever."

—F. Scott Fitzgerald, *The Great Gatsby*

Now the wren has gone to roost and the sky is turnin' gold
Like the sky my soul is also turnin'
Turnin' from the past, at last and all I've left behind
Could it be that I am finally learnin'?

—Ray LaMontagne, "Old Before Your Time"

If life gives you limes, make margaritas.

—Jimmy Buffett

PROLOGUE

Mina, South Dakota, October 25, 1999

The ghost flight lost its right engine first and banked gently to the east as if preparing an approach to land. The left turbofan quit next. The slender nose of N47BA, a white Learjet 35 trimmed in gold and gray that carried six people and a thirty-pound golf bag, pitched in the direction of the South Dakota prairie more than eight statute miles below and began to fall, half a continent from where it was supposed to be, at 12:11 p.m. central standard time on October 25, 1999.

For the two pilots and their four passengers, the morning began with a smooth morning ascent over central Florida into faint winds and forever visibility. The airplane reached twenty-three thousand feet. An air traffic controller in Jacksonville instructed the crew to climb to thirty-nine thousand, swing west, level its wings, and cruise to Dallas Love Field, where it was supposed to unite the reigning U.S. Open champion with an old friend from college, and then deliver him later to the last golf tournament of a resplendent season. But no one replied to that last command, and the aircraft made no change in heading. It just kept rising and rising.

Sometime after 8:27 a.m., when the controller last spoke with the pilots of N47BA, the cabin lost pressure, starving everyone aboard of oxygen until they lost consciousness, as if they slept to their eventual death. The military sent fighter pilots to examine the aimless Learjet. The aviators reported frost inside the cockpit windows and no response to their radio calls. Television networks broke from programming with scant details about a rogue business jet flying up the middle of America with a famous golfer inside. A question arose: Where and when would this Learjet come down? Shortly after noon, a group of pheasant hunters crunched through dormant cornstalks near Aberdeen and noticed a streak that looked like lightning.

The question now had its answer.

Here. Now.

N47BA was airborne for three hours and fifty-four minutes, most of that time on autopilot, to a score of bells, alarms, chimes, and claxons that no one heard. It covered fifteen hundred miles over eight states. US Air Force and Air National Guard pilots from three different installations intercepted the Learjet on its northwesterly journey as aviation experts calculated end-of-flight scenarios that took into account airspeed, fuel capacity and consumption, weight, heading, thrust, the direction and velocity of the wind, and vulnerable populations below.

The Learjet touched an astounding altitude of forty-eight thousand feet, the ceiling for an aircraft on the ragged edge of an aerodynamic stall, and there it bobbed like a porpoise at 540 miles an hour. In the thin air of the upper stratosphere, the temperature hovers at sixty-nine degrees below zero, with little turbulence, meaning the aircraft cruised surely and steadily, locked under its own command, until the two Honeywell TFE371s on the aft fuselage exhausted the fuel tanks on the tip of each wing. As N47BA gathered speed and neared the earth, an effect called *Mach tuck* pulled the nose of the Learjet farther and farther down, until the aircraft was nearly vertical.

It was a quiet scenario that, from the time the engines wound down to impact with the ground, took less than a minute to complete. The episode that killed Payne Stewart, who had reached a personal and professional apogee in 1999, commenced with no violence until, as the world watched and waited to see how it all would end, his aircraft, twirling downward like the stripe on a candy cane, met the prairie at nearly the speed of sound.

For decades, professional golfers have flown thousands of miles to compete. Air travel allows them to spend more time at home, more time practicing before tournaments, more time at lucrative appearances between official starts, and less time in a car subject to speed limits and traffic. Tragedies are rare. Until Stewart boarded N47BA, no high-profile golfer had died aboard an aircraft since 1966, when a Beechcraft Bonanza carrying the effervescent Tony Lema crashed the day after the PGA Championship at Firestone Country Club in Akron, Ohio. Like Stewart, the charismatic Lema, who was thirty-two when he died, lived and played boldly and vividly, so much so that when he won the 1962 Orange County Open, he treated the entire press tent to champagne. Lema enjoyed his best season in 1964, when he won five titles, including a five-stroke victory over Jack Nicklaus in the Open Championship— known more commonly in the United States as the British Open—at St Andrews in Scotland. Lema and his young wife, Betty, were traveling to a two-day exhibition in Illinois when their charter encountered engine trouble, clipped the ground near the border with Indiana, and exploded in a golf course lake. Lema often credited Betty for the happiness in his life. She was a flight attendant. They met on an airplane.

Payne Stewart left his home in Orlando early on that October morning in '99 for a quick business trip and his last tournament of his best season in years. He had an appointment in Dallas to discuss the design of a golf course for the teams at Southern Methodist University, his alma mater. He planned to go to Houston next. He was in the Tour Championship with twenty-nine other players at Champions Golf Club. He planned to spend the off-season with his family in Florida.

It had been a redemptive return to prominence for Stewart. He'd earned more than $2 million that season. He'd won his tenth and eleventh PGA Tour tournaments, including his third major championship, in a twenty-year career that included eight other victories worldwide. He'd played on the American team that won the Ryder Cup matches that September against Europe over a regrettably contentious three days in Brookline, Massachusetts. His victory in February at the AT&T Pebble Beach Pro-Am had come four years after his last win, ending a slump that was so frustrating he considered quitting the game.

Stewart had won no tournaments between the summer of 1995 and the winter of 1999. He'd finished second a few times, third a few more. He'd made piles of money, but money no longer motivated Stewart the way it once had. He'd sometimes lost interest in competing. He'd found it hard to believe in himself, and when he should've been working on the putting green or the practice tee, he'd poured himself another drink, lit a cigar or put in a pinch of smokeless tobacco, and sat on the dock behind his mansion on a small chain lake in Orlando, trying to remember what had once made him one of the greatest players in the world, which is what he would become again in magical and magnificent 1999.

His performance that summer at the U.S. Open at Pinehurst, where he endured challenges from a new wave of younger and stronger PGA Tour stars playing equipment that made the game simpler, ranks as one of the epic demonstrations of grit and resolve in the history of American golf. So does, for entirely different reasons, the final day of the Ryder Cup. Stewart and his eleven US teammates were down 10–6 after two days of team matches at The Country Club in Brookline, a suburb of Boston. They built one of the biggest comebacks in sports that Sunday in singles play. It was the last time Stewart would produce that signature swing in front of massive galleries and an international television audience, and he took the final shot of the matches: a splash from a bunker on the eighteenth hole, captured in a photograph that hangs under a light in the august men's locker room at The Country Club. A month after that picture was made, he was on a business jet that leaned east over South Dakota.

Stewart was the brash and unapologetic dandy of his day: a Jay Gatsby among the indistinguishable Tom Buchanans pounding Titleists on practice tees. He wore shortened, bloused pants known as plus fours, patterned shirts bearing National Football League mascots, elegant white golf shoes with gold tips, argyle hosiery, a flat cap, an occasional smirk. He was a colorful and complicated presence on the golf course. He was a peacock, the Missouri showman, someone who wanted to be heard and noticed and remembered and admired. He was loud in a sport that valued silence. He was cocksure in a game that promoted humility and modesty. He was too much for some of his peers who preferred less. He blamed exterior forces for interior faults. He often spoke before he thought. He acted before he thought. Then came the 1998 U.S. Open in San Francisco, where Stewart lost a golf tournament but won respect in ways that foretold the story of the summer of 1999. He was about to turn forty-two, find a new kind of peace, and, as he'd suggested in an interview that year, arrive at the conviction that his best golf, and his best life, was yet to come.

Stewart learned golf from his father in the early 1960s. Bill Stewart was a traveling salesman and the father of two daughters and a son in Springfield, Missouri, at the edge of the Ozarks, about an hour north of the Arkansas state line, down in the hills and the woods. The elder Stewart was a two-time state amateur champion in the '50s and a fixture on the amateur tournament circuit, and he considered a go at professional golf until he and his wife, Bee, determined that he didn't have what it took to play the game at that level. He soon brought his young son to his country club and taught the boy to use his eyes, hands, and feet to feel and execute a good swing.

The Stewarts had excellent golf clubs, but this was long before equipment became such a sophisticated and specialized industry. Their tools were much more demanding than the ones golfers know now. They were made with steel shafts, oiled persimmon-wood heads, forged-steel blade irons, and balls wound with rubber bands inside covers of balata rubber. Tolerances were looser. Shots were less predictable. Drives didn't travel as far. The players hitting them had to do a different kind of work to control them and score well. Their way of moving a golf ball through space required a sense of refinement and finesse, a mastery of hand-eye coordination, and an element of artistry that seems as anachronistic as the slashing swings, hickory-shafted niblicks, and woolen suit jackets of the eight men competing in the first Open Championship in 1860 at Prestwick on the Firth of Clyde.

The year of Stewart's death corresponded with a wave of dramatic change in golf, a confluence of coincidences, a murmuration of starlings that for a second form a perfect funnel. Along with advances in clubs and balls, players at the time could learn more about their swings through emerging technologies that are as commonplace today as a hazard stake. They were learning more about the roles of fitness and diet. They were starting to understand, and harness, the psychological dimension of golf. They were becoming athletes in ways Stewart and players of his era hadn't been.

That new generation, led by an emergent Tiger Woods, was beginning to dictate a way of playing that involved soaring shots with enormous titanium drivers and superior golf balls that cut the wind and carried bunkers or trees protecting the inside corner of a dogleg. These players attacked the ball with faster, harder swings. They fretted less about shots that wandered from the fairway because their strength minimized the penalty of the longer grass in the rough. If they were closer to the green, they could use shorter clubs, like higher-lofted wedges, that were easier to hit higher and more softly. The great Jack Nicklaus and Bobby Jones and Ben Hogan never pictured this kind of golf when they were in their primes. A younger Stewart didn't, either. The developments beginning to take hold in 1999 created the game spectators see now when they watch Dustin Johnson or Brooks Koepka or Rory McIlroy ravage once-sturdy golf courses with modern balls, clubs, bodies, and minds.

The 1999 season was a season of loss for golf. It brought the death of a player and a manner—*his* manner—of playing.

Golf invites such fables. The game welcomes its new legends and celebrates its emergent heroes with stories held on the three legs of perseverance: distress, acceptance, and survival. Jones, the vaunted amateur and founder of Augusta National Golf Club, managed debilitating emotional swings, from anxiety to anger, to capture the four then-major championships of golf in 1930. Hogan, the indefatigable Texan from the dusty caddie yards of Fort Worth, rose almost mythically from a head-on collision with a Greyhound bus in West Texas to win the 1950 U.S. Open, three years before the season when he won every major but the PGA. Nicklaus, still the greatest player the game has known, conquered time itself to win the 1986 Masters at the age of forty-six.

Payne Stewart engaged his own toughest opponent in 1999, a year of reckoning and loss.

He faced the man he had been, who was no match for the man he'd become.

Part One

OLYMPIC

*Eighteenth green, Olympic Club, San Francisco,
California, June 19, 1998*

CHAPTER ONE

No one agrees on the number of hills there are to climb in San Francisco. Everyone acknowledges the famed original seven, among them Russian and Telegraph and Mount Davidson and the Twin Peaks, but there might be as many as forty-two in and around the city. Merced Heights, the hill nearest the Olympic Club in nearby Daly City, rises five hundred feet above sea level on the other side of California Highway 1 from the site of the 1998 U.S. Open, which is where Payne Stewart did plenty of climbing over four days that June. Dimpled with testy pitches and slopes and boomeranged angles, the Lake Course at Olympic made the best players of the year work diligently and patiently at the national championship of golf, particularly at keeping their balls from peeling through fairways and into the rough, dense and long and cruel, like beads of water on wax. Those golfers in 1998 certainly saw more than just forty-two hills, and all of them felt like threats. How many hills are there in San Francisco? It depends on how the climber defines the climb.

Payne finished the first round and signed his scorecard: a 66. He had one more hill to walk that Thursday, but he was happy to do it. An official with the United States Golf Association fetched him for post-round press interviews, in the clubhouse many steps above the eighteenth green, to answer questions about how he'd played such an unforgiving golf course in four strokes under par.

Payne remembered how it felt in 1991, when he'd gotten to explain to reporters how he'd won his first U.S. Open. He remembered the losses, too, but he now embraced this moment at Olympic, which was such a charmed place to him. His father had played the 1955 U.S. Open at Olympic as an amateur. Bill Stewart missed the cut, but knowing he had played these holes gave Payne another reason for gratitude. He bounded up the hill to join the reporters, many of whom he knew by name but hadn't seen in years. While Payne hadn't always been interested in talking to them, and many of his interviews had ended poorly before, this time would be different. He knew what to expect from them, and he knew what to expect of himself.

He appeared.

The crowd in the room watched William Payne Stewart stride to his seat, his six-foot-one-inch frame still lithe but not as limber, and smooth his smudgy blond hair, darker now than it was in his youth, and shorter and thinner, with less of a feather now and no more bangs. When he spoke, people still heard the hills of southern Missouri in his high-pitched voice, the twang of the Ozark Mountains, a relic of what some called, inelegantly and dismissively, a hillbilly or a Missouri mule. Here was a man who once had imagined a Fitzgeraldian life of fame, wealth, and happiness through golf—a temporal existence made possible by the moment of impact of steel on rubber. He always had been a man motivated by moments. Moments lived *in*. Moments lived *for*. He had made his decisions in the ephemeral, and some of those decisions had cost him, and now he no longer wanted to be the same man with the same values who pictured the same future. The Payne Stewart who sat down in San Francisco on June 18, 1998, had suffered. He regretted the decisions that dictated the way people saw him, just as he understood and accepted that they were not altogether wrong to see him in the way they did. It had taken him a long time to see what they had seen. It had taken reflection, and now he felt a new commitment rising in him, a dedication to change while there was still time to make changes. He didn't like who he had been. But he liked who he could become. He could start now, after this round of golf at the Olympic Club. Payne sensed a fresh moment. This one felt permanent. It felt important.

He faced the room.

No one knew what to expect when Payne addressed the professional golf media. After a poorly played round or a lost tournament, he could be abrasive and churlish, even mocking. He privately had felt unfairly criticized over the course of his career for things he said and did. He had long felt like the media made more out of his antics and words than they really deserved, to the point that he flinched when he saw a headline that seemed too harsh or twisted. But this, too, had changed. Payne was beginning to accept the role of the reporters who wrote about him. It wasn't their job to promote him. It was their job to portray him. It stung sometimes to read about himself, to see in black ink his own actions and voice, but when he settled down enough to think clearly, he had to admit that he deserved it sometimes. The press held a mirror, and if that mirror didn't reflect truth and fact as he saw it, Payne acknowledged that it reflected, at the very least, how reporters saw him.

Those at the Olympic Club tried to recall when he had last been interviewed at a U.S. Open—or any major championship. It had been a while. Years. Les Unger, the USGA media official, had managed many press conferences in his career in sports, and he understood the delicate dynamics of an interview with an athlete, so he eased into the exchange by congratulating Payne on his round. He said it was nice to see him again. He noted that Payne hadn't been recently to a U.S. Open press conference.

"You never invited me," Payne said, pretending indignation. "I would've come."

"You have to do something to be invited," Unger said.

Payne smiled. Of all people, he surely knew a well-earned barb when he heard one.

"That's a good shot," he said. "I will take it. I deserve that."

The room brightened. The atmosphere at a U.S. Open, the second major championship on the golf calendar, can tend to feel charged given the difficulty of the conditions: the constricted fairways, the speed of the greens, the expectations both real and imagined, the pressure, the opportunity, the fear, the ghosts. Players could be tense. But the playful start to the interview drained some of the formality of this occasion as Payne, now forty-one years old, described how he made five birdies against one bogey to be sitting in front of the media again after a long time away with a one-shot lead in a major championship.

There was a lot to discuss and dissect that afternoon in Northern California. The meaning of this tournament seemed even larger, and it surpassed the routine concerns of scores, shots, and million-dollar purses. The field included Casey Martin, a twenty-six-year-old Stanford graduate from Oregon who'd successfully sued, under the Americans with Disabilities Act, for the right to use a riding cart on the PGA Tour. Martin suffered from a circulatory ailment in his leg. The condition impaired his ability to walk a golf course, especially hilly Olympic. The federal court decision, announced in February, had divided the tour, a place where social issues rarely occupied time in a press conference. Sides had to be picked: rally behind a man with a disability or forsake him in the name of tradition and competition. Perception mattered. But rules were rules. Arnold Palmer and Jack Nicklaus had testified in favor of the tour, which argued that allowing Martin to ride in a cart would give him an unfair advantage over players who had to endure the stress and strain of walking. There was little room for nuance.

"Are you, in particular, interested in that or over it?" Payne was asked.

"I am a supporter of Casey Martin, and I always have been," Payne said. "Let him play."

A younger Payne might not have been so magnanimous. The Payne of the past could be ugly and shrill, selfishly consumed with personal gain to the point that his peers in the game thought of him as a self-absorbed brat. Now here he was, after a long absence from prominence, saying that golf should change its position on what it was "because the game is bigger than that."

Attention returned to his play in the first round. Payne answered routine questions about putts, pin placements, distractions, focus, expectations, the slope of the greens, and a rather inane attempt to clarify what he thought of his four-under 66 ("It was really good," he said). No one brought up Baltusrol in 1993, when rounds of 70-66-68 had positioned Payne a shot behind the third-round lead. In that U.S. Open, Payne had trailed Lee Janzen, a quiet and assiduous man of twenty-eight, who wore muted tones on the golf course and rarely made the newspaper headlines. He was nearly the opposite of Payne, who was eight years older and full of flourish, but Janzen actually admired Payne. The former all-American at Florida Southern appreciated the fact that Payne also hadn't played for a top-tier college program, and he saw parallels in the way he and Payne had taken long and winding paths to the PGA Tour and to the final round of the 1993 U.S. Open in Springfield Township, New Jersey.

Paired that Sunday in '93 for the first time in a major, Payne and Janzen had nipped at each other throughout the hot and humid day. Neither player made much of a move early. Payne sacrificed a crucial shot on the seventh, when he had to play a left-handed shot from the base of a tree trunk. Janzen, meanwhile, kept making workmanlike pars. Then luck made its cameo. On the tenth hole, Janzen hit a shot right through a tangle of branches to save himself from disaster. He holed an improbable chip from the rough for birdie on the sixteenth. His drive at the next hole, a long par-five, ripped through a maple and bounded into the fairway. Janzen's mistakes cost him nothing, and all Payne could do was watch. His even-par 70, typically a fine score in a U.S. Open, wasn't enough. Janzen clipped him by two. The champion called it destiny. Payne called it another lost tussle with fate.

Janzen was in the field again in 1998 at Olympic, but he shot 73 in the first round, seven distant shots behind Payne. He left that day without a visit with Unger and the gathered press. Payne, meanwhile, fielded questions about the penalizing slopes of the Lake Course, where drives to the middle of the fairway might carom into long grass in low spots. He had prepared for that frustrating possibility. He and his instructor, Chuck Cook, spent a few days the week before at Isleworth, one of Payne's home clubs in Orlando, rehearsing the curving shots dictated by the Lake Course. On holes that moved left to right, Payne drove with his fairway metal, a shorter club he felt most comfortable drawing into the camber of slope, rather than along it. On holes that flowed the opposite direction—draw holes that move right to left—he used a driver. Payne could cut a driver at will. Cook picked up Payne's balls in the fairways of Isleworth and placed them on uneven lies for the approaches. Payne didn't hit a shot from a flat stance the entire time in Florida. He was ready for San Francisco and its hills, those large and small, both metaphorical and actual.

A reporter finally asked Payne to reflect: In what ways was he a better player than he was in 1991?

Payne took a moment to think about the '91 U.S. Open at Hazeltine National near Minneapolis. He was thirty-four then and unstoppable. He was a two-time major winner, a couple of years removed from his PGA Championship title in Chicago, a flaming success from the Ozarks of Missouri. He was the famous celebrity in the knickers and the vintage cap, someone even casual fans of golf could recognize in silhouette. But that moment in Minnesota also represented the beginning of a struggle he now, after the first round at Olympic, had begun to solve. *Was* Payne better? The question seemed innocent enough. But it was more meaningful than anyone knew.

"I'm probably a more mature player," Payne said finally. "I feel that I probably am a more complete player. Things went real good in 1991, so you can't complain about that. But I just think I am, you know, older. And wiser."

In the second round, Payne started with three straight birdies to reach seven under par through twenty-one holes. Stretching his lead to five, he now had made six consecutive birdies: the sixteenth, seventeenth, and eighteenth on Thursday and the first, second, and third on Friday. He tied a U.S. Open record set by George Burns in 1982 and by Andy Dillard a decade later. Payne knew he was on an unsustainable pace. The course was just too severe. In practice rounds earlier in the week, his caddie, Mike Hicks, had repeated over and again that par was a good score at the Lake Course.

"The key to winning a U.S. Open is staying away from the double bogey," Hicks had reminded him. "You're going to get a few birdies. You're bound to make some bogeys. But stay away from losing two at a time."

Payne obeyed. But he encountered complications inevitable in a U.S. Open—losing tee shots to the sharp angles of the fairways, making bogeys instead of pars. The course was toughening, just as the USGA wanted it to. As the anticipation of the weekend grew, spectators began to rally—around their favorite players and against their favorite villains. Colin Montgomerie, the Scotsman with a reputation for being fragile, left a putt a foot short on one hole. "Why don't you cry about it, Colin?" rose a voice. Montgomerie marked his ball and waited dramatically for silence. The USGA later dispatched additional security to his group. Payne, meanwhile, tried to play smart golf with an impenetrable focus. He didn't care how the gallery treated Colin Montgomerie. He was abiding to the plan he'd rehearsed in Orlando.

But he just wasn't quite as sharp as he had been Thursday. Even the tee shots he played with his one-iron—like many players of his aging generation, Payne still carried a one-iron, the hardest club in golf to play with skill—seemed to leave an impossible approach. He came to the eighteenth hole at even par for the round, still in the lead but teetering.

He drilled a two-iron on the short finishing hole to wedge distance. He carved the approach to ten feet. His ball stopped to the right of the hole, which was cut deep in the pitched green and near the left edge. It was the correct, mature play. It eliminated a miss to the left—the dreaded short side, which on increasingly firm U.S. Open greens like Olympic's would mean certain bogey or worse. Payne marked his ball and tried to parse its path to the cup.

He clearly could see the side-hill slant. Hicks recommended he play it gingerly, allowing for a cautious line with more break. He later regretted the advice. Hicks wished he'd told him to hit the putt boldly. Payne applied a gentle stroke to the ball. It missed the hole by three inches and kept going, tumbling for a half minute like a leaf in a breeze, as Payne, indignant and scowling, followed along with his arms crossed. His ball stopped some twenty-five feet downrange. He missed the return putt for par.

Hicks watched him closely. He looked for signs that Payne might be boiling. The Payne he knew—Hicks had carried his bag since 1988, through good seasons and bad ones, through harmony and distress—had a way of personalizing the vagaries of golf. That Payne Stewart could turn a bad break into self-destruction. It was something Payne tried to limit. But it also was who he was. He had a hard time accepting chance in all its forms. His fragile temperament had cost him tournaments before, and it had shaped his legacy, which is what hurt and frustrated Hicks the most. He wanted Payne to rise above his misfortune, not revel in it.

On this Friday, Payne swallowed whatever resentment roiled inside, signed his scorecard, and, because he held a one-shot lead in the championship, reported to his post-round interview with an evenness that both surprised and buoyed his caddie. Unger, the media official, elected to open the interview by mentioning the birdie-birdie-birdie start. "Can't birdie them all unless you birdie the first three," Payne said.

The mood of the room felt like it had the day before: loose, light, jovial. Even when a reporter inevitably brought up the eighteenth hole, Payne avoided criticism that might seem petty and generate the wrong kind of headline. He told a television reporter earlier that the hole position was "bordering on ridiculous." That much was true. Jack Nicklaus had made a forty-foot putt there to make the cut—the last time he would play the weekend in a U.S. Open. But other players suffered as Payne had. Frank Nobilo faced thirty-five feet for birdie on eighteen and, after his putt failed to reach the hole, twenty-five for par. He missed. He called it "the worst pin I've ever seen in a major." Tom Lehman required four putts to finish the hole. He seethed.

"Give me a half hour," he told a reporter after he finished, "or I might kill somebody."

The demonstrative John Daly, whose soaring drives at the 1991 PGA Championship had hinted at the kind of golf that was yet to come, also dropped a shot on the final green. "People watching on TV probably thought we were idiots," he said. "That's not golf, and it's not fair. It was absolutely stupid." The usually agreeable Kirk Triplett, who knew he was going to miss the cut anyway, grimly planted his putter behind his ball, halting its roll and incurring a two-shot penalty from the USGA. He didn't appear to care.

"I suspect he was trying to make a statement," said USGA executive director David Fay.

Fay would later admit the hole placement was a mistake on one of the smallest greens in championship golf. The USGA knew that only the front half of the eighteenth was in manageable shape, he said, but cutting the hole there all four days would've created problems of its own. The number of footprints and spike marks would've maimed the surface by Sunday afternoon, when the drama was at its deepest. Fay and the USGA took a risk. They watered the back of the green and cut it at a higher height. They expected the back-left hole to be hard. It became a monster. Fay called it a "miscalculation."

Payne remained steady in the interview room. He waited for the questions about the eighteenth green to end. When they did, a reporter asked about Janzen, who was on the course, crafting a round of 66, moving into position to play with Payne in the last group on Saturday.

"If I've got to play with somebody, it might as well be somebody I know," Payne said.

Another reporter asked about the mechanics of Payne's swing, which had long been a model of impeccable timing, supple rhythm, and flowing grace. Payne wanted to tell everyone in the room that the struggle since 1995 hadn't been his swing. The struggle had been with his own creeping indifference, and that had started with his equipment. Locked into a binding and lucrative sponsorship deal that required him to use clubs and balls that didn't suit the way he learned and liked to play, Payne was beginning to accept that he needed to make changes.

But he kept that to himself among the reporters. He had learned it was bad form to complain.

Unger said there was time for one more question. Someone inquired about focus. Did Payne still care as much about winning golf tournaments?

"I have got a beautiful wife and two lovely kids that I am really enjoying spending time with," Payne said. "And as I'm getting older, it is getting harder and harder to go out and do the grind out on the PGA Tour."

It felt good to be honest. The reporters appreciated it, too. It gave them context and perspective that informed their accounts of birdies, bogeys, and holes bordering on the ridiculous. Many players they wrote about kept a shield around their lives, as if explaining their personal values might prevent them from playing better golf. Payne was like that once. He was done pretending. He had made the decision to pare down his schedule so he could spend more time at home in Florida.

Payne had one more thought to share before he left to prepare for the weekend: "There is more to life than playing professional golf."

CHAPTER TWO

The Lake Course at the Olympic Club opened in 1924, in the early years of the golden age of golf-course architecture, a period when bold and taxing tests of golf were being routed by Donald Ross at Pinehurst No. 2 and Seminole and Oakland Hills, Douglas Grant and Jack Neville at Pebble Beach, George Crump at Pine Valley, A. W. Tillinghast at Winged Foot, George Thomas at Riviera, Alister MacKenzie at Cypress Point, and MacKenzie and Bobby Jones at Augusta National. Architects of the golden age employed dramatic bunkering as both fortresses to penalize poor shots and beacons to show the way for good ones. They created greens that heaved and flowed with the contours of the surrounding topography. They saw no point in trying to fashion a golf hole that looked out of place. Their work became timeless.

Designed by Willie Watson and restored by Sam Whiting after a terrible winter storm in 1925, the Lake at Olympic wound through forty thousand cypress trees in the southwest corner of San Francisco, near enough to the Gulf of the Farallones that Payne could glimpse the Golden Gate Bridge from the tee of the third hole. The course was not long, but it was bunkered fiercely, and the pitch of the fairways—the hills of San Francisco in miniature—demanded so much of the greatest players of all time that it had become, by the summer of 1998, a cemetery of broken hopes.

Ben Hogan lost to unheralded Jack Fleck there in 1955. Arnold Palmer wasted a seven-shot lead there with nine holes to play in 1966, pretty much gifting the championship to Billy Casper. Tom Watson got beat there in 1987, when he failed to protect a one-shot lead with five holes left and Scott Simpson won by a stroke. Now here was Payne, reporting Saturday to the par-five first hole, in the same tenuous predicament. He led by one over Jeff Maggert and Bob Tway, and by two over Janzen, Lee Porter, and the amateur Matt Kuchar.

He hammered his drive. (Payne used his driver just twice that Saturday, on the par-five first hole and the long par-four seventeenth, a converted par-five. ("Driving statistics don't mean diddly to me," he would say later that afternoon. "I'd like to be in more fairways.") He chose a five-iron on his second shot. He floated it to twenty feet and banged in the putt for eagle. He was on his way to an even-par 70, and a four-shot lead, with one round to go.

But Payne wasn't at his best. Chuck Cook, his swing instructor, who already had gone home to Austin, watched the round on television and thought that Payne had lost some of his crispness from his first two rounds. His iron play looked suspicious. Payne missed the third green with a six-iron and made bogey from a bunker. He missed the ninth green: bogey. His seven-iron approach on the fifteenth finished in another bunker: bogey again. Cook attributed the sloppiness to a lack of post-round practice. Payne had played late Friday and Saturday, giving him no time to correct his emerging flaws on the range after his obligations in the media room with Les Unger and the reporters. A late start, especially on the weekend, meant a player was in or near the lead. It was a blessing in that way. But it came with its own set of problems.

Payne gave no hint he was concerned. He said in his press conference that he remained confident. He said he was ready.

"If I come out tomorrow and play the way Payne Stewart can play, I'll win the golf tournament," he said. "If I don't, I'll deal with that then. But there's no reason why, in my mind, I don't believe that I'm not capable of winning."

He was asked what it would mean to win. It was the kind of question players like Payne, familiar with the lead, had grown used to answering.

"It would prove a point to myself that I still have the ability to compete in major championships," he said. "There's no reason why I shouldn't believe that."

Payne thought about his wife and children. They were back home in Florida. His young son, Aaron, and his daughter, Chelsea, were getting ready to go to summer camp. Tracey, his wife, was helping them prepare while their father was trying to win a second national championship. There was a time when Tracey, Aaron, and Chelsea traveled with him. Now they had other interests.

"I said this yesterday," Payne added. "It's hard to motivate yourself to come out here, year in and year out, and work at it. I don't want to blink and see my kids are in college, because I know once they're in college, they'll probably never live under our roof again. So, if I have the opportunity to spend time with them ... that's what I'm going to do."

It was nearly dark when Payne left Olympic. He would play the next afternoon with Lehman, a scrappy and tough thirty-nine-year-old veteran from Minnesota who'd risen through the minor tours in Asia and South Africa. Lehman had won the British Open in 1996. It was his only major championship. But he'd been close in the last three U.S. Opens: a finish for third in 1995 at Shinnecock Hills, a share of second in '96 at Oakland Hills, and third again in '97 at Congressional. He'd played in the final pairing on all three Sundays. Those who paid attention to golf wondered if it just might be Lehman's time.

Lehman liked Payne. While not close—given its solitary nature, the PGA Tour didn't exactly foster close relationships, at least not until events such as the Ryder Cup, and only then when chemistry and the moment conspired to do so—Lehman considered Payne one of the colorful personalities that made the tour compelling to fans. Lehman admired the tempo and timing of Payne's swing, how liquid it seemed, long and loose. He knew of Payne's reputation as a mercurial and sometimes insufferable loudmouth. Everyone did. Lehman wondered if it was fair. He wondered if other players were jealous of Payne: his good looks, his fluid swing, his bold ensembles, his undeniable grace on the golf course. Lehman had seen Payne and his wife on the putting green after rounds. He watched them work together, often in silence, and respected the implicit partnership in their marriage. He remembered when Payne had changed his equipment. The move surprised him, as it did many players. It felt like a sellout. It had led to a long, languishing slump. And now here Payne was, in the last group of the national championship, with one of the steadiest U.S. Open players in the last decade: Lehman.

Like Payne, Lehman was a feel player who played a finesse game. He and his generation, made up of players born before 1960, surely wanted to hit the ball hard, but pure length hadn't become the grail it soon would. They didn't try to bludgeon the ball. They sought to caress it, to will it through the air with an arc and apex that fit the exact result they had in mind. Lehman learned and peaked in the game as Payne had, with persimmon woods, wound balls, and forged irons. They conjured the spirits of Ben Hogan and Byron Nelson and Sam Snead, even Bobby Jones, men who, in the primes of their careers, never knew the piercing concussion of titanium on the solid-core balls that were becoming standard now on the professional tours. They never enjoyed the ease of playing a cavity-backed iron cast with melted steel; they did their work with smaller irons that were hammered and bent, as the blacksmith once forged the pickax, from a glowing ingot.

From a commercial standpoint, there was a lot to like about the state of golf in the summer of 1998. The new balls were designed to make shots more predictable, especially in wind. Graphite shafts and metal woods rendered long holes simpler to manage. The blockier, cavity-backed irons were less demanding of a perfect strike. Golf was getting easier for a greater number of people. But that welcome development robbed the ancient game of some of its art. Payne, Lehman, and their generation didn't need technology to make shots. They made their own. They were the last true shot-makers of the millennium.

And there stood Lehman and Payne on Sunday afternoon, tugging at their shirts and fiddling with their gloves, as the starter announced their names at the first hole.

Paul Azinger, the winner of the 1993 PGA Championship, had taped a note to Payne's locker that morning. "Stay in the present and enjoy the walk," it read. The words meant a lot to Payne. He and Azinger were close, and years earlier, when Azinger was sick with cancer, Payne saw in him a kind of bravery, faith, and perspective that made him question the way he conducted his own life. Through his illness, Azinger had helped Payne confront his own priorities and choices. Azinger changed Payne by example.

Ahead on the Lake Course, Bob Tway had begun the fourth and final round in a tie for second with Lehman at one over par. Nick Price and Lee Janzen were plus two. At thirty-three, Janzen was the youngest player within five shots of Payne's lead, but he believed in careful, conservative, and thoughtful golf like the older men ahead of him. The field included the younger stars on tour—David Duval, Phil Mickelson, and Tiger Woods among them. None of them would pose a threat. On a cloudy, gloomy, and still afternoon in Northern California, the national championship would come down to who could feel the right shots for the slopes and slants of the Lake Course.

Payne made straight pars on the first three holes. His first bogey came at No. 4, where he drove into the rough. He could accept a bogey, just as he could accept straight pars: par was a good score, bogeys would happen. *Just stay away from losing two at a time.* Janzen, meanwhile, had dropped shots to par on the second and third holes. He recovered with a birdie on the fourth and then drove a four-metal into a cypress on the fifth, where his ball got stuck in its branches. The rules of golf prescribed a shot-and-distance penalty for a lost ball. Janzen and his caddie began the deflating march back to the tee. *This isn't right,* Janzen thought. *I've just made birdie to turn things around. Now I'm going to be lucky to make double.* Then chance made its return appearance to the final round of a U.S. Open involving Lee Janzen and Payne Stewart. A breeze rose, and the ball in the cypress plopped to the ground. Janzen punched a recovery shot to the fairway and flew the green with a six-iron. He chipped in for par.

Payne absorbed his second bogey at No. 7. It was no time to panic. No one was making a run on the front nine—Lehman, Price, and Tway were over par and in retreat—while Payne and Hicks were keeping their own damage to an acceptable level. They finished the first nine at plus two. Janzen holed a nice birdie on the seventh to complete the front at even par, but he was still three strokes behind Payne. A birdie at eleven nudged him closer, and as he was rolling in another birdie putt at the thirteenth, Payne and Hicks, still in the lead, prepared to play No. 12.

How a major is remembered can hinge on a single turn of a ball. If his green-side bunker shot bends one rotation to the left on the last hole at Inverness in 1986, Bob Tway watches his ball glance off the flagstick instead of hitting it squarely, and the PGA Championship goes to a playoff with Greg Norman. With one more roll at the 1992 Masters, gravity drags Fred Couples's tee shot on the twelfth into Rae's Creek. With a harder rotation to the right at the seventeenth green at the 1994 British Open, the eagle putt Nick Price made at Turnberry misses the hole wide.

Now, on the twelfth at Olympic, Payne drew a three-metal into the heart of the fairway. "That's a beauty," NBC broadcaster Johnny Miller told his audience. But the ball settled in a fresh divot coated in sand, 137 yards from the hole. Payne shook his head. ("The first fairway I had hit in a while, and sure enough I was in a bunker," he would later say.) He champed furiously on his gum. His mind raced. He tried his best not to dwell on his misfortune, but he also couldn't help questioning his luck again.

Raymond Floyd, the 1986 U.S. Open champion who also was on the broadcast team for NBC, told viewers, "That is the worst divot. I mean, you're right in the middle of it."

One turn of the ball separated a predictable lie from doubt.

Payne pulled a club. He rehearsed a swing from other divots nearby and worked through his emotions. Arms crossed over his chest, he conferred with Hicks about the shape of the shot, the strategy, the target, the feel. An approach of this distance rarely complicated a professional golfer's thinking, even in a U.S. Open. The divot introduced all manner of dark possibility. Payne needed to think it through.

He selected a nine-iron. He made two more practice swings, retreated behind the ball, and confirmed his line. He settled into his stance.

Ahead, Janzen had laced a five-iron to five feet at the thirteenth. Another birdie. He made a par on No. 14. The championship now was his or Payne's.

Two holes behind him, Payne swung. The ball rose from a cloud of debris.

"Sounded like he hit it clean," Floyd said on the broadcast.

"Actually, he got it a little heavy," said his NBC colleague, Roger Maltbie, "and it's going right."

The ball dove into a deep bunker near the front-right edge of the green. Payne understood the consequences of the shot the moment he watched it land. He faced a nearly impossible play: a high, soft splash over the inner wall of the bunker, to a flagstick a few feet away.

"That just wasn't good," Floyd said.

Then it got worse. Payne saw USGA rules official Tom Meeks walk toward him on the twelfth fairway.

"You just got a bad time," Meeks said.

Payne had taken more than forty-five seconds to play his approach from the divot, and now his pairing was out of position in relation to the group ahead. Another bad time could mean a one-stroke penalty, which no one could afford in circumstances like these. The ruling irritated Payne. The shot itself had required more calculation than a routine play. The swarm of media—photographers and camera operators competing for vantage points—had made keeping pace difficult. But more than that, Payne was annoyed that the USGA seemed unconcerned about the stakes. This was the final round of the U.S. Open. This was the last group on the course. He and Lehman had a lot to play for. So what if they were a few minutes behind?

Everything seemed to happen so fast now. The ball in the divot in the middle of the fairway. The impossible bunker shot to a short-sided hole. The ruling from Meeks. The chance of a penalty. Payne tried to slow his breaths. He reminded himself that he had six holes to play, that he still had time. He had taken a look at a leaderboard at the tenth hole. He had seen that Janzen was one under par. He could feel him closing on him as he had in '93. He evaluated his lie in the bunker, planted his feet, and screwed the soles of his shoes into the sand. His ball stopped ten feet from the hole. He missed the putt.

Janzen made five consecutive pars to finish his round: a two-under 68, good for a composite score of even-par 280 over four hard days at hilly, persnickety Olympic. Payne was never the same after the debacle at twelve. He made another bogey at thirteen.

"Hang in there," Hicks told him on the walk to the fourteenth tee. "Your swing is fine." But it wasn't really. And he wasn't, either.

Payne played the last six holes at plus one. He had a twenty-foot putt to tie Janzen on the seventy-second green. It peeled away a foot from the hole.

Payne dreaded the march up the hill to his fourth post-round interview of the week. There was so little good to remember this time, so little good to say. He had carried the lead all week and lost the national championship in the last six holes. He knew he would be asked about the situation on twelve, both the sand-covered divot and the warning from the USGA. He wondered if he might be asked to talk again about the speed of the green on the eighteenth in the second round. He prepared himself to explain how he'd committed five bogeys and managed only one birdie in the most important round of his career in a very long time, maybe as long ago as 1993 at Baltusrol. He thought about blame. He thought about fault. He sat down and waited for the questions about failure and luck.

Unger, the moderator, opened the interview with a question about the divot on twelve and whether it foretold defeat.

"Did you get any feeling that maybe this wasn't meant to be?" he said.

Payne ignored the question. He wanted his first words to address the final day as a body of work—full of flaws, to be sure, but not isolated to one random revolution of the ball. He reminded the gathered reporters of what he'd told them the evening before, when he'd said he was confident in his play, and that if he continued to think clearly, remain calm, mitigate mistakes, and make good swings, he could win.

"And I didn't do that," Payne said.

The divot did bother him now, but not just because it possibly had cost him one of his 281 shots that week. It was bigger than that. Payne believed a sand-filled divot should be played as "ground under repair," a golf term that describes conditions influenced by an effort to fix a problem. "If they're going to come out and physically try to repair something, in my opinion that's ground under repair," Payne said later in the interview. He said players deserved a free drop from situations like that, just as they do when their ball lands in an area actually under repair, like where a drain is broken or dead turf has been replaced by sod. The grounds crew that filled the divot with sand after play Saturday tried to repair something, he said. "But the USGA and the PGA Tour don't see it like that."

He was asked about the warning for slow play. Payne accepted responsibility for that. He wanted to defend the time it took to think through the shot from the divot, wait for the media to be still, and simply try not to hurry with so much at stake, with no one behind him and plenty of time left until NBC had to end its broadcast. But he didn't. There was no use. The tournament was over, and warring with the USGA over rules, especially in a public forum, would bring nothing but more attention to the perception that Payne could be a baby.

"I'm still going to be able to sleep tonight," Payne said. "There's some disappointment, but I think the reason why I'm in here, and the reason you're viewing me differently, is that I've matured, and I understand what this job is about. I understand what playing golf for a living is all about and how I'm supposed to handle myself, and that's what I'm doing. I really feel that I've got a better grip on that."

A younger Payne Stewart might not be as willing to face those questions. The man he used to be might be quick to pillory all that had gone against him. That man might've allowed the scalding frustration of three years without a win to turn a press conference into a self-serving referendum on chance, fairness, rules, and, without his even knowing it, his own insecurities.

But a different Payne sat down that Sunday after losing the U.S. Open with unexpected grace. He was climbing hills no one else could see.

CHAPTER THREE

Hicks waited outside the clubhouse. He looked at the other scores. Casey Martin had tied for twenty-third. Azinger shot 65 and tied for fourteenth. Mark O'Meara, one of Payne's friends in Orlando and himself of the shot-maker era, finished with a handsome 69. Hicks had witnessed the five-over 75 that Lehman shot, giving a tie for fifth: another near-miss at the national championship. It never would be his time at the U.S. Open.

Hicks thought about lost chances that day and regrets of his own. He missed the singular joy of fetching a flag from the stick on the eighteenth green after victory—the duty of the caddie for a champion, to preserve the glory of the day. He thought about how close he'd been to doing that on the darkening amphitheater of cypress and grass below where his man had missed the putt to tie.

Payne appeared finally, wearing the gray long-sleeved shirt he'd chosen for the final round and the smart navy plus fours. He looked content.

"You OK?" Hicks asked him.

"I'm OK," Payne said. "We did accomplish one thing."

"What's that?"

"I know I can win again."

Hicks never really knew how Payne would handle defeat. At times, he seemed to accept it well and move on. At times, he wanted to wear it like a weight. Hicks had seen Payne act like a child after losing a golf tournament, like when he had lost the 1989 Nabisco Championship at Hilton Head and refused to grant Tom Kite, the winner, a proper handshake. But Hicks saw something at Olympic that gave him hope. He liked to hear Payne say that he knew he could win again. It meant he was dwelling on the future, not the past.

Payne drove to the airport to get on a private business jet to Illinois, where he and two other players, Justin Leonard and D. A. Weibring, were committed to a charity outing before the Motorola Western Open, which would begin that Thursday. Leonard and Weibring were in their seats when Payne arrived, ready for a drink.

Leonard expected Payne to sulk. He didn't know him well—not yet, anyway—but he knew his reputation. Instead, Payne produced a bottle with a proof label from one of his bags and poured for everyone aboard. The three players drank and told stories about the U.S. Open all the way to Quincy. The flight landed without incident. Leonard was beginning to like Payne as he got to know him away from the golf course. A former U.S. Amateur champion from Texas, Leonard had been on tour for only four years, but Payne treated him on the flight like an old friend, like a fraternity brother. They arrived at the hotel late. Payne wasn't about to let the night end. He dialed Leonard's room. Leonard picked up the receiver and heard Payne's voice.

"Throw some jeans on," Payne said. "We're going out."

The group raided a bar owned by someone Weibring's caddie knew. The owner locked the doors and told the golfers and their guests to have fun. Leonard kept the bar. Payne warmed the grill. It was four in the morning by the time they went to bed. After that night, Leonard was joining Payne in practice rounds on the tour. ("I liked being around him," Leonard would say years later. "He was a nice mix of homework and analysis and feel.") They were alike in that way: contemplative about golf but intuitive in the end.

Payne tied for fifty-seventh at the Motorola at Cog Hill, outside Chicago. He missed a couple of cuts in the second half of the season. One of them came at the PGA Championship at Sahalee Country Club near Seattle, where Vijay Singh of Fiji won by two. Meeks served on the rules crew, and he found Lehman to tell him he regretted the situation at Olympic. Lehman understood. He knew Meeks was just doing his job. Meeks wanted to have the same talk with Payne, but the U.S. Open runner-up shot 76-74 and was gone, and not likely to be in the frame of mind for that kind of conversation anyway. Meeks promised himself he would have that talk with Payne someday. He wanted Payne to know that giving him a bad time after a lousy break in the final round of the national championship was as hard a decision as he'd ever had to make.

It had been a nice year of golf for Payne. He'd played twenty-one tournaments, with two second-place finishes, a third, and six inside the top ten. He'd nearly won the Greater Vancouver Open two weeks after Sahalee, and he'd had a chance again in Williamsburg, Virginia. He played three more times after that. Then it was November.

He'd earned $1.19 million. Payne always seemed to manage to win lots of money, with the exception of 1994, when he'd made only fifteen cuts for a relatively meager $145,687 and tended to brood too much. That was the worst year of them all. That was when Payne questioned everything and had answers for nothing. Now, after so many good signs in 1998, he felt good about his life and his golf. He sensed he was on the brink of a professional renaissance and personal fulfillment: a summit of some kind. But first he wanted to go home. He was ready to spend a lot of time there with Tracey and Aaron and Chelsea at his mansion in Orlando with the boat dock out back.

The boat dock was where Payne could think. He used to sit there and smoke and drink and fight doubt. But that fight was over now. He'd won it.

Payne wasn't just looking forward to 1999. He thought '99 could be a season of salvation.

In every sense, the boat dock behind the house was a long way from Springfield. So were Bay Hill, Isleworth, and Orange Tree, the exclusive golf clubs in Orlando where Payne practiced and played. Fame and prosperity had given Payne the means to live an extraordinary life in Florida, including private school for Aaron and Chelsea, a palatial house with a swimming pool and a basketball court behind the iron gate with the big *S* on a secluded road lined with trees, a Porsche in the garage, anything he and Tracey wanted. But wealth hadn't fundamentally changed Payne as a person, and there were occasions when he used his wealth to help other people, like when he gave his entire first-place winnings to a children's hospital. As his father had been, Payne was generous with his money, the kind of person who wanted the check after dinner. He cut a debonair, sophisticated figure on the golf course, but Payne was and would remain an uncomplicated man from the hills of southern Missouri.

His father joined Hickory Hills Country Club before he and his wife, Bee, started their family. Hickory was the old, established club in Springfield, the third-largest city in the state, about an hour north of the Arkansas line, and home to Southwest Missouri State Teacher's College (now Missouri State University), where Bill Stewart had lettered in football, basketball, and golf. The club incorporated just east of downtown in 1934. It was a good year for golf in Springfield: Horton Smith, who often played at Hickory and competed on five Ryder Cup teams, won the first Masters Tournament in '34. Twelve years later, another golfer from Springfield and a member at Hickory, the stern Herman (the "Missouri Mortician") Keiser, would win the spring invitational in Augusta, making Springfield, home to about seventy thousand people in the middle of the century, the smallest city in America to claim two Masters champions as residents.

Hickory was famous for little else. Though it opened in the golden age, it was not, in its earliest form, a notable test of golf. The club retained Robert Charles Dunning, a professional golfer from Kansas City and former semipro baseball player, to renovate its course to modern standards in 1962, about the time Bill Stewart began to take his five-year-old son to Hickory. Bill and Bee brought their three young children to the course and let them play along as much or as little as they wanted, so long as they kept quiet, stayed out of the bunkers, and behaved themselves around the adults. Payne clearly found something in the game that touched him. Using cut-down adult clubs his father had given him, he sprinted to the ball as he squirted it along the tumbling fairways. His father surmised that he had indeed found a lifelong partner in golf.

Bill Stewart shaped his son more than anyone else in Payne's life. He remained a source of deep motivation and inspiration for Payne's entire career. He encouraged the young Payne to believe in himself; failing that, he should always give the impression that he did. He urged his son to adopt a sartorial style, and he set his own example. Bill Stewart wore loud, brightly colored blazers and distinctly patterned ties to his sales calls. *Clients would remember him that way*, he thought.

He spent a lot of time away for his job as a traveling salesman for Leggett & Platt, which manufactured mattresses and box springs. The task of raising Payne and his two older sisters, Susan and Lora, fell to their mother until her husband came home from his sales territory in Iowa and Missouri and the five of them could go back out to Hickory. The family lived in a one-story ranch house on South Link Street. It was a modest dwelling in a shady neighborhood teeming with kids on bikes who kicked hedge apples that fell from Osage orange trees and looked for something to build up, tear down, or hit with sticks. William Payne Stewart went by his middle name. It was a way to set him apart. As one of the younger boys in the pack of children in their part of Springfield, he needed to find ways to be noticed.

Louder than most boys his age and as rambunctious as a puppy, Payne was an otherwise unexceptional midwestern youth, uninterested in art or books or politics, uneasy in solitude, blissfully unconcerned with gas rations, Nixon, Saigon, or anything else the grown-ups discussed after church or in the bleachers of his baseball games. He was a social marvel, a figure the boys at school admired for the way he moved easily and confidently through space and someone the girls swooned over for the way he feathered his hair and smiled their way in the halls.

Payne craved the company of those people, of all people. He loved to entertain and be entertained. He was at his best when he was the focus of attention, and the larger the crowd, the better.

Payne was a magnet among flecks of steel at the Greenwood Laboratory School near the campus of Southwest Missouri State University. His peers were drawn to his charisma, charm, and command of the confusing assemblage of the evolving hierarchies among cliques and friend groups. He seemed always to be in charge. It seemed to require no effort at all. Payne sensed that people his age admired him, and he learned to perform the roles they implicitly assigned to him, from the jock of jocks to object of awkward romantic impulses to the prince of clowns. He understood at an early age that people wanted to be around a winner. Payne saw himself as a winner at everything. He didn't create his image. He became it.

Springfield was a quiet, clean, uneventful place in the 1960s and '70s. It gave the Stewart children an idyllic, but also sheltered and limited, existence. The Stewarts went to Grace United Methodist Church, but not every Sunday morning, and the youngest of them wouldn't discover meaningful spirituality for many years, which he would regret as an older man. Sports and games and competition were what he worshipped as a boy, one who never outgrew his penchant for mischief and play. He pitched for his Little League baseball team, played point guard for the basketball team, and was an agile, confident, strong-armed high school quarterback. But golf was his truest love.

His father won a lot of amateur golf tournaments, so he ended up with a surplus of credit at golf course retail shops. (The rules of golf allowed amateurs to win so-called shop credit but not actual money.) Bill Stewart's accumulated shop credit provided plenty of Christmas gifts at the Stewart house. The clubs under the tree barely resembled the crude, wood-shafted instruments Francis Ouimet had used to win the 1913 U.S. Open at The Country Club in Brookline, Massachusetts, an achievement credited with kindling America's interest in watching competitive golf. But they weren't far, in form or in function, from the equipment Ben Hogan, Byron Nelson, and Sam Snead had played two decades earlier to launch the popularity of tournament golf in America and to become familiar names at places like Hickory Hills Country Club in Springfield.

Equipment companies were just beginning to change golf in ways the game had never seen. Steel shafts had replaced hickory in the late 1920s, and Billy Burke became the first player to win a major championship with them at the 1931 U.S. Open. Steel was more predictable and resilient than hickory. Club builders could more reliably tune and match steel shafts throughout a set, giving players the sense that each of the fourteen clubs in his or her bag felt the same as the others. Because steel flexed less than hickory, better players like Bill Stewart could make stronger, faster swings for longer, more powerful shots.

In January 1966, the proprietor of a small Arizona company called PING returned from the Los Angeles Open with an idea. Karsten Solheim had designed a number of putters already. But none of them achieved the popularity of the Arnold Palmer signature blade putter, similar to the Wilson 8802, that he'd seen so much of that week in California. Solheim sketched his idea on the sleeve of a 78 rpm record. His rendering became one of the most played, copied, and revered putter designs of all time: a heel-to-toe balanced blade with a goose-necked hosel and a lower center of gravity than the Palmer putter, which promoted a quicker forward roll. Solheim decided to call his new invention the "Answer" putter. But his engraver couldn't fit all six letters on the cavity, so Solheim dropped one. He introduced his Scottsdale Anser in February. The putter was a runaway success. George Archer used it to win the 1969 Masters. The design was here to stay.

So was the cavity-back iron. Similar to the Anser in its design with a carved-out rear section, the irons distributed the weight of the steel on the perimeter of the head instead of uniformly behind the face, a concept that corrected mishits. They were far less demanding than the forged blade irons used by Hogan, Nelson, Snead, and other skilled players who preferred the way blade-style irons could be used to shape shots in different directions and flights. But they were ideal for recreational players. What they lacked in feel they made up in forgiveness. Weekend players loved them. Tournament players said they felt dead.

Bill Stewart played forged-blade irons, which meant his son did, too. The evolving young player with the blond hair, now a fixture on the fairways at Hickory, was learning to flight golf shots with balata-covered balls, wound inside with rubber bands, that soared over tall trees, hugged the ground under their low branches, drew right to left, and faded left to right, curving around them like homing pigeons.

Bill Stewart taught his son everything he knew about golf. He later handed him over to Sam Reynolds, the longtime head golf professional at Hickory Hills and an excellent tournament player in his own right. A stern, ball-cap-wearing, and cigar-smoking pro's pro from Wichita Falls, Texas, Reynolds helped his young charge build a swing that started with the hands. The move he taught Payne led the grip into the takeaway as the head of the club dragged slightly behind. Reynolds called it the *pullback motion*, compared it to a bullwhip, and insisted everyone who took lessons from him at least give it a try. It was a relic from the era of hickory shafts, when an oily tempo distinguished a good shot from a poor one, when power and force gathered in the swing like an elastic band being stretched. The pliability of hickory mandated a smooth, almost quiet blow to the ball. The best players of the hickory era, ones like Bobby Jones, rarely had poured their entire being into the golf swing, even if it looked to the untrained eye like they did. They coaxed shots. They delivered them. They *had* to feel them, to sense the bend and lean of the hickory in their hands. The invention of steel shafts changed that. But it didn't change the way teachers such as Sam Reynolds helped his students build a golf swing, an action that began with the first move away from the ball. Reynolds said the pullback motion prevented a player from yanking the club away from the ball. "It's a golf *swing*," Reynolds liked to remind Payne and his other pupils. The pullback motion became the swing trigger for the rest of Payne's life.

Reynolds had a daughter, Cathy, who was six months younger than

Payne. Cathy went to a different school, but she became one of Payne's closest friends, and a bit of a sporting rival, through the junior program at Hickory. Payne liked to hear Cathy tell stories about shagging balls for her father at Firestone in Akron or Indian Wells in Palm Springs alongside Arnold Palmer and Lee Trevino. He liked to compete against her with their putters and wedges. Payne and Cathy became two of the best juniors in Missouri, and when Cathy qualified for the U.S. Women's Open at the age of fifteen, Payne was both proud of his friend and likely motivated by a healthy tinge of envy. Sam Reynolds had taught his daughter the pullback motion, too. She would leverage it into a college career with Nancy Lopez at Tulsa and seventeen years on the LPGA Tour, including a victory over Betsy King in 1981.

By his teens, Payne had a swing that made the members at Hickory stop what they were doing and marvel. Exceedingly flexible and loose of limb, he moved the club through space as if poised on a fulcrum, from the slight rightward tick of the grip in his hands to the soles of his feet, which shifted his weight like a seesaw. He kept a straight but relaxed left arm to the top, with an imperceptible pause there, a comma in a perfectly balanced sentence, a trace of Hogan and Jones. His downswing continued to set the cock of his wrists, storing power all the way to the ball, culminating with a full and high finish until the middle of his shaft rested on the nape of his neck. ("A *classic* swing," said the great Johnny Miller, never one to sprinkle compliments. "He could hit *any* shot.") Payne's long arms created width and kinetic energy with little forced effort. His supple hips rotated as if greased. The physics of his move through the ball matched his body in a way that meant he rarely had to work at it by the time he became a scratch player who shot par almost every time he teed his ball. Bill Stewart met privately with his son's golf coach at Greenwood Laboratory School. "Payne knows how to play golf," the father advised. "He doesn't need any help. Please don't mess with his swing."

Payne learned to see shots in his mind before he executed them. Sam Reynolds emphasized the importance of balance and footwork.

"All rhythm is created from your feet," Reynolds told Payne, repeating a tenet he had learned from his own teacher in Kansas City. Later, when Payne was contending at U.S. Opens at Shinnecock Hills and Hazeltine and Baltusrol and Olympic, he wouldn't even address his ball until he had a sense of the shot through the soles of his shoes and a clear, crisp picture of the way he wanted the shot to look and feel off the club. While that's true of many golf champions, Payne and players of his generation and before became shot-makers because their equipment dictated it. They were forced to play with what they called *feel*—a subjective and personal sense, developed through hours and hours of time on the practice range, of making shots through the essential connections between the eyes down to the fingertips and the soles of feet, the tactile representation of Hogan's conviction that the secret to golf was there to be discovered, through discipline and repetition, in the dirt.

Payne churned a lot of dirt at Hickory. By the time he was ready to graduate from high school and play golf in college, he was beginning to wonder if he could make a living by feeling and making shots on the PGA Tour.

CHAPTER FOUR

Payne qualified for the U.S. Amateur in the summer of 1975. He didn't do well in the championship, won by future Augusta National chairman Fred Ridley at the Country Club of Virginia, but he did meet another recent high school graduate at a reception before play began. Payne and Lamar Haynes, of Shreveport, Louisiana, had much in common. Both of them loved golf as much as they did a good time and a loud laugh. They also learned they would be teammates in college.

Haynes and Payne would be going to Texas in the fall to play golf for Southern Methodist University. In many ways, SMU was perfect for Payne. Because it was a relatively small school, Payne and his parents figured he could get to know his professors and not get lost in the crowd. Because it was right in the middle of Dallas, Payne would get a taste of city living. Playing for SMU got him out of Missouri and broadened his impression of the world. The program wasn't one of the big powerhouses like Houston or Wake Forest or Oklahoma State. Payne hoped he would have the chance to play right away for Earl Stewart, the head coach.

Like many players of his era, Earl Stewart was a former club professional who'd set out each summer to compete on a circuit that was not yet known as the PGA Tour. The so-called PGA Tournament Bureau, the tour's precursor, ran a series of events that attracted names like Dow Finsterwald and Lloyd Mangrum and Lefty Stackhouse and Lew Worsham and Jack Fleck, slayer of Hogan. They played for little money and a lot of pride. They caravanned around the country, three or four of them to a Buick, their canvas bags in the trunk carrying forged blades and wood-headed drivers with chromed steel shafts that might be tarnishing if it were July or August. Most of them played the tour only to make a name for themselves so that they might get better club jobs, which was how golfers made a living in the game. PGA Championship and Masters winner Jackie Burke Jr., for example, could earn about $10,000 on the tour at stops such as the Rio Grande Valley Fruit and Vegetable Open in Harlingen, Texas. And that was for a good year. His club-professional job at Winged Foot in Westchester County, New York, paid him three times as much. Television changed everything. The first tournament to appear on live TV was the 1953 Tam O'Shanter World Championship north of Chicago. That was the year prize money rose to a half million dollars. Five years later, purses paid $1 million for the first time. Golf could be a living, and a good one.

That was long after Earl Stewart, the 1937 and '38 Texas high school medalist from Dallas, won the 1941 NCAA individual title at Louisiana State University. A career club professional until his years at SMU, he won the 1953 Greater Greensboro Open, the 1953 Ardmore Open, and the 1961 Dallas Open Invitational at Oak Cliff Country Club, where he ran the pro shop, kept inventory, and gave lessons to members just taking up the game and tour players mastering it, including Mickey Wright, one of the greatest players of all time, a future member of the Ladies Professional Golf Association Hall of Fame. Wright and Stewart were on the Wilson Sporting Goods staff when Stewart became the first host professional in history to win a tour start at his home club in that summer of '61. He beat Arnold Palmer by a stroke.

He became the golf coach at SMU when his playing days were over. He created the women's team in 1975, the same year Payne, who was unrelated to his college coach, joined the Mustangs men's team. Earl Stewart was built like a boxer, lean and rippling, and if it didn't make sense, he didn't like it. He smoked unfiltered cigarettes as he watched Payne, Haynes, and his other players shape shots around the courses of Dallas. A municipal course on Mondays. Country clubs, including Royal Oaks, where a young Justin Leonard was learning the game, on Tuesdays and Wednesdays. A daily-fee course on Thursdays.

They spent little time on the range proper. There were no drills, swing aides, alignment sticks, distance-measuring devices. The SMU golf team practiced by playing, like Ben Crenshaw had done at Texas, where his great teacher, Harvey Penick, just sent him to play Austin Country Club with three new balls as preparation for his three future individual NCAA championships for the Longhorns. Up at SMU, the head coach admired the way his freshman from Springfield handled his Kenneth Smith persimmon driver, a menacing black implement with a white insert in its face, on the tight holes that frustrated his other players.

"He can make the ball bleed," the coach told his friends.

He didn't mess with that swing from Missouri, either.

"Just trust it," he would tell his ball-bleeding player from Missouri.

College golf in 1970s was nothing of the scope and scale of the modern sport. The SMU team played most of its tournaments in Texas: the All-American Intercollegiate in Houston, the Morris Williams in Austin, the Southwest Conference Match Play in Texarkana, the Border Olympics in Laredo. The Mustangs traveled by automobile. They slept in modest motels. They played their tournaments on hardscrabble golf courses, many of them open to the public, which meant that, in addition to opposing teams, they had to compete with scruffy greens, manifold divots, baked-out bunkers, and other relics of the relatively primitive state of heavily used golf courses in the hot, arid American Southwest. There was little elegance or opulence in college golf then. But there was the essential esprit de corps that turned teammates into lifelong friends.

Payne went to college for the companionship, not to complete some grand career plan involving a profession other than golf. Effervescently social and always eager for a good time, he joined the Phi Gamma Delta fraternity and rarely did anything without his fellow Fijis, Lamar Haynes, or his other friends from both on and off the golf team. He started smoking. He liked to drink. He liked to date. He worked just hard enough in his courses to keep his eligibility to play golf and remain in satisfactory standing with the dean of students. He lived in every moment and never looked too far beyond—a trait Earl Stewart saw as a weakness—as a reason Payne might not ever be as good at golf as he could be. For his restive freshman from Missouri, college seemed to be just another way to enjoy whatever life had to offer, in all its vividness.

Payne qualified for enough tournaments to earn a varsity letter. He returned to Dallas for his sophomore year and completed the mandatory questionnaire required of all SMU athletes. "Hobbies?" His listed hunting, fishing, and water skiing.

"What has been your biggest sports thrill?"

"Making a hole in one."

"What's most important to you: Winning or playing your best, and why?"

"Winning," Payne wrote. "That is what you are out here for."

"Your favorite athlete?"

"Myself."

Payne finished sixteenth as an individual that year in the NCAA championships. He won nothing as a junior. He was named captain of the team for his senior year, tied for eighth in a tournament, went home to Missouri for the holiday break, and told his father he planned to enter the qualifying tournament for the PGA Tour, known as Q School, at the end of 1979. Bill Stewart didn't have a problem with his son's goal in the abstract. It was the kind of idea he might've pursued three decades earlier, had he and Bee not become parents so early. The problem, Bill Stewart thought, was that his son hadn't won even one golf tournament at SMU.

"You haven't done anything in college but have fun," he told him.

That changed when Payne returned to Dallas for his last semester in the spring of '79. He won his first collegiate tournament, the NTSU Invitational, in March, and a week later, he beat a stellar field in Austin at the Morris Williams Invitational. He and Fred Couples of Houston tied for the Southwest Conference Championship at Briarwood Golf Club in Tyler, Texas. In the playoff, Payne won on the first hole. He credited Earl Stewart for toughening his attitude.

"For the last couple of years, I didn't understand, or didn't want to understand, the way he was coaching," Payne said in Tyler. "He's been a big help this semester."

As conference champion, he was invited to play in the 1979 Colonial, his first exposure to the PGA Tour. He shot 74-76 and missed the cut by five. But in three months, he'd won three tournaments. He'd still had fun, but he'd also learned to win. Payne graduated in May with a degree in business. He had no plans to use it. After "he wasted three and a half years of his golfing career" not caring enough about golf, as his coach complained, Payne was ready to pour himself into the game.

"I just decided to play to win," he said. "I used to get down on myself and get mad. I don't do it anymore."

Payne entered and lost a number of amateur tournaments in the summer of '79. He qualified for the 156-player field in the Missouri Golf Association amateur championship at Wolf Creek Golf Links, a sturdy and male-only private club in Olathe, Kansas, across the state line from Kansas City. He won the low-score medal in stroke play— five-over 149—and roared all the way to the match-play final. His opponent: Jim Holtgrieve, ten years older than Payne, the reigning Missouri Amateur champion, a man who had qualified for the 1978 U.S. Open and had just played on the winning Walker Cup team with Hal Sutton that beat the Europeans at Muirfield in East Lothian, Scotland. Payne was neither intimidated nor impressed.

"If I didn't think I was the best player in the state, I wouldn't be out here," he said.

Holtgrieve was one of the finest amateur players in Missouri, a man who would later play in the Masters and on the senior tour, and captain Walker Cup teams in 2011 and 2013. He knew and often competed against Bill Stewart and the other great players in the state. Like the Stewarts, Holtgrieve was a shot-maker at heart. He learned the game at Westborough Country Club in St. Louis, a tight course hard along a railroad track, a place where he had to think his way through a round. He was skilled enough in 1979 to consider the one-iron the best club in his bag. Tom O'Toole, a future president of the USGA, carried that bag at Wolf Creek.

On the eve of the final match, Payne saw Holtgrieve and his caddie walking through the Wolf Creek parking lot.

"Bring your Walker Cup game tomorrow, fat boy," Payne barked.

The remark didn't sit well with Holtgrieve or O'Toole. Words were exchanged, and O'Toole had to defuse a potential fistfight. The episode hinted at the side of Payne that would color his reputation for many years on the PGA Tour. It violated the decorum of golf, that spirit of grace and gallant sportsmanship perpetuated through the generations by the public examples of Francis Ouimet, Bobby Jones, Byron Nelson, Arnold Palmer, Jack Nicklaus, and Tom Watson. Holtgrieve had seen the seamy side of Payne in his semifinal match against Mark Hanrahan, an SMU teammate with Payne, the day before. After winning his own semifinal, Payne had caddied for Hanrahan in the four sudden-death holes of his semifinal match. He'd laughed at Holtgrieve's poor shots. He'd cheered even passable ones by Hanrahan as if he'd just won the national championship.

The tension carried over to the next day. It was a hundred degrees outside and humid. Payne reported to the first tee for the final match, looked Holtgrieve in the eye, and said, "I'm going to beat you today, and I'm going to beat you bad." It was poor form, to be sure, but Payne did what he said he would, winning the first five holes and beating Holtgrieve by the astounding match-play score of eight and seven. Holtgrieve admitted that Payne had rattled his focus. He would always regret that lapse. Sometime later, Bill Stewart told Holtgrieve, "I'm sorry it happened that way." The father had regrets of his own.

Bill Stewart had won the Missouri Amateur in 1953 and '57, finishing his career with a 45-18 record in match play. Regardless of his behavior, his son was the champion now. The achievement meant even more when Bill Stewart captured the Missouri Senior that year. Bill Stewart looked at his son and thought he saw the kind of future he had had to sacrifice for his family. He hoped the twenty-two-year-old man he'd raised could accomplish in golf what he wished he'd had the talent and time to try. He hoped, also, that he would learn to do it with humility and grace.

Payne failed to qualify that fall for the PGA Tour, which at the time granted the twenty-five lowest scorers and ties in Q School membership for the next season. He returned to Springfield, worked a couple of retail sales jobs, and kept his game sharp with Sam Reynolds, Sam's daughter, Cathy, and the other better players at Hickory who didn't blanch at a hefty Nassau and some side bets. Payne considered a return to the PGA Tour–qualifying tournament in the spring. But he was too impatient to wait. In February 1980, after his father and five other men formed a syndicate to finance his trip overseas, Payne left the Missouri Ozarks for an eleven-week tournament schedule in Asia, where he would learn to travel, broaden his world, meet his wife, and win. It was the best decision he could've made.

Payne joined a handful of other American players on what was known as the Asian Golf Circuit (it later became the Asian Tour), including Terry Anton, a fellow prankster and a former University of Florida golfer Payne had befriended over the summer in Arizona. The two of them often roomed together in distant exotic cities as the tournament circuit swept through Hong Kong, India, Indonesia, Malaysia, the Philippines, South Korea, Singapore, Taiwan, and Thailand. They competed each week for a $10,000 first prize, playing in the presence of kings and fearing the appearance of cobras, bellowing the theme song to the campy 1960s television show *Gilligan's Island* on a charter bus to tour the Taj Mahal, making a lot of noise and fun wherever they stepped. The tournaments they played were attended well. Golf was a curiosity in those countries, where only the elite were entitled to the few courses, all of them private, and spectators were eager to see how and why men with sticks swatted balls through the jungle to faraway holes. Payne and Anton usually finished high in the money. And Payne, especially, learned a different and necessary kind of golf for an aspiring PGA Tour player. He'd grown up in a part of the world with bent grass greens—the softest and most uniform putting surface a boy with a talent for the game could ever experience. Bent grass held golf shots like no other grass. The way Payne learned to play, the game was an airborne puzzle to solve, and shots unobstructed by low-hanging limbs were played high, even the short ones close to the green. If he could, Payne wanted to watch the ball float.

But Asian golf asked for something else. Early on the circuit, Payne noticed how players from Asia or Australia played low, running shots into the greens, better to stay out of the wind, and better to eliminate the many risks of trying to loft a pitch when bumping a chip with a lower-lofted club would do. His competitors played a ground game. Payne decided he should be able to, too. He and Anton practiced piercing little shots that scampered to the hole instead of flying to it. They studied contours and slopes for clues to how their balls would roll on the grainy greens of Royal Calcutta in India or Royal Selangor in Kuala Lumpur. The new shot made them better, it made them more complete, and it prepared them more to make the step from the Asian Golf Circuit to the PGA Tour.

Payne won no tournaments that year in Asia. But he did meet a twenty-year-old Australian named Tracey Ferguson, who was on a three-week holiday with her older brother, Michael, who played professional golf on the Australian Tour. Michael Ferguson entered the Malaysian Open and invited his sister along. They went to a cocktail party before the tournament. Tracey saw Payne across the room. She followed him to Singapore the next week.

Payne had had serious girlfriends, but something about Tracey was different. She had a silly side, as Payne did, but she seemed more grounded than he was and more of a realist. She calmed him. She exuded a sense of reason and a temperament of evenness that he craved. She impressed him as rational and reasonable, with immense commitment, dedication, and patience. Sometimes Payne found it hard to think past the next morning. In Tracey, he found someone who didn't just take the long view. She lived for it.

Tracey returned to Australia, and Payne returned to golf. He finished the season with enough points on the Order of Merit to qualify for a kind of Asian Circuit Tour championship in Japan. He still hadn't won when he left Japan, but his game had matured, and he felt good about another run at Q School. He entered in the fall of 1980. He failed again. He told a family friend that he wanted to give it one more try. Then he set out for Australia.

Payne played the Australian Tour in October and November, partly for the competition, partly so he could see Tracey again. She joined him in Sydney, introduced him to her parents on the Gold Coast, and caddied for him at the Australian Open, where another dashing and charismatic golfer with a future on the PGA Tour won at the Lakes Golf Club in New South Wales. Payne couldn't compete yet with the likes of Greg Norman. He finished well behind him in his first Australian Open. But he was less absorbed by that than he was his affection. "We make a good team," he told Tracey that week.

Payne invited her home. He drove her from Los Angeles to Springfield to spend Christmas with his family. Her introduction to Payne's father was harsh; Bill Stewart wanted no distractions to keep his son from playing better golf and from preparing for that last effort at Q School in Lake Buena Vista, Florida. He considered a woman a distraction. When he looked at Tracey, Bill Stewart didn't see a source of happiness and inspiration for his son. He saw a threat.

"Don't think you're anything special," he told her. "Payne has had plenty of girlfriends."

But those girlfriends didn't go back to Asia with Payne Stewart in the winter of 1981, which is exactly what Tracey did. A wedding now seemed inevitable. Payne proposed to her over dinner in Malaysia. Her new fiancé won twice: the Indian Open and the Indonesian Open, his first big four-round titles as a twenty-four-year-old professional. When he left the Asian Golf Circuit for another Q School that June, Payne had enough in earnings to pay his debts to his sponsors in Missouri, enough confidence to arrive at the Palm Course at Walt Disney World ("Where dreams come true!") with the conviction that he could earn his tour card, and the grade of game it would take to do it. He went

74-69-70 in the first three rounds. He shot 69 in the last. Anton shot 71. Both of them finished at six-under 282, two shots inside the qualifying number. The friends who'd traveled across the world to play tournament golf would now travel to Bay Hill, Colonial, Doral, Harbour Town, Pebble Beach, Riviera, and, with a little luck, U.S. Open venues like Oak Hill, Olympic, Shinnecock Hills, even Pinehurst No. 2.

The symmetry of his career had been established. Payne would make his last PGA Tour start right where it began: at dream-delivering Disney, three days before he would rise early, kiss his children goodbye, drive to the Orlando airport, and carry his golf bag to the Learjet 35 with N47BA painted on its tail. His 465th tournament on tour would bring another spray of public controversy, contrition, and humiliation. It also would be remembered as the last time a golf audience, and many of Payne's friends on tour, saw him alive. Payne was to become a starkly different man by the end of that crowning season of golf.

But now, after he signed his fourth-round scorecard for Q School and reflected on what he had done that day in 1981, Payne thought about his father.

He thought about his friends at Hickory Hills, and his first teacher, Sam Reynolds, and Cathy Reynolds, and Charlie Adams and Lamar Haynes and Mark Hanrahan from SMU. He imagined what it would be like to scatter a bag of practice balls next to Nicklaus or Palmer or Watson, to see a locker with his name on it, to hear the starter announce his presence to polite applause, to mark a birdie putt on the seventy-second hole with everything at stake, maybe even a Masters jacket or a Claret Jug. It was a good time to think and imagine. The end of Q School was the place for that kind of innocence, but only for the fortunate few. Payne had failed twice. He now was one of them. He dialed Tracey and took a breath.

"I made it," he said when she answered the telephone on the far side of the world. "We're on the PGA Tour."

Part Two

PEBBLE

Third round, Pebble Beach Golf Links, Pebble Beach,
California, February 6, 1999

CHAPTER FIVE

Payne rushed home to Springfield. He gathered his sponsors, who agreed to provide $1,000 a week for travel, hotels, and tournament entry fees. Payne hoped to play fourteen tournaments through October, starting right away. He submitted his entry into the Danny Thomas Memphis Classic, once known as the Memphis Open, and he and his fiancée set out for Tennessee.

The PGA Tour of the early 1980s was no place for the weak of will. The tour had no full exemption for graduates of Q School, so they had to try to qualify each week on the Monday before each tournament: an eighteen-hole, win-or-go-home grind from which only a handful of players earned a spot in the field. The stakes were paralyzing. While every shot certainly mattered in a seventy-two-hole tournament over four days, a sloppy pitch or a botched three-foot putt in a Monday qualifier meant the difference between the chance to earn enough money to cover expenses that week or earning nothing—which, to a young rookie like Payne, meant losing money he couldn't afford to lose. Professional competitive golf always had been a pristine meritocracy. The men and women who built careers in the game did so through sustained excellence under immense pressure with uncanny concentration, with only themselves to hold to account. A player who didn't do everything well—from executing shots to maintaining confidence to managing ever-swirling emotions—was a player who didn't last. Payne thought he understood that as he drove that June across Missouri to Memphis, just as he understood another sobering fact of the PGA Tour: Only the top sixty players on the tour earnings list were exempt from one-round qualifying on Mondays. They and the men who won.

Payne felt sure he would win, and soon. But he was about to learn that winning the Missouri Amateur or the Indian Open guaranteed nothing on a merciless PGA Tour led by names like Jack Nicklaus, Arnold Palmer, Gary Player, and Tom Watson. Payne failed to advance from the Monday qualifier in Memphis. He failed a week later to advance to the Western Open in Chicago. He qualified for the Canadian Open in early August but missed the cut. He remained optimistic. He believed in himself. He remembered what his father told him about confidence. Two weeks after his missed cut in Canada, he walked to the first tee of the Monday qualifier in Hartford, Connecticut, with purpose.

Payne qualified that week, too. He also paired rounds of 71-68 to make the thirty-six-hole cut at the Sammy Davis Jr. Greater Hartford Open, his first time playing the weekend as a professional. He finished with a share of fifty-first place. He won $715.50 for the week. He never failed to advance from a Monday qualifier for the rest of the season, and while he missed five cuts, he also tied for fifteenth in Massachusetts and ninth at the Southern Open, a tournament he led by three shots after two rounds, in Columbus, Georgia. Payne made bogeys on the final three holes at the Southern. J. C. Snead passed him to win. The young, chain-smoking Missourian with the blond hair had learned a lot, but not yet how to win. He made $13,400 for the year. He was 160th on the tour earnings list, meaning all that 1982 promised was the numbing reality of Monday qualifiers until he played consistently well enough to earn top-sixty money. He returned to Missouri to plan his wedding and his first full schedule of Mondays on the PGA Tour.

The Stewarts married in Australia, honeymooned in Tahiti, and set out in January for the tournaments on the West Coast. They drove, which gave them time to talk and dream and imagine. Tracey saw herself as an unconditional advocate for her husband: his chief motivator, his source of counsel and confidence, his voice of reason and logic, and his ballast. She was perfect for the man he was. Payne, now almost twenty-five, was supremely talented, but he was not yet a complete player. He tended to be rash, impetuous, moody, juvenile, obstinate, mentally and emotionally scattered. He didn't yet have the maturity required of a champion golfer. She was the counterweight he required. He needed her maturity and wisdom and calmness, especially after missing the first four Monday qualifiers of the season in Arizona, California, and Hawaii.

"We'll get it next week," he told her on a long drive to another Monday qualifier. "We'll work harder."

It was a different kind of work, this pursuit of a career on the unforgiving PGA Tour. It wasn't like it was at SMU. Payne couldn't just ignore his studies and run out to Plano Municipal with Charlie Adams, Mark Hanrahan, and Lamar Haynes with a pack of cigarettes, a sack of beer, and a sleeve of balls to play eighteen holes with abandon, as if nothing mattered, because nothing at that time really did. It wasn't like playing in Asia. The Asian Circuit had great players, but the PGA Tour in 1982 was a special kind of great. Johnny Miller won in San Diego with rounds of 65-67-68-70 on the sturdy South Course at Torrey Pines, drilling his forged irons through the Pacific breeze. Tom Watson, who would go on that summer to win the U.S. Open at Pebble Beach, battered Riviera with rounds of 69-67-68-67 to win the Los Angeles Open. These were serious shot-makers playing divine golf on hostile courses. The symmetry of their tournament scores awed Payne. Their workmanship from tee to green seemed ethereal, like draftsmen with their triangles and scale rulers, but with flourish derived from that delicate sixth sense they called *feel*. Their consistency on the golf course was matched only by their even-tempered deliberation, especially in times of peril. Payne was a long way from Johnny Miller and Tom Watson. Their worst golf was nearer to his best.

Payne was plenty long enough with his steel-shafted wood driver to compete with the Millers and the Nicklauses and the Players and the Watsons. His average drive in 1982 traveled 269 yards—a hefty wallop for the time that ranked ninth on the PGA Tour. But he tended to spray those crucial setup shots more than the best scorers in the game. He missed nearly half of the fairways he played. He missed too many greens in regulation—one in three that year—to have the same number of birdie putts those men had, meaning he leaned far too much on the considerable artistry and range of his short game, diversified in Asia, to get up and in for par. Par wasn't good enough at Torrey Pines or Riviera. Not against shot-makers like Miller and Watson.

Worse yet, Payne wasn't a tour-class putter. His wife recognized that, and she insisted on long hours on the practice green, where she would arrange her husband's wound Titleist balls in a circle around the hole and fetch them—sometimes from the hole, often not—as Payne made his grim way around. He frequently had to force himself to comply with his wife's idea. The monotony and relative inertia of putting practice taxed his attention. He wanted to go out and play, like he did at SMU, when practice felt more like fun than work. But those evenings on the putting green also meant time with his new wife, and her buoying presence made him want to, in his words, work harder. He would learn later to cherish that little putting-circle game with her. That little game would, in 1999, mean everything.

Payne qualified for his first start of 1982 in Miami. He missed the cut. A week later, he advanced to the weekend at Inverrary Country Club in Lauderhill, Florida, in what now is known as the Honda Classic. Payne shot 70-71 to tie for forty-second place. Hale Irwin, another shot-maker from Missouri, shot 67-66 to win. Payne made enough to pay his hotel bill and fill the tank of his Grand Prix. Irwin earned $72,000. Eight strokes—two a round in a four-day tournament—separated Irwin and Payne on that weekend in March: the difference between a couple of drives lost in the rough, one more missed green, and a few mismanaged putts of five or seven or ten feet like the ones Tracey insisted he practice while fighting boredom and dangerous daydreams. Payne was quickly beginning to appreciate the preciousness of a single swing of the club. On to the next Monday qualifier he went.

He was one of fifty players to make the cut in April at the Magnolia Classic, the tournament in Mississippi opposite the Masters. He shot 65-67 in the dense pines of Hattiesburg Country Club.

"My game is just starting to come around, and I'm glad it is," he said.

The newspapers adored him. Wearing his flowing hair parted neatly down the middle (Payne had not yet adopted the signature flat cap and plus fours) and his feelings for all to see, he was a refreshing and intriguing character, animated and demonstrative, and he spoke his mind. "The tour needs more blond-haired, blue-eyed guys," he said in an interview in Hattiesburg—a sure sign he was searching for a way to distinguish himself in the pack. Even after a one-over 71 on Saturday, which put him three strokes behind the leader, the *Clarion-Ledger* in Jackson put his picture on the cover of the sports section. More than six thousand spectators flocked to the tournament to watch the handsome, charismatic Missouri showman lash his way through the final round.

They bore witness to his best. A galvanized Stewart made up five shots on the leader, a faltering Bruce Douglass, with birdies on the sixth, seventh, and eighth holes. He won with a three-under 67. In his first post-round interview as a champion, he didn't mention realized dreams, cosmic meanings, or the culmination of hard work.

"I've got $14,822 and twenty-eight cents," he told the press, citing to the penny the prize for first place.

Because the tournament was scheduled opposite the Masters, the PGA Tour didn't recognize the Magnolia as an official victory, a policy that would later be changed. That meant Payne, even with a trophy of his own, either had to petition sponsors for exemptions at future tournaments or keep entering those exhausting Monday qualifiers. The qualifiers helped to shape him as a player. They required a certain win-or-go-home aggression on the golf course, but also a composite of discretion and acceptance. Payne was still learning how to calculate risk in competition. He was still learning the meaning of a shot that could keep him in a tournament, a shot that could eliminate him altogether, and a shot that could win—the distinctions made, in the right place and at the right time, by champions. Payne was beginning to narrow the important difference between the three.

He continued his good play for the rest of the summer. He missed qualifying for only one tournament and made seven cuts in a row, including a tie for ninth in Memphis, where he had made his professional debut the season before. He began wearing the jaunty plus fours that would define him for the rest of his career. He'd recalled what his father, the salesman, had said: "If you stand out when you go to sell somebody something, they'll remember who you are. But if you come dressed in a boring, navy-blue suit, you'll just be another person in the crowd." Payne wasn't interested in selling anything beyond the impression that he was his own man, confident and assured. The new look was his signature, his brand. It was a bold move for a twenty-five-year-old player who hadn't won an official tournament and struggled to find fairways and convert important putts. But Payne wanted to be noticed. He wanted to be known. And, as his father emphasized, he wanted to be remembered. He ordered his first set of plus fours from a boutique in California. The shipment arrived in time for the final round of the tournament that May in Atlanta. Payne chose lavender, shot a snappy 67, and finished with a share of sixteenth place. Reporters asked him what was behind the new look.

"Clothes help your attitude," Payne said.

These clothes, this new look, would become his signature ensemble for the rest of his days in tournament golf. He certainly appreciated the historical reference to the golden age players like Bobby Jones, but Payne wasn't trying to fool anyone into thinking he was an old soul or a man born too late. He was neither. He was, in fact, a man who lived in and for the moment. The plus fours and flat cap were a costume, a stage ensemble Payne could wrap himself in when it was time to perform and strip when the show was over. He was, in his resplendent garments, a superhero: famous and infamous in character, anonymous when not. The locker room was his telephone booth.

The Stewarts traveled to Coal Valley, Illinois, that July for the Quad Cities Open. Payne was especially excited because his father would be there. He wondered what the man who told him to be remembered would think about the plus fours. He believed he would approve. To really make a statement, Payne decided that week to wear a flat cap. His ensemble was complete.

He opened at Oakwood Country Club with a 66. He shot 71 in the second round to make the cut with ease.

He finished the third round with a clean 68 and a chance. Payne was two strokes behind the three players who held the lead.

That night, he set out his plus fours—lavender, just like the ones that he thought had brought him luck in Atlanta, with matching argyle socks—and tried to quiet his mind, which was a cacophony of doubts, hopes, and self-defeating impulses. He thought about the Magnolia. The victory in Mississippi felt to him like second place, since he'd earned no exemption for winning a tournament opposite the Masters. He was glad the same rule didn't apply to the British Open, which was being contested that week at Royal Troon. Most of the top players were in Scotland, but that didn't bother Payne as much as the nagging impression that his Magnolia Open title was somehow invalid. He went to sleep hoping to validate his second season on the PGA Tour.

Rain fell that night and into the morning. Payne welcomed it. A softer course took pressure off his driver, which he still tended to spray. He birdied the first hole. He made the nine-hole turn at minus three for the final round, eight under for the tournament. He told himself on the eleventh tee that twelve under would win—and that's what he shot, tying the Quad Cities Open record with a 63 that included a streak of birdies at the fifteenth, sixteenth, and seventeenth. Bill Stewart found his son on the eighteenth green, and the two of them cried.

Payne had his validation. He also had his exemption. He would play no more Monday qualifiers in 1982, or ever again. He won $36,000, an original painting, a silver plate, a crystal trophy, and a pendant for his wife. The tournament also gave him a Rolex watch, which he would be wearing on his wrist seventeen years later, when he boarded the Learjet. The trophy, valued at $2,000, was an eagle in flight.

"We live in a car," Payne told reporters after his round, "so I don't know what we'll do with that."

"That's all nice," Tracey added, "but all I was thinking about was the exemption."

Her husband would never wonder again about where or when he could play. The Missouri showman had his stage.

Payne finished the 1982 season thirty-ninth on the earnings list, assuring his exemption for '83. Using his childhood home in Springfield as their base, the Stewarts set out in January to play every tournament through the end of March, completing the swings in California and Florida. Their decision was a good one. Payne had five top-twenty-five finishes, including the tournaments at Pebble Beach and Lauderhill, Florida, where he would continue to enjoy great success. He qualified for his first Masters Tournament. He played in his first PGA Championship. He missed the cut that week at Riviera, won by Hal Sutton, with whom he was becoming friendly, given the proximity of their lockers, assigned alphabetically each week. Payne tied for third in Milwaukee and fourth in Columbus, Georgia, and won the October tournament in Orlando—at Disney again, that good-luck golf charm for Payne—with rounds of 69-64-69-67. He no longer needed a wardrobe to be noticed. The showman from Springfield was now being remembered for his scores.

The Stewarts moved to Orlando, a city popular among professional golfers for its abundance of private country clubs, agreeable year-round climate, and ease of travel from its airport. They purchased a house along the twelfth hole at Bay Hill. Payne's father disapproved. He thought the couple should stay in Springfield, where the Stewarts were from, after all. Springfield was home, Bill Stewart insisted, for him and his sisters and his lifelong friends at Hickory Hills. He felt abandoned by his son. He felt threatened by his Australian daughter-in-law, who seemed, to him, to be pulling Payne from his Missouri roots and distracting him from being an even greater golfer. But his son wasn't being pulled. He was pulling himself. Now an established tour star, he wanted everything the life of a star could offer, and he had the means to make it happen. Tour stars didn't live in Springfield, Missouri. They lived where the other stars lived and played and reveled in their own communal celebrity.

Payne played another fine season in '84. He failed to win, but he came close at the Colonial, the Memorial, and the Buick Open, and he finished third in Las Vegas. His best chance came in Fort Worth, where he led by a stroke on the seventy-second hole at Colonial Country Club but pushed his drive badly to the right. He made bogey. He lost in a playoff to Peter Jacobsen, who'd told reporters the day before that he was playing for his father, who'd been diagnosed with cancer. When he shook Jacobsen's hand, Payne pulled him close and told him, "That one was for your dad."

There were unpredictable and untenable sides to Payne, now twenty-seven years old and consumed with himself and his image, but also touchingly sensitive to the personal crises of others. His peers on the tour saw him as an attention-monger and self-promoter. His closest friends and family knew him as a convivial soul with a good heart and little social restraint. While not yet the enigma he would become in his thirties, he projected a chilly aloofness in the heat of competition, but unlike other steely and self-absorbed players in the game—Ben Hogan, famously—his preening flamboyance and air of grandiosity made it hard for his peers to accept him, especially because he hadn't established a record deserving of their respect. Players admired Hogan for his intensity. They respected his quiet, grim countenance on the course, where he wore muted grays and no expression on his face. Hogan didn't seek to be noticed or remembered. He'd sought only to win, and he had: sixty-four times, with nine major championships. Payne had won only three trophies on the PGA Tour. And only two of them counted.

Professional golf celebrated amplified personalities, but only on the condition that they win, especially in the four majors. Walter Hagen arrived at tournaments in a Pierce-Arrow with an open bottle of champagne between his legs. He won forty-five times, and eleven majors. Arnold Palmer built an entire legacy through his gregarious, welcoming warmth. He won sixty-two titles, including seven majors. The debonair Seve Ballesteros, one of the most imaginative and intuitive players in the history of golf, won fifty-nine tournaments worldwide, among them two Masters and three British Opens. He was a menace to the Americans in the Ryder Cup.

Payne had the Quad Cities Open and the Disney. He had never factored in a major or earned consideration for a Ryder Cup team.

A month after his son's loss at the '84 Colonial, Payne's father was told he had cancer. It was a devastating form of the disease: in his bone marrow, the cause of a chronic sluggishness Bill Stewart had been feeling. The prognosis was poor, with no cure, and by the time Payne told him that Tracey was pregnant with their first child, his father was two weeks from death.

Payne chose to confront the loss of his father—the man who'd introduced him to golf, taught him to shape shots, and impressed upon him the importance of being remembered—by not really confronting it at all. He didn't cry at the funeral. He didn't mourn with his wife. He retreated into his golf. It was all he knew to do. Out on the range at Bay Hill, Payne worked through his grief by pounding balls, the one experience he'd shared all his life with the most important person in his life. Payne could be with his father through golf. He could feel his presence on the course. He would long regret that his father never again got to see him win, especially in 1999.

The next two seasons on tour expired without another title for Payne. He made plenty of money, enough to keep his exemption. But he couldn't win.

He rallied in the final round in 1985 at Pebble Beach for a share of fifth. He tied for fourth in Houston. In May, at the Byron Nelson in

Irving, Texas, he brought a two-shot lead to the last hole, but made a double-bogey six with two shots out of bunkers and three putts on the green. The three putts alone were hard to accept; putting, again, had contributed to the self-inflicted sabotage. But what really bothered him was the decision, born of inexperience and hubris and pride, to attempt an aggressive play from the fairway bunker. He'd fired right at the flagstick. He'd found another bunker. He would, in time, learn the value of prudence, but he was still too stubborn and reckless in 1985, still enamored of the reward and dismissive of the risk. Payne lost on the first hole of the ensuing playoff to a Bob Eastwood bogey. The CBS television cameras followed him and Tracey, holding hands and barely speaking, as they trudged through shin-high grass. It was a picture of despair for everyone to see.

"There goes Payne Stewart," said Pat Summerall, the hole announcer at the eighteenth. "Do you think that's not a lonely walk?"

"Defeat," said Ken Venturi of the CBS broadcast team, "is always a lonely walk."

Later that season, Tracey called an old friend in Orlando. Paul Celano, the director of golf at Grand Cypress, had known Payne since 1983, when he and other tour players, such as Greg Norman and Nick Price, would come to Celano's course to practice and play. Celano knew a lot of people in golf and a lot about golf. Tracey thought he might have answers her husband needed.

"What are we going to do?" she asked him.

Celano introduced Payne to E. Harvie Ward, the 1955 and '56 U.S. Amateur champion who also lived in Bay Hill, and while Payne wasn't exactly searching for a teacher, he soon knew he'd found the one he needed. Ward reminded Payne of his father. He was of the old school, the feel era: all feet and eyes and fingertips. He didn't clutter Payne's mind with angles or positions or complicated sequences that felt to Payne like white noise. ("He had a swing like a Rolls-Royce," Ward would tell friends. "All you had to do was be sure that the water and oil levels were right, and that there was gasoline in the car.")

Ward learned soon enough that Payne resisted changes to his swing. But he was willing to work on his attitude. He struck Ward as immature. He seemed to take the game too lightly, as if it were one of those weekdays in Dallas when he was at SMU and the only stakes were beer money. Payne wanted to have fun when he should've wanted to work. Ward tried to help Payne see golf as his job. "Like a doctor who goes to the hospital to operate on somebody," Ward told him.

Ward also introduced him to Dick Coop, a professor at the University of North Carolina and one of the early golf and sports psychologists, who suggested to Payne they work to better channel his focus, attention, and concentration. Celano knew Coop from his time as a golf professional in North Carolina. He respected him for being caring but blunt. In their first meeting, Coop told Payne he was "prickly, cocky, arrogant, and brash." Payne did not quarrel with the doctor. He asked Coop what he could do to be less provocative and more purposeful. The two began work on a pre-shot routine.

Coop believed Payne had some form of attention deficit disorder. Without a system or structure, Payne had nothing to guide him into a shot, no pattern or process to lock his wandering concentration the same way every time. Coop suggested he find a spot on the ground—a random blade of grass, an old divot, an abandoned tee—a foot or so in front of his ball and aim for it. That intermediate target gave Payne a focal point, a specific goal, to quiet his mind.

The lonely walks mounted as he tried to incorporate this new and unfamiliar structure. He tied for fifth in the U.S. Open. He missed two short putts late in the British Open at Royal St. George's and lost by a stroke to Sandy Lyle. He took second in 1986 at Pebble Beach and, as he had two years earlier, Colonial. He played his way into the last pairing at the U.S. Open at Shinnecock Hills. His fellow competitor: Raymond Floyd. He wilted in the presence of the forty-three-year-old veteran known for his imposing glare. Payne tied for sixth—another top-ten finish in a major, and yet another loss.

"I'm going to be around a long time," he told reporters, who were unsure if Payne really believed his words. "If I keep contending in these major events, I'm going to eventually win."

Payne had three second-place finishes that year, sixteen in the top ten, and $535,389 in earnings, a tour record for most money earned without a victory. He had the reputation of someone who could play well enough to keep his exemption on the PGA Tour, but not well enough to win. Jack Nicklaus, his Ryder Cup captain in Payne's first appearance in the matches in 1987, criticized him after the US team lost at Muirfield Village. "Look at you, Payne Stewart. You make all this money on tour, but how many tournaments have you won? Why don't you win more?" Payne had no answer. Even his wife questioned his flagging desire. She confronted him after he missed the cut at the Canadian Open.

"Why don't you just quit if you're not happy?" Tracey asked.

He actually considered it. Payne thought about taking off the second half of the '86 season, to get away from the lost chances and the lonely walks and the scalding glare of those who thought he underachieved. He was tired of being known for not winning. It wasn't enough anymore to simply be remembered. But golf was all he knew.

Validation returned in the spring of 1987. After a pair of second places at Pebble Beach and the Honda Classic in Lauderhill, Payne traveled to Orlando for the tournament at Bay Hill, his home course. He paused each day at his house on No. 12 to kiss his sixteen-month-old daughter, Chelsea, through the wrought-iron fence in his backyard. He shot 69-67-63-65 to win by three. There was no lonely walk now.

Payne later donated his entire first-place earnings of $108,000 to build a home in Orlando for families of cancer patients. It was a gesture made in the spirit of his father, but it also changed the way he was perceived. George White, a reporter with the *Orlando Sentinel,* wrote: "A lot of people talk about helping others. Few actually do something about it. Occasionally one of those really concerned is an athlete." White went on to praise Payne as a "doer." He mentioned the memory of Bill Stewart.

"I wanted to do something that would show people how much I thought of my father," Payne told him. He added, "I wanted everyone to know that golfers are people, too. We can be as thoughtful as anybody."

Payne was on the verge of greatness. He believed it. His wife believed it. Other players sensed it.

"Payne Stewart is the fiercest competitor on tour," Mark Wiebe said.

"Payne Stewart is this game's next great superstar," Fred Couples said.

"The man's game has no weakness," Lee Trevino said.

Payne made twenty-five cuts in twenty-seven starts in 1988. He signed a three-year, $675,000 contract with NFL Properties that covered his flat caps, plus fours, shirts, socks, and rainwear. Payne joined a band, Jake Trout and the Flounders, with Peter Jacobsen, Larry Rinker, and Mark Lye, and played harmonica, not so much with skill but with zest (the pop singer Huey Lewis, whose music Payne liked, once called Payne an "eighth-handicap" on the instrument). The band filled a role in Payne's life. It gave him another, literal, stage. It gave him another way to perform, another crowd to entertain. In 1988, Payne also became a father. He and Tracey had their son, Aaron, and now it was getting harder to leave home for long stretches. He missed a month of competition early in 1989 after doctors in California found degenerative disks in his back, a chronic condition related to a fall from a diving board as a child. He withdrew from the Pebble Beach Pro-Am and Los Angeles Open. He committed to an exercise routine.

"In the past I exercised only if I was hurting," he told a columnist in Dallas. "Now I'm doing it every day."

Then he won again. He shot 65-67-67-69 in the 1989 MCI Heritage at Harbour Town, the coastal South Carolina course designed by Pete Dye and both celebrated and despised for its small greens and exacting shot values. It was the kind of venue that brought out the best in the shot-makers, these men now in their thirties who could see, in the younger players rising to the tour, that a new, more aggressive way of playing was nigh. Payne already had made one concession to the changing times—he'd adopted the Wilson Whale driver, one of the earliest oversized drivers on the market. The club, manufactured by Louisville Golf but sold under the iconic Wilson badge, dwarfed the other persimmon drivers on tour, more reminiscent of the titanium drivers to come than the solid-block heads like the Wilson Staff. Payne won the MCI with the Whale and its distinct red Fire Stick graphite shaft. He would never go back to steel shafts and small wooden drivers.

As the season wore on, Payne, thirty-two, kept nipping at the lead. He took third at the Memorial. He shared second in Michigan. He tied for eighth in the British Open at Royal Troon—club motto: "As much by skill as by strength"—where Payne completed three rounds two shots out of the lead but let another major slip on the last nine holes. His wife said nothing to him for most of the drive back to their rental on the Ayrshire Coast of Scotland. And then:

"When is this nightmare going to end?"

Tracey was tired of watching her husband lose majors on Sundays. She demanded more out of him at those career-defining moments. Her words stayed with him. He wondered if he could keep his momentum and earn a spot on his second Ryder Cup team. More than that, he tried to convince himself that his legacy should mean more than a flat cap, plus fours, and failure in the four tournaments that mattered the most. In August, feeling fresh and energized and empowered by the ambitions of a man who fancied that luck was about to touch him in a colossal way, he and his Wilson Whale struck out for suburban Chicago and the seventy-first PGA Championship, the last major of the '80s.

CHAPTER SIX

The PGA of America issued more than six hundred media credentials for its marquee championship in '89. It was a record for the PGA. Interest was high because the last major of the season, typically contested at older and pedigreed private clubs, had been awarded four years earlier to Kemper Lakes, a public daily-fee course that had been open for less than a decade. It was a big, broad-shouldered, and contemporary golf course with 7,197 yards of bent grass fairways and bluegrass roughs, humid and marshy, with massive greens. Water occupied more than one hundred acres on eleven of its eighteen holes. Some honey locusts grew on the margins, but Kemper Lakes generally was more open than most PGA Championship venues, making it vulnerable to the wind. Some players in the field thought it lacked the prestige becoming of a PGA Championship. Others enjoyed the novelty of playing a modern course in greater Chicago, which had last hosted a PGA in 1961. "We like to move around to exciting golf courses," PGA president Mickey Powell said when Kemper Lakes was awarded the championship.

Larry Mize, the 1987 Masters winner, arrived early to play a practice round on the Sunday before the championship. Mize was thirty, on the younger end of his generation, a wily player who drove the ball with accuracy but not length, hit a lot of greens in regulation, and scrambled well when he didn't. Kemper Lakes suited a player like Mize. The spacious green complexes in particular required deft shot-making, soft hands, and creativity. Their distinct tiers, lobes, and petals favored the player who knew how to hit his spots.

"I like it, and I'm looking forward to playing it again," Mize observed after rain chased him from his practice round. "It's got a couple of real good holes coming in at sixteen and seventeen."

The closing holes at Kemper Lakes wandered through, along, and into water, which roiled in whitecaps when the inevitable gusts rose. A harassing lake lined the right edge of the fairway at the par-four sixteenth and curled around the green of the par-three seventeenth. The par-four eighteenth, a contemporary version of the classic cape hole, wrapped around the water like a thrown boomerang, with bunkers on the far side of the fairway, both for aiming purposes and for penalizing drives that missed their marks. It was target golf from the tee.

That style of golf favored veteran players like Mize, Payne, and others of their era who were trying to win the last major of the decade.

The week before, Payne had played two days of good golf in Memphis, posting rounds of 67-69 at the St. Jude Classic. He faltered on the weekend. He shot 75-76 to drift into a tie for fifty-third. But he didn't fret. He'd been in contention all summer. He'd improved his driving accuracy to the point that he was in the fairway 70 percent of the time, and he now ranked thirty-second on tour in greens in regulation. He was putting well, too. His scoring average hovered around 70, one of the five best on tour.

He opened the championship with a 74. No one paid much attention. The afternoon belonged to Arnold Palmer, who dazzled his gallery with five straight birdies, seven in total, and a first-round score of four-under 68, two shots behind the leaders, Leonard Thompson and Mike Reid. It felt like time had been rewound. Palmer was fifty-nine and slowing. He hadn't played a full season in years, and he'd made only one cut on the tour since 1986. He'd last won in 1973. That was his sixty-second title in a career that included four Masters wins, two British Opens, and a lone U.S. Open. He'd never won the PGA Championship in thirty-one attempts. Now he was in the post-round interview room, being asked if this might, miraculously, be the year.

Palmer told reporters he doubted it. In fact, he said, he'd considered skipping the championship because he'd been playing so awfully.

"I thought about not playing and taking someone's spot," Palmer said. "But I felt I could contribute something. When I can't, I won't play any longer."

The first round at Kemper Lakes in '89 was a legitimate occasion for true fans of American golf to celebrate, to flirt with possibilities. There was Palmer, in his straw fedora, with his first sub-70 score in the PGA Championship in a dozen years. Tom Watson shot 67. Three weeks from turning forty, he had eight majors but, like Palmer, had never won the PGA. A stroke behind him: Jack Nicklaus, who would turn fifty soon. Spectators watching his play that day wondered if he possibly could reprise his Sunday at the 1986 Masters. The grounds rippled with anticipation for Friday morning.

Rain returned for the second round. The tournament was delayed for nearly two hours. Palmer faded. Watson and Nicklaus played well enough, but too many others in the field were better, and the two titans never factored on the weekend. Reid stretched his lead to two. Payne shot 66 to climb to within seven.

He followed with a clean 69 on Saturday. He had ten players ahead of him with a round to go. It looked like another good finish without a win in a major for the showman in the plus fours and flat cap who couldn't explain why he didn't win more.

Payne chose the colors of the Chicago Bears for the final round. He played the front at even-par 36, capped by three irritating putts on the ninth that put him five strokes behind Reid. Payne saw Jerry Pate, who was broadcasting on the course for ABC, on the walk to the tenth tee.

"If I can shoot 31 on the back nine, I could have a chance to win this thing," he told Pate.

It seemed like another bold pronouncement, another empty assertion, another case of spouted words he could not back up. That chance would depend on luck: a calamitous, uncharacteristic collapse by Reid.

The thirty-five-year-old from Utah, one of the shortest drivers on tour (247.4 yards off the tee) but also the most accurate (almost eight of ten fairways on average, ranking second on the tour), played a cautious, reserved style of golf with his bag full of Wilson forged blades, Hogan Apex persimmon woods, and balata-covered balls. Payne would need big mistakes from a man who didn't typically make them.

Payne shot that 31 on the back nine at Kemper Lakes. He birdied four of the final five holes. Three groups behind him, Reid bogeyed the 469-yard sixteenth after his drive found water and doubled the seventeenth with a poor pitch and pitifully rushed short putt for bogey. The two holes Mize had noted after his rainy practice round a week earlier had turned the championship in the favor of Payne, who rolled a twelve-foot putt for birdie three on the eighteenth hole and crouched in celebration as his ball tumbled into the cup.

"Never a doubt!" ABC color analyst Bob Rosburg told his audience as the putt fell. "Right in the middle!"

For the first time in his career, Payne had the clubhouse lead in a major. Now he had to wait.

But Payne did more than wait. The cameras followed him to the scoring tent, where he made a spectacle of himself as Reid, one shot behind Payne, prepared to play the final hole. Payne flitted among the officials in the tent, giggling and gesticulating with nervous energy, practically performing for the cameras. Reid drove to the fairway. Payne motioned to the Chicago Bears logo on his shirt and made a face. Reid struck his approach, a five-iron to eight feet. Payne raced to the cooler and gulped a cup of water, chewing something furiously. He seemed unable to stand still. When Reid missed his putt to tie, Payne rushed outside.

Paul Azinger, who'd missed the cut, was watching the broadcast while talking to his father on the telephone.

"Does this look as bad as I think it looks?" he asked. He already knew the answer.

Back on the eighteenth green, Reid could barely process what had just happened. But he saw Payne ahead, between the green and the scoring tent, and thought about the scene at the Byron Nelson in 1985, after the playoff loss to Bob Eastwood. The image of Payne and his wife on their lonely walk through the shin-high grass gave Reid an odd sense of comfort. He convinced himself that Payne deserved this moment and marched to sign his card. He and Payne embraced. "This is what the game of golf is all about," Rosburg told his television audience.

At his post-round press conference, a tearful Reid had to pause six times to gather himself. Part of his anguish came from his memories of the Masters that year. He'd held the final-round lead until the fifteenth hole, where he dumped his third shot into the water and, eventually, lost to Nick Faldo. Part of it came from the way he'd lost the PGA Championship—with a ball in the hazard on the sixteenth from the second-most accurate driver on tour, after all, and a short putt on the seventeenth missed in careless haste—and part of it came from the swiftness of his collapse. But another part of it had to have come from watching Payne celebrate so lustily at his expense.

"Sports is like life with the volume turned up," Reid told reporters.

He sighed often. He seemed damaged but determined to mask it as best he could. Richard Mudry, a columnist for the *Tampa Tribune,* would return to his desk and write: "I've been around some great collapses in recent years—Greg Norman, Seve Ballesteros, and Tom Kite coming most to mind—but never had I seen a player more publicly devastated than Reid."

"Life goes on," Reid said. "One of these days I'll get there."

But he wouldn't. The quiet, reflective Reid, who spoke in almost a whisper, never would win a major championship. He later would recall the final round at Kemper Lakes with a wistful resignation, not so much about his late-round loss but about the way Payne further damaged his reputation by acting up for the television cameras in the scoring tent instead of conducting himself with more restraint. ("He wasn't being his best self then," Reid would say, nearly twenty years removed from that day.)

The reporters gathered for his post-round interview watched Reid leave the room and felt the weight of his own culpability remain like a scent. It was clear to them that this was a tournament outcome dictated by negligence: it was a story of failure more so than success. Payne had shot a spectacular 67 to finish four rounds at twelve under par. That score won. But there was a sense among the press, including many veteran reporters who admired Payne for his golf but not his personality, that Reid was more responsible for that winning score than Payne was.

And then the winner bounced in.

"Man!" Payne announced. "This is unbelievable!"

His tone chilled the room. It seemed out of place, like a prank at a funeral. While answering questions, Payne said he felt badly for Reid and that he was as surprised as anyone by his double bogey five on the seventeenth hole.

"But I'm not going to kid you about how I feel," he said. "His misfortune is my gain."

The reporters were aghast.

Payne finally had his first major. He'd won $200,000, secured his place on the Ryder Cup team, and avoided another lonely walk. But when he admitted that he'd prayed for victory—"Lord, how about some good stuff for Payne Stewart this time?" he said he'd petitioned while cavorting in the scoring tent—the mood in his press conference darkened even more. An hour earlier, Payne had the chance to begin to repair his image. Instead, he'd damaged it more.

Peter Jacobsen, who'd tied for twenty-seventh at Kemper Lakes, found Payne later at a private reception for the winner of the Wanamaker Trophy. They'd become friends since their duel at Colonial and closer through their gigs as Jake Trout and the Flounders at golf tournaments. Jacobsen had seen all the sides of Payne, from his touching gesture after the playoff in Fort Worth to his donation after Bay Hill to the uneasy scene now at Kemper Lakes. He felt he needed to intervene.

Jacobsen asked Payne to meet him in the men's room. He locked the door. He grabbed Payne by his shirt collar and pressed him into a wall.

"Stop!" Jacobsen demanded. "Look. You did not win this tournament. Mike Reid lost it."

Payne flew to Oregon hours later for the Fred Meyer Challenge, a popular charity golf outing at Portland Golf Club hosted by Jacobsen and attended by the glitterati of golf. Payne took to the stage for an auction Monday night after too many cocktails and too much haughtiness in his glow of glory. Holding the trophy he'd won the day before. He looked directly at Palmer and said, "Arnold, don't you wish you had one of these?"

Palmer and the rest of the room forced a laugh.

Payne rarely spoke of the lecture he got from Jacobsen at Kemper Lakes, but it left the impression Jacobsen intended. Many years later, Payne would approach Reid at a tournament and confess his regret. He would say he wasn't the champion he wanted to be when he'd gotten caught up in the moment at Kemper Lakes. He would say he still needed to work on the man he wanted to be.

Payne played on his second Ryder Cup team in September. He lost his singles match to José María Olazábal, the US team tied Europe, and the cup remained overseas for the third consecutive session, now six years running. In October, at the season-ending tour championship (known then as the Nabisco Championship), Payne shot 66 in the final round at Harbour Town with a three-putt bogey on the last hole. He went to the fifth playoff of his career, this one against Tom Kite, the only player who could pass him for the season earnings title and the $175,000 bonus that came with it. Payne missed a four-foot putt in sudden death. He was so incensed by the effort that, in self-absorbed haste, he barely shook hands with the champion, mustering only a half-hearted grasp. It was another stain on his fragile reputation for substandard sportsmanship and another lonely walk after coming so close. Payne won $376,000 for being runner-up and finished the season with $1,201,301 in earnings.

"Ain't life a mess," he said. "I'm complaining and I just made $376,000."

Payne did an interview at the end of 1989 with his hometown newspaper, the *Springfield News-Leader*. Even though he was growing more mistrustful of the local and regional media along the tournament trail, he made a point of talking to the Springfield reporters, now that he lived so far away, so his friends from the neighborhood and from Hickory Hills could hear straight from him what it was like to be a famous celebrity golfer winning millions of dollars in fanciful outfits no one else dared wear.

He mentioned to reporter Scott Puryear his deep regrets about the Ryder Cup tie. He called his disappointment at the Nabisco one of the worst of his career. But he also said he anticipated the coming season in a way he hadn't in many years. He said he'd lost fifteen pounds that season through exercise. He'd been at home in Orlando since the Nabisco, considering new sponsorship deals and other business invitations that typically come the way of a major champion, especially one so telegenic and popular among the public. He planned a full schedule in 1990: twenty-six starts, from January in California through October in Texas, where the tour championship would be played that season. Payne was feeling good, playing well, and happy with his life, even if it meant less time at home with his wife and growing children. He felt he had no choice if he wanted to be the best. Such was the sacrifice of playing to win on the PGA Tour.

"I think it could be my time," he told Puryear. "It's like, hey, I am better than everybody. So why can't I beat them all the time?"

He thought for a moment.

"I think the '90s could be really awesome," Payne said.

Payne tied for tenth in the first event of the new decade, the Tournament of Champions in Carlsbad, California, where winners from the previous tour season played for a purse of $750,000. Paul Azinger prevailed, which pleased Payne. If someone else had to win, it might as well be someone he liked.

Payne and Azinger shared a certain kinship on the tour, but they weren't the close friends some in the media made them out to be. Like many players, Azinger could take only so much of Payne. But Payne was a loyal friend, and Azinger appreciated that, even if he seemed to be (and often acted like) a puppy. Loyalty sometimes could make up for poor form. It could make up for bad taste and an inappropriate comment or gesture. It was the measure of their friendship that Azinger thought of when Payne did or said something dumb.

They had met on the practice putting green at the Magnolia Classic that Payne won in 1982, when Azinger, who was three years younger than Payne and just getting his start, motored from tournament to tournament in a camper with his wife, Toni. Like Payne, the quick-witted Azinger enjoyed a well-timed joke and a well-placed barb, and he exuded a poise and self-assuredness that Payne liked to think he projected, too. Lean and angular, Azinger also was a play-by-feel shot-maker. He used to borrow his mother's MacGregor irons to learn the game when his family lived in New Jersey, but Azinger learned to play on a variety of courses. His family moved often. His father was an officer in the air force. The set of forged Hogan Producer irons and oiled woods he gave his son in junior high accompanied him all the way through college at Florida State University to Hattiesburg, where he finished seventh behind Payne.

Azinger expected a great deal of himself in 1990. He'd been a force the previous season, winning in Hartford, taking second at two other tournaments, and playing himself into the top fifteen at the Masters, U.S. Open, and British Open. Azinger missed the cut at Kemper Lakes. But, as Payne had for him at the Tournament of Champions, he rooted for his friend as Payne made that scintillating run through the final five holes in suburban Chicago. A month later, they were Ryder Cup teammates for the first time, connected even more deeply now by a layer of fellowship and shared purpose through the strongest bond in men's golf.

The new season was a time for the shot-makers to shine. Azinger won only once, but he collected a dozen top tens and nearly a million dollars in earnings. Jacobsen won the Bob Hope. Ben Crenshaw won the Colonial. Hal Sutton, whose relationship with Payne continued to build through their locker-room proximity and rising status, endured a poor year by his standards, but he contended in Los Angeles and

Milwaukee, among other starts. Mark O'Meara won twice. He played his best golf at two golden age courses: Pebble Beach and Oak Hills Country Club in San Antonio, an A. W. Tillinghast design where both nines concluded with a par-three hole. Davis Love III, who was seven years younger than Payne but embodied the same manner of play, took the International. Tom Lehman, who'd nearly accepted a job to coach golf at the University of Minnesota but decided to give professional golf one more chance, beat a field of much younger upstarts to claim his first tournament on what was then known as the Ben Hogan Tour.

Payne won twice that year. He defended his title at Harbour Town, where he'd won the MCI Heritage the spring before and lost the tour championship in the fall, in sudden death with Larry Mize and Steve Jones. Payne thought about his loss to Kite as the playoff was about to begin. *Look, this is the '90s,* he told himself. *All those playoff losses were in the '80s.* He dropped an eight-iron shot to a foot on the first sudden-death hole to eliminate Jones. His long birdie putt on the second dispatched Mize. Three weeks later, Payne won the Byron Nelson: redemption for the lonely walk five years before. He tied for second at the British Open in July.

He reported to the PGA Championship that August in exquisite physical form. He had played beautiful golf in 1990, missed only two cuts, and won his sixth and seventh career titles. He'd committed to the pre-shot routine he and Dick Coop created to lock in his concentration. The defending champion was certain he would keep the Wanamaker Trophy after four rounds at Shoal Creek Country Club outside Birmingham, Alabama.

"There's going to be one champion," Payne declared in his pretournament press conference. "I don't see why that can't be me."

But the PGA Championship at Shoal Creek wasn't yet about what it would take to win. Bigger conversations were happening the week before the championship. The founder of the private club, Hall W. Thompson, had granted an interview earlier that summer to a reporter with a Birmingham newspaper who inquired about the membership at

Shoal Creek. Thompson said the club welcomed women and people of Jewish faith, but not African Americans. "We don't discriminate in every other area except the blacks," Thompson told the newspaper.

It was a clear affirmation of racism. Reaction was immediate. The Reverend Joseph Lowery, president of the Southern Christian Leadership Conference in Atlanta, immediately called on the PGA of America to reconsider the venue for its championship.

"To cooperate with evil is to affirm it," Lowery said. "This honest man, Mr. Thompson, has exposed the sophisticated layer of deceit and hypocrisy that veils the racism that still exists in our society today."

The revelation mobilized activists and journalists. A survey conducted by the *Charlotte Observer* found that seventeen other clubs where the PGA Tour played had all-white memberships. Four companies canceled their plans to advertise on ABC during the PGA Championship. The PGA Tour, which had a television package with the CBS network worth more than $20 million, announced that it would consider diversity and inclusion when evaluating potential tournament sites.

"We are saying that if we haven't been attuned enough to the situation in the past, now we are going to be," tour deputy commissioner Tim Finchem said.

While it had no jurisdiction over the PGA Championship, the United States Golf Association also took a position. "The Shoal Creek issues are not new or confined to Alabama," said Grant Spaeth, president of the USGA, which conducted the U.S. Open, U.S. Senior Open, U.S. Women's Open, and many high-level amateur competitions. "So however distressing one finds this firestorm, I conclude without question that open debate and decision-making is long overdue."

The SCLC and other civil-rights groups announced plans to picket the PGA. They canceled the demonstrations after Shoal Creek invited a black businessman to become an honorary member a week before the tournament. The PGA of America announced a new policy on Wednesday: Starting in 1995, clubs that excluded minorities no longer would be eligible for its championship. Contestants, including Payne, heard question upon question about the topic.

"I think the whole thing's been blown out of proportion," Payne told reporters. "That's something you guys are pretty good at, blowing things out of proportion."

Then he added, "The players have probably made more jokes about it than anything else."

It was a careless, flippant, perfunctory postscript that resonated deeply in the setting of the Jim Crow South. It implied that Payne and others in the field didn't take seriously the festering, tacit discrimination that still permeated golf and, in some quarters, the perception of it. It was one thing to emphasize that players just wanted to talk that week about the PGA Championship, the Shoal Creek course, and their strategies to play it. It was quite another to dismiss abject racism at the club by suggesting it wasn't being taken seriously in its locker room.

Some in the press repeated Payne's remark to other players. "I don't think that's a joking issue," said Jack Nicklaus.

The championship nonetheless began on a blistering Thursday in north-central Alabama. It was so hot a car window burst. Players complained about the Bermuda grass rough, five inches deep in spots, more like a U.S. Open than a PGA Championship. The rough length annoyed Payne, who shot 71-72-70 and played in the final pairing on Sunday with Wayne Grady of Australia. Payne observed that recovery shots from beyond the fairway dictated a sand wedge back into play.

"It's the most boring play in sports," Payne said.

Payne wore the green and gold of the Green Bay Packers for the fourth round at suffocating Shoal Creek. He took a triple bogey on the eleventh hole, shot 79, and tied for eighth, ten strokes behind Grady. Azinger also failed to break 70, finishing thirty-first. Sutton shared forty-ninth place, Love fortieth, O'Meara nineteenth.

"I'm just glad it's over," Payne said.

Scott Korzenowski, a columnist for the *News-Press* of Fort Myers, Florida, tried to capture the mood of the week. "Someday the 1990 PGA Championship may be known for something other than racial elitism, thick rough, hard greens, and the confirmation that nobody other than Green Bay Packers—at least, not Payne—should wear green and gold in abundance," he wrote.

The 1990 season neared its end, with a handful of tournaments left in the next three months, none of which Payne would win. Three of the four major championships had gone to foreign players. (Nick Faldo, the steely Englishman, won his second Masters and British Open titles in 1990.) Hale Irwin, forty-five, had become the oldest champion of the U.S. Open at Medinah. Payne and the other Americans of his generation looked now to 1991.

Their sport was shifting. The coming year would show them another way to play their game. Feel players like Payne, shapers of the golf ball, sensed the threat. Payne couldn't wait to confront it. He was going to dominate the '90s, he still believed. He was going to be remembered.

CHAPTER SEVEN

Payne wobbled through the first four starts of the '91 season. He hurt his neck in February and missed the entire month of March. Doctors found a bone chip that required him to wear a neck brace as it healed. The time away from the game gave him a lot of time to think, and for the first time since the missed cut at the 1986 Canadian Open, he had to contemplate life without golf. It terrified him. Five years earlier, after the missed cut in Canada, he had won only twice, and he'd confronted the possibility that he wasn't as good as he'd always told himself he was. But now, in the early spring of '91, he was a seven-time winner on the PGA Tour with a major championship and dreams of playing his best golf in the '90s, and he was partially immobile. Payne watched the Bay Hill tournament from his patio on the twelfth hole. He barely could turn his head to follow a shot. He'd never felt more dispirited.

Payne tried to return for the Masters. His instructor, Chuck Cook, met him in Augusta early in the week and watched him on the range. "Your swing is perfect," Cook told him. But Payne doubted he could sustain it through four rounds at Augusta National, given the chronic weakness in his left arm, which was one of the effects of the bone chip. He withdrew and wondered again if the '90s would be the peak of his career or the end.

The realities of a career in sports were weighing on Payne in profound ways. He was only thirty-four, but he had been swinging a golf club for most of his life, and the stress on his body—three decades of torsion, force, and split-second violence—seemed to be eroding him from the inside. He understood the seriousness of a spinal injury, even a minor one, to a professional golfer. The psychological affect alone could prevent him from swinging with abandon, with freedom, and without fear. He knew he might never be the same.

But he was cleared to play after a strength test in late April. Payne registered for the tournament at Harbour Town, where he was defending champion. He tied for fourth. A week later, he shot three good rounds and one mediocre one in Greensboro. Each swing gave him new hope. His confidence returned with every strike of the ball. He began to think about the U.S. Open.

The national championship returned in '91 to Hazeltine National Golf Club in a southwest suburb of Minneapolis. Designed by Robert Trent Jones and christened in the early 1960s, the course had been the site of the 1970 U.S. Open, whose contestants uniformly derided Hazeltine as unfit for competition. They criticized the severe doglegs, poorly placed trees, and lack of definition of the holes. They saw it as yet another example of a modern routing—a premium on length, more penal than strategic—that failed to meet the high standards of symmetry with nature established by the architects of the golden age. Dave Hill, the 1970 runner-up to Tony Jacklin, famously observed, "Just because you cut the grass and put up flags doesn't mean you have a golf course." Hazeltine was redone eight years later. It was not the same course Payne and the rest of the field had faced in '91.

Payne raced to a one-shot lead after rounds of 67-70. Hazeltine pummeled other shot-makers; Azinger, O'Meara, and Sutton missed the cut, while Love followed a 70 on Thursday with a dreary 76 a day later to slink into the weekend. For the third round at Hazeltine, Payne presented the colors of the Miami Dolphins: nautical aqua plus fours, a striped orange shirt with banded sleeves, with a matching green flat cap. As he drilled balls on the range before his afternoon starting time, a broadcast reporter approached. Payne turned, smiled, and leaned on his club.

"How's your back?" the reporter asked.

Payne said he was wearing a brace. He said he had been sleeping well. He said he didn't mind the stirring wind on that Saturday in Minnesota. He smiled a lot and tried not to say something that could be construed in the wrong way and put him on defense. He said he planned to lean on his experience five years before at Shinnecock, where he'd allowed the menacing countenance of a charging Raymond Floyd to strip his confidence on the last six holes of the championship.

"I learned quite a bit from that day," Payne said.

The reporter let the statement hang without explanation. Payne returned to his swing. He wanted to forget about Raymond Floyd and Shinnecock.

He shot one-over 73 in the gusts. Scott Simpson, the champion of the '87 U.S. Open at Olympic, tied Payne for the fifty-four-hole lead with an even-par 72. No one broke 70.

"I think the USGA got what it wanted today," Payne told reporters after his round.

ROUND 3 GOES TO HAZELTINE, read the headline the next day on a column in the Minneapolis *Star Tribune*.

Simpson led Payne by two shots with three holes left in the final round, a warm and windless afternoon on the prairie. Simpson lost the lead with bogeys on sixteen and eighteen, and the two of them completed play at minus six. The tie meant an eighteen-hole playoff on Monday. Wearing a red, white, and blue shirt with the logo of Super Bowl XXVI on his chest, Payne didn't play his best golf, but he played better golf than Simpson did. He hit a ball into a lake on the par-three eighth. It struck a rock and bounced back into play. He again fell two shots behind Simpson with three holes to go, birdied the treacherous par-four sixteenth, and won his first national championship. Thirty thousand spectators watched Payne ignore his ailing back and gamely hole a four-foot par putt on the final hole.

"To win championships, you have to have some good breaks," Payne said after the round.

Dave Anderson, the august sports columnist for the *New York Times*, noted that Payne had become the first champion of the U.S. Open to wear plus fours since Gene Sarazen in 1932. An impressed Rick Reilly filed his long story for next week's *Sports Illustrated*. "You showed us something new, Payne Stewart," he wrote. "You showed us something courageous."

No one in the media could besmirch this victory. This wasn't the '89 PGA at Kemper Lakes. Through dull pain and the ensuing fatigue of a fifth round in five days, Payne had earned this major, not been gifted it by the collapse of another player. It was validation on a higher plane: the realm of Jones and Hogan and Nicklaus.

"This means so much," Payne said. "I'm as good as I thought I was going to be."

It was a curious and revealing assertion from someone so outwardly sure of his own ability and skill. It seemed uncharacteristically vulnerable, as if Payne needed tangible evidence, like the lowest score in a U.S. Open and the attention that came with it, to prove his greatness, even to himself. He remembered what Perry Leslie, one of Sam Reynolds's assistant golf professionals at Hickory Hills, had once told him when his arrogance had become overbearing: "America doesn't want to hear how good you think you are. What they want to hear is that it could happen to anyone. They want to hear that the dream exists for them. They want to hear humility." There was a scrap of humility in Payne at the conclusion of that grueling playoff that June '91. It was another side of the showman from Missouri, subtle but telling.

It also was fleeting. The U.S. Open at Hazeltine elevated Payne's profile even more. He lapped up the new level of celebrity and status like it might expire if he didn't. He set out for Europe and the British Open, the Irish Open, and the BMW International in Munich. He beat Bernhard Langer by nine at the Dutch Open. He played with Prince Rainier of Monaco in a pro-am before the Torras Monte Carlo Open, where he performed for Princess Stéphanie on harmonica, his instrument of choice in the band with Peter Jacobsen. His fame as a U.S. Open champion was his identity now, and it was intoxicating.

The fans wanted his handshake, his rococo autograph, his picture, his smile, his charming wink. The directors of golf tournaments wanted his entry form. The press wanted his opinion whenever and wherever he played. He was desired. He was important. He felt reborn and limitless.

He believed again, as deeply as he ever had, in the fate of the '90s.

Payne qualified easily for his third Ryder Cup, soon to join his friends Azinger and O'Meara on the team, along with other veterans such as Fred Couples, his competition in the Southwest Conference Championship long ago, and Hale Irwin, Lanny Wadkins, Corey Pavin, and Steve Pate.

Payne made newspaper copy before the captain Dave Stockton even announced his two captain's picks. Payne had been asked at the Buick Open in August if Nicklaus, the winner of the 1991 U.S. Senior Open but who had last played on the team in 1981, deserved consideration as one of Stockton's two selections. Payne said he doubted Nicklaus had the stamina to play two matches in one day, which is what Ryder Cup players might have to do in foursomes and four-balls at the Ocean Course at Kiawah Island, South Carolina.

"I wouldn't pick Jack Nicklaus," Payne said. "Intimidation is the major reason why you'd pick Jack Nicklaus. But he'd be good for one match a day. What if they needed him to play thirty-six holes? The man is fifty-one years old. I don't know if he's capable of playing thirty-six holes. I don't think intimidation is that big of a factor anymore in golf."

Headlines portrayed Payne as a heretic. PAYNE SAYS JACK'S STARE ISN'T ENOUGH FOR RYDER CUP SPOT, declared the August 1 edition of the *News-Press* of Fort Myers, Florida. The implied disrespect toward Nicklaus triggered yet more criticism of Payne for arrogance, cockiness, and belligerence. Payne blamed the media, as he had at Shoal Creek, for stirring up controversy.

"It was printed a bit differently than the intention in what I said," he explained a week later, before the PGA Championship in Carmel,

Indiana. "Jack Nicklaus is the greatest golfer that ever lived. I grew up modeling myself after him. It came out that I was knocking him, but that's not true. I'd like to let this all rest."

The last major of the '91 season brought Payne to Crooked Stick Golf Club in a suburb of Indianapolis. The PGA Championship was the first big professional tournament at Crooked Stick, a bold and brassy Pete Dye design that opened in 1964 with spacious fairways, sinister European-style pot bunkers, and Dye's signature railroad ties, used as bulkheads around bunkers and greens. The 7,289-yard course intrigued some players, especially the longer drivers on the tour. Fred Couples, who averaged 277 yards in driving distance that season—behind only Greg Norman and John Daly, a little-known, sunburned, twenty-five-year-old from Arkansas with a mullet—said on the day before the tournament, "There are going to be long hitters who think they have a good chance."

Even with his enormous Wilson Whale, Payne was just a passable driver of the golf ball, both in distance (an average of 264 yards, good for sixty-fifth that year on tour) and accuracy (69 percent of fairways, ranking him seventy-sixth). Sheer length at the expense of control had never been important to him, or to any player of note in his thirties. Feel players learned a more holistic approach to managing a golf course, and that started with avoiding par-threatening conditions such as rough and trees outside the security of the fairway. But Payne was beginning to appreciate the evolving role of driving distance in the professional game. Courses were getting longer. Clubs were getting better. It was getting easier, and indeed more necessary, to launch drives of dimensions Jones and Hogan never thought attainable.

Daly was the ninth alternate in the field at the PGA, notified that he would fill the spot vacated by Nick Price, who withdrew because his wife was expecting. The former Arkansas Razorback was a tour rookie who'd missed eleven cuts in twenty-three starts in 1991. But he drove his Maxfli golf ball a stunning distance: more than 287 yards on average, rarely straight but far enough downrange to negate the inaccuracy by resulting in shorter, easier-to-hit clubs into greens. His fans marveled. His fellow competitors envied his ability to convert long holes into scoring feasts. It was everyone's first glimpse of the future.

Daly ravaged Crooked Stick that week. He averaged 303 yards off the tee through four rounds, which he finished at minus twelve, three strokes ahead of runner-up Bruce Lietzke. Daly hit the ball higher than anyone had ever seen, shots that stayed in the air like comets. Swinging a Cobra driver with a composite Kevlar head, Daly carried bunkers 270 yards from the tee, a feat never seen by the older players who tried to fit their drives around them. He played the 453-yard tenth hole with a booming drive and a soft wedge. He eagled the par-five ninth from two hundred yards with a six-iron to three feet. His one-irons sailed past the driver shots of men who had won U.S. Opens and Masters Tournaments. "Good gracious, what a coil," Nicklaus said when asked, as he often was, for historical comparisons. "I don't know who he reminds me of. I haven't seen anybody who hit the ball that far."

Facts were facts. No one had ever averaged more than 300 yards in four rounds on tour, let alone won hitting the ball like that. More telling: Daly came into the PGA at Crooked Stick ranked 186th in driving accuracy. It suddenly didn't matter where a drive went, as long as it went a long way. "You talk about the next Mr. Nicklaus," noted Kenny Knox, a fine putter but weak driver. "I think they're going to be talking about the next Mr. Daly in the next twenty years."

Payne had played solidly: 74-70-71-70, for a share of thirteenth place. He told reporters he was exhausted after his whirlwind season, which also included a few rounds in Scotland with friends, and that he had a mountain of mail to answer back home in Orlando. Hal Sutton tied for seventh, Davis Love III thirty-second. Mark O'Meara missed the cut. Azinger had withdrawn. The ninth alternate beat them all and the rest of the shot-makers in the last major of 1991.

A new calculus ruled golf now. Everyone wanted to drive the ball like Long John Daly.

* * *

The US team won the Ryder Cup that fall in a bitter, raucous, and tense three days of golf on the Ocean Course at Kiawah. Payne again lost his singles match, this time to David Feherty of Northern Ireland, but he'd contributed two points in foursomes play with Mark Calcavecchia, and now, on his third team, he'd experienced victory. He was completely romanced by the idea of the Ryder Cup, from the fellowship and unity of team golf to the patriotic, even militaristic, subtext of the biennial competition. Payne was so carried away after the joyful closing ceremony at Kiawah Island that he helped his teammates to throw their captain, Dave Stockton, into the sea.

Payne played twenty-three tournaments in 1992. He made the cut in most of them but never factored in the majors, and the closest he came to winning was at the Memorial in Columbus, where he tied for third. He admitted that he was trying too hard to be a player he was not. He was listening to too many people with good intentions. A friend suggested he add more structure to his practice. It didn't work. Chuck Cook, his swing instructor, tried to get him to change his takeaway. That didn't, either.

"It was very mechanical," Payne said. "That's not how I played golf for thirty-four years. I played by feel."

At the 1992 U.S. Open at Pebble Beach, Payne thought a return to one of his favorite courses, and one he played well, might induce a rally in the second half of the season. Oddsmakers gave him a four-to-one chance to defend. He shot a miserable 83 in the last round and tied for fifty-first.

"I thought I would enjoy being the [U.S.] Open champion a lot more," Payne told reporters that week, "until I realized I was putting too much self-imposed pressure on myself to *be* the Open champ. I thought I had to perform at that new, high standard."

It looked like 1993 could be another encouraging season like '89 or '91. Payne lost the Memorial on the last hole, when Azinger, the best sand player in golf, clipped his ball perfectly from a greenside bunker and holed it to win. The turn of events rattled Payne so much he missed a three-footer for second. He then hugged his friend and called him a champion.

"I wasn't up to the challenge," Payne said. The *New York Times* called him "admirably philosophical in defeat."

Payne had nine top tens before the U.S. Open at Baltusrol, including a share of ninth at the Masters. Then luck touched the slender shoulder of Lee Janzen on the last nine holes in New Jersey. That August, Azinger won the PGA Championship at the Inverness Club in Toledo, Ohio, where Payne tied for forty-fourth. Payne was thrilled for his friend, and also relieved. He understood what it'd meant. Azinger, now thirty-three, had been tabbed as the best player in the game without a major.

"I didn't resent that," Azinger told the press after his round. "But that being the case, I felt more pressure today."

The 1993 season ended for Payne with four runner-up finishes, more than $982,000 in earnings, and another berth on the Ryder Cup team. The matches returned to the Belfry in the English Midlands, where the United States had lost four years before. The Americans coasted through the tricky four-ball and foursomes matches with no irreparable damage. They sailed through singles. Payne won his match over Mark James, Davis Love III beat Constantino Rocca, and Azinger halved with Nick Faldo. The United States won again.

Payne and Azinger played in the annual Skins Game in November. He chartered a Beechcraft King Air business jet to Los Angeles after the exhibition in Palm Springs and invited Azinger and his family to join him on the flight. As they waited to take off, Azinger showed Payne an MRI scan of his shoulder, which had been bothering him for months. Payne pointed to a dark spot on the image.

"What's that?" he said.

"I don't really know yet," Azinger said.

"I hope you're all right," said Mike Hicks, Payne's caddie.

"I'll be fine," Azinger said.

A biopsy the next day revealed that he wasn't.

Azinger disclosed his lymphoma diagnosis on December 8. He said he would miss up to seven months of competition and, should his doctor's optimistic prognosis prove true, defend his PGA Championship title in 1994 at Southern Hills in Tulsa, Oklahoma. He said he hoped to be hitting golf balls again in six months, after six chemotherapy treatments and five weeks of daily radiation. He planned to recuperate at home in Florida.

The announcement shook Payne, who immediately thought of his father, who'd died soon after his cancer was found. But there were reasons to hope. Azinger's doctors predicted a good chance for a full recovery. Media reports reminded him that Gene Littler, an eight-time winner on the Senior PGA Tour, had been stricken by the same type of cancer in 1972, and he'd won four more tournaments after his cure. Payne thought about Azinger's wife, Toni, and their two young children, Sarah and Josie. He thought about the little bond he'd formed with Azinger since the Magnolia Classic in Mississippi more than a decade earlier, a relationship tempered by bravado and bluster, their common journey to the tour, the heat of competition, a boyish zeal for practical jokes, the tempestuous Ryder Cup matches, the bunker shot at the '93 Memorial, and an unspoken but mutually assumed presumption that they would being playing each other, and beating each other, for a long time to come.

Like many friends on the PGA Tour and throughout professional sports, Azinger and Payne sustained their friendship at the cosmetic level. It was genuine and felt, but it wasn't the kind of profound relationship built on shared secrets or bared souls, true of Payne's nature in every relationship outside of his family. Payne liked Azinger for his jocularity, swagger, and ability to play great golf when it mattered the most—the holy trinity, in Payne's estimation. Azinger could take a prank. After he'd won the Memorial Tournament with that holed bunker shot, Payne sneaked to the Muirfield Village Golf Club locker room and filled Azinger's street shoes with mashed bananas. He'd once procured a set of fake teeth, broken and disfigured, and fooled Azinger into believing he'd been ambushed by muggers. Azinger, who was more warmly regarded on tour, once was asked what he saw in Payne, given his friend's proclivity to offend.

"He always said he was sorry," Azinger replied.

Now, in the early months of 1994, the two friends faced new emotional territory. While a number of professional golfers expressed concern and high hopes for Azinger, none of them spent the kind or quality of time with him that Payne did. They often met at Azinger's home in Bradenton, south of Tampa, and fished the Manatee River for redfish and snook. They never talked about cancer. They never talked about faith, death, or heaven. But Azinger sensed that Payne was exploring those concepts in his own quiet way, just by being in his presence. ("I was staring my mortality down," Azinger would say many years later. Through him, Azinger would surmise, Payne was, too.)

Payne staggered through a lackluster 1994 season on tour, managing only a pair of top-ten finishes and more missed cuts—seven, with one withdrawal—than in any other year he could remember. He shot 78-78 in the Masters and told reporters that he'd decided then and there to withdraw from the MCI, a tournament he'd won twice on a course that favored a pure feel player like him. He didn't feel like a shot-maker now.

"I'm not going to benefit by playing there and they're not going to benefit by having me in their golf tournament," Payne said.

He added, "I'm not having fun. I won't come back until it's fun for me."

He took off four weeks and missed the cuts in Dallas and Columbus. He gained weight. He avoided practice. He tried to quit tobacco. He harassed and howled at referees (and sometimes players) at Orlando Magic games from his season-ticket seat behind the bench. Nearby spectators at Orlando Arena thought it was funny at first, *Payne being Payne.* Then it just seemed pathetic.

Payne and his wife bought secluded five acres in southwest Orlando on Pocket Lake. They built a dock, hired a famous architect to design a new house, and directed him to include six bedrooms, six baths, a swimming pool, a spa, a fitness room, a billiards room, an indoor putting green, a tennis court, and a bar. Payne acquired a boat, and then another, as friends and family worried he was devoting his time to the wrong things. He'd missed the cut in three of the four majors. He'd fired Mike Hicks, his caddie of six years. He'd spent a lot of time angry. He'd been drinking too much.

"Every time Payne Stewart opened his mouth, the words got angrier, the sarcasm thicker," Melanie Hauser, the golf writer for the *Houston Post*, wrote from the Masters Tournament. "He was past the point of mad. He was fed up. His stare was cold and hard; his words pointed. His actions? Even he had to admit they were embarrassing. He wasn't talking anymore, just snapping. It had passed the point of turning his clubs into whirlybirds and kicking trash cans."

Payne was quietly desperate. He'd lost belief, a misery compounded by a lack of trust in the instruments he used to play his sport. When his contract with Wilson Sporting Goods expired at the end of '93, he'd signed a new endorsement package with Spalding, a company that sold clubs and balls under the Top-Flite brand. Spalding agreed to pay him $9 million to play its equipment and display its name on his bag for the next five years. The money alone was seductive. Payne had a house to pay for. He wasn't going to do that by missing cuts.

The new contract required Payne to play Spalding irons and a Spalding ball. The irons were cast instead of forged, and they were cavity-backs, not blades. The steel was harder. The grooves were a different shape. The design of the club head made it more difficult for Payne to actually experience a shot, from his fingers to his feet, because it transmitted less information at impact to Payne's sensitive hands. The feel player no longer could feel. The Spalding ball behaved differently, too. It spun more than the Titleist three-piece wound ball that he had played with so much success. Now nothing made sense. Payne had switched his ball and clubs at the same time, meaning he never knew what to blame when one seven-iron shot flew 135 yards and the next one flew 180. It was hubris again. He thought he was good enough to win with anything. He was dead wrong. But he'd made a deal. He'd signed his name to it.

So there he was, cloaked in a gaudy ensemble of marigold plus fours and black argyle socks one afternoon in 1994, filming a television commercial for Spalding staged on a busy practice range, his new Spalding bag positioned perfectly for viewers to see the brand name. "Recently, I started playing the Top-Flite Tour irons," Payne told the camera in his lilting country affect. He pointed to a so-called ballast bar in the cavity of the clubs—a narrow band of steel horizontally connecting the sole and the topline of the iron. "It makes them feel better than any clubs I've played," Payne said of the bar. He sounded convincing enough.

"But the real reason? Let's face it. If you're going to dress like this, you better be able to back it up."

Back it up. Payne spoke those words but wasn't living them. Two seasons without a win. Nothing since the U.S. Open. He wore his costume and made enough money to keep his playing privileges on the PGA Tour, but the stage hadn't been Payne Stewart's in a very long time. The new clubs and ball might change that, he figured, but he would be wrong about that, too.

He made $145,687 in 1994, an abject disaster of a season for someone of Payne's talent and touch. He was too stubborn to switch his equipment to suit the way he played golf and too loyal to try to break his contract with Spalding. He reflected on the year with indifference. His wife challenged him again. "You've played golf since you were four years old," she told him when he offhandedly mentioned quitting, as he had years earlier after he'd missed the cut in Canada. "You've always wanted to play golf for a living. What else are you going to do?"

Tracey's words stung. Her blunt candor had a way of resetting Payne whenever he felt sorry for himself or was frustrated or impatient. They pushed Payne into 1995 with his new clubs, the new ball, and new drive to be the player his wife knew he still was. He tied for fourth in the Phoenix Open and, a week later, finished in fifth alone at Pebble Beach—consecrated ground, where he had played some of the best golf of his career. He almost won the Players Championship in March. In April, he was the benefactor of Scott Hoch's losing a six-shot lead with nine holes remaining in the Houston Open. The two went to a play-off at twelve under par, and the adrenaline Payne hadn't felt in months pulsed again.

This is the time to be a champion again, Payne told himself. He holed a four-foot putt to beat Hoch on the first hole of sudden death.

It was his only victory of '95. It wasn't a bad year by numbers, especially when Payne considered his scoring average of 70.23, good for seventeenth on the tour, and he'd made more than $866,000. But he was spent. He'd fired his teacher, Chuck Cook, after sleeping through an appointment to work on the practice range at the U.S. Open. Cook refused to adjust his schedule that day to fit Payne in. Cook told Payne he was committed to helping another player. That player, the shot-making Corey Pavin, won his only U.S. Open that week at Shinnecock.

Payne finished outside the top twenty in the national championship. He had one more decent tournament—the Buick Open, where he took eighth—but he missed five cuts and failed to make the Ryder Cup team for the first time in eight years. He didn't win, but the year wasn't a complete loss. Payne ranked twelfth on the money list, thanks to his win in Houston. Paul Azinger had indeed recovered from cancer treatments to defend his PGA Championship, and competed in twenty-three tournaments in '95. The 12,275-square-foot house on Pocket Lake was finished. Payne had all the money he and his family required. He was still the showman, thirty-eight now, in the jaunty flat cap and the plus fours, with the Paramount Pictures face and the same flowing swing that made Johnny Miller swoon. But he couldn't help feeling that 1995 was another mystery, a nice sentence with a missing word. The '90s were not the '90s he had pictured.

The Stewarts decided in 1996 to put their children, now seven and ten years old, in private school affiliated with the First Baptist Church in Orlando. Aaron and Chelsea came home each afternoon brimming with excitement about their lessons. Payne hadn't been serious about faith in years, but as he got older and saw the enthusiasm in his children about the Bible, he began to feel new interest in spirituality and the notion of returning to church. He joined a men's group at First Baptist. It filled a hole in his life he wasn't aware he'd had.

Payne had one second-place finish in 1996. As he had in the lean years, he played well enough to make cuts and good money, but still he wasn't winning, and that frustrated him. He remained wary of reporters and anyone who wanted something from him, even though his overall poor play since 1992 meant he was less in demand for interviews and quotes. He sometimes allowed that mistrust to bubble, like when Jayne Custred, a journalist from Houston, traveled to the Players Championship in March of '96 to report a story about Payne for the Houston Open. She found him as he was walking to the locker room at TPC Sawgrass.

"Payne," she said. "I need a few minutes. Anytime today, tomorrow, whenever you want to do it. It's for the cover piece of the Shell Houston Open."

"I'm doing a conference call with them Monday morning," Payne said without stopping.

"I understand that, but they want some more in-depth stuff, and I'll be on an airplane at that time," Custred said.

"Well, I guess you have a problem, don't you?"

Payne left Custred there and disappeared. But he found her later and apologized. They did the interview.

Two weeks later, after he missed the cut at the Masters, he and his wife were leaving the clubhouse when a spectator asked him for his autograph. Payne mistakenly thought he was in a restricted area, where autographs weren't allowed. The spectator persisted.

"I'm not allowed to," Payne told the man, who explained he wanted the signature for his son.

"Get away from me," Payne snapped. "I told you I can't."

The exchange left Tracey cold and embarrassed for her husband. Payne saw it in her face. This time, he didn't apologize. But she did.

The 1997 season was another march of mediocrity. Payne didn't qualify for an invitation to the Masters, so he joined forty-four million other television viewers to watch Tiger Woods win his first major championship with a Masters-record eighteen under par. It was an astounding display of power and finesse. He drove the ball 323 yards on average, 25 yards longer than anyone in the tournament. The longest club he hit into a par-four that week was a seven-iron. Woods had practiced for the tournament with an old MacGregor Eye-O-Matic, a persimmon driver with a face more curved than those on the metal drivers that were now common on the PGA Tour. That horizontal curvature, known in golf as *bulge*, helped Woods produce a right-to-left draw, the preferred bend at Augusta National. The vertical curvature, known as *roll*, helped him groove a swing that would flight a shot higher on the face. After two starts at the Masters, Woods knew what the champions with the green jackets knew: Chance favored the player who could execute a high draw. Woods was only twenty-one years old, but he knew he wanted luck on his side. He didn't need much. He won by twelve. The evidence was clear: On the PGA Tour, the long ball no longer was the exception. It was the rule.

Payne saw signals of better golf late in the '97 season: four top tens, from Vancouver to Disney. But he missed qualifying again for the Ryder Cup, and while US team captain Tom Kite considered Payne for a captain's pick—Payne even had flown to Spain to play the Valderrama Golf Club in an effort to impress Kite with his pluck—those picks went to Fred Couples and Lee Janzen.

The US team lost. Payne decided right then that he would earn his spot on the 1999 team. He reunited with Chuck Cook, his former teacher. He rehired Hicks as his caddie. The '90s were supposed to be the defining decade of Payne Stewart, and now he had two years to make them so, which is how he ended up preparing the next summer at

Isleworth with Cook for the hills of the Lake Course, leading through three rounds of that 1998 U.S. Open with Hicks on his bag, missing the putt on the seventy-second hole, admitting to himself that he alone was responsible for another loss, and leaving the Olympic Club grounds on that Sunday in June—one more lonely walk—with the conviction that he could, and would, win in '99.

CHAPTER EIGHT

Payne played his last golf tournament of 1998 in November. He'd fulfilled the five-year term of his endorsement contract with Spalding, and the only new equipment deal he signed for the coming season was with Acushnet, the company that made the Titleist Professional three-piece wound ball he wanted to play in 1999. He was done with unpredictable balls that spun too much for his swing. He knew what a wound ball would do every time he struck it.

He spent the next two months at home in Orlando, considering the clubs he would play in his eighteenth season on tour. He had options. The realm of golf equipment was much more advanced and diverse than it had been the last time he'd had the freedom to choose. He settled on a Titleist titanium driver, an Orlimar fairway metal, a Cleveland wedge, and a Scotty Cameron putter like the PING Anser 2 model he'd used in the '89 PGA Championship and the '91 U.S. Open. His old friend Lamar Haynes, a teammate and roommate at SMU, shipped him a set of Mizuno MS-4 irons that Payne had given him a decade earlier. Simple and sleek, the narrow forged blades reminded him of the irons he'd played before the allure of endorsement money polluted his better judgment. He bought a black golf bag with no corporate logos at an Edwin Watts Golf retail store in Orlando. It cost him $130. It lacked the prestige of the big staff bags like the ones Tiger Woods or Phil Mickelson or David Duval had, but it did carry fourteen golf clubs, plenty of balls, a rain suit, and an umbrella. It arrived in California on the first day of February for the Pebble Beach National Pro-Am, Payne's third start of 1999.

The season had begun with optimism. Payne traveled to Austin before the Bob Hope Classic in La Quinta, California, to practice for three days with Cook. He played a money game at Barton Creek, one of the clubs in the capital city of Texas where Cook taught his players. Payne hit a lot of golf balls and rolled putts for hours. He recorded his full swing on video for the first time. Cook was relieved to see that Payne was playing equipment he could control. He was encouraged by his attitude, which carried none of the apathy or pessimism that had poisoned previous seasons. Their work involved recognizing the swing that used to win and committing to it. It almost was like his college coach, Earl Stewart, was leaning in between pulls on a Camel to whisper in his ear, *Trust it.*

Payne tied for eighteenth in La Quinta and eighteenth in Phoenix before he met Hicks and his plain black bag at Pebble Beach. It felt good to be back on Carmel Bay. No matter what the state of his game was, Payne played well at Pebble, one of the great golden age courses that seemed to bring out the best in the shot-makers.

It also brought out dark clouds and rain slickers. Since moving his festive "clambake" to Pebble Beach in 1947, Bing Crosby, the original benefactor of the tour stop on the Monterey Peninsula, had seen his pro-am interrupted time and again by rain. It couldn't be helped. Scheduling was the culprit. The tour wanted the pro-am to be part of its winter West Coast swing, which happened to coincide with the time of the year—November through March—when an average rainfall of sixteen inches visited that part of California. Any other tournament might've been marred by a lack of participation by the tour players, given the lousy weather and hassle of playing in it. But the Crosby Clambake, as it was informally known among celebrities, wasn't any other tournament. Tour players enjoyed the three courses and the one-of-a-kind pro-am format, which gave them the opportunity to play golf for official money with Hollywood stars.

"This is my week for vacation," Lloyd Mangrum, the 1946 U.S. Open champion, once said. "A fellow can't get serious about his golf when Crosby and his gang are around. I do not expect to do very well on the scorecard." But he did. Mangrum, a gambler and World War II hero with a pencil mustache, won the 1948 Crosby by five strokes. His three-round total of 205 was a record score that stood until he broke it in 1953 with 204.

The previous year, known around Monterey as the Big Blow of '52, brought all manner of mayhem to the peninsula. It poured. It howled. Jimmy Demaret, the garrulous head professional at River Oaks in Houston who could croon like Sinatra, finished his round with his partner, Bob Hope, before gusts of forty-five miles an hour scraped the coast. "It's a little breezy," Demaret noted, "but in Texas we'd consider this a wonderful day for a picnic." Cary Middlecoff of Memphis complained that he couldn't even keep his ball on the tee at the sixteenth at Cypress Point. He was reminded that there was nothing in the rules of golf that required shots to be played from a tee. That night, biblical rains washed out the next day's contest.

Between 1974 and 1986, three Pebble Beach Pro-Ams were abbreviated by weather to fifty-four holes. Many more rounds were played in showers not severe enough to suspend play. The courses were so wet in 1995 that players weren't even allowed a practice round. Sheets of persistent rain canceled the third round of the '96 tournament. The CBS Sports television crew panicked: How would the airtime be filled? A group of amateur celebrities, led by Bill Murray, proposed a spontaneous seven-hole match in the drizzle. Tommy Smothers, John Denver, Glen Campbell, and Kevin Costner joined Murray. CBS had its television. The sideshow was a hit.

Between March and November, the peninsula was glorious, and never more so than the day Payne invited Cook, his teacher, to the 1992 U.S. Open media day, an occasion for reporters to see the course and interview the defending champion. After he finished his obligations, Payne and Cook had dinner, which turned into cocktails, which turned into a late night and an idea to go outside. The two of them took the U.S. Open trophy out to the famous seawall on the eighteenth hole, sat down, and listened to the surf. Payne rarely looked deeply inward in conversation with friends, but on that night, he did. He told Cook things he had never told anyone else. He admitted how insignificant the trophy seemed to him right after he'd won it in '91. He said it didn't even seem important now.

"I worked all my life for that trophy," Payne told Cook in the dark. "That was the tournament I always wanted to win."

The sky was clear, blinking stars.

"But then, all of a sudden, everybody was gone and I'm just there," Payne said. "And it doesn't mean that much."

Payne slopped through a practice round on that Wednesday in '99 in typical Crosby rain and a spitting wind off the sea. His putting was dreadful on the Poa annua greens of Pebble Beach. After lunch, he ventured outside and saw Hicks toying with an odd-looking putter from a new company called SeeMore. The SeeMore was completely unlike, in form and in function, the Cameron and Anser putters that Payne had used for most of his career. It looked like a block with two white alignment lines and a red dot on the top, with the shaft right in the center. But the center-shafted block with the lines and the dot worked. Payne holed putt after putt, like he was finishing another circle game with Tracey from a foot away.

"I think it's got to go in the bag," Hicks said.

"I think you're right," Payne answered.

He shot 69 at Pebble on the first day of the tournament, three shots out of the lead in temperatures in the fifties and no precipitation, the calmest conditions the players would face that week. On the second day, he played Poppy Hills, the newest of the three courses the contestants played with their celebrity amateurs and one sheltered from the elements by the tall Monterey pines of the Del Monte Forest. He shot a blistering round of 64 that began with an eagle on the par-five tenth. He birdied the next hole, and the next. He was four under par through three holes with three putts—from twenty, eighteen, and ten feet—with the SeeMore putter. He made a sixty-footer on the sixth. He missed two fairways and two greens in regulation during a bogey-free round that lifted him into a three-shot lead halfway through.

Tour officials escorted him to the post-round interview room, where he saw many faces he recognized from Olympic. Reporters again noted a level of honesty and warmth in the loquacious Payne, as they had the summer before in San Francisco. Some of them wondered if the seven-year slump had made him humbler. (Bobby Jones used to say that he learned more from losing than from winning.) Some remembered the U.S. Open the previous year, when he'd talked about achieving peace through faith and his family. ("There is more to life than professional golf," Payne had said after the second round.) One reporter asked Payne if he felt at ease because Pebble Beach, where he had come close to winning so many times, owed him.

"I think you create your own destiny," Payne replied. "I didn't play well enough to win, you know? So be it. I'm going to see what I can do this week."

He said no more about destiny. He did discuss his lack of an equipment contract, his plain black bag, the practice session in Austin, the three courses on the peninsula, and his new putter. He didn't mention the taxing years, during which he'd won only once, and only then because Scott Hoch lost that big lead in Houston. He didn't say anything about the doubts. He didn't say anything about the temptation to quit. He didn't place blame: on bad luck, on his bad back, on his clubs, on reporters, on how golf nowadays was more a test of length and strength instead of feel, shot-making, and the capacity of the mind's eye. Payne did say he was at a place in his life where he felt more needed at home than at a golf tournament. He said it was refreshing—restorative, even—to take a two-month break from golf between his last tournament of 1998 and the Bob Hope.

"I didn't really touch the golf clubs," he said. "I went home and was a father. It was wonderful."

Payne woke up Saturday and heard rain lashing the windows of his room. He was glad that bag from Edwin Watts had pockets for a wind shirt and extra towels. He would be playing the third round on Spyglass Hill, another inland course protected by the forest, so he could at least hide from the worst of the weather. He was grateful he'd played Pebble Beach in the first round. Payne knew the players on Pebble faced an ambush.

He was right. None of the sixty contestants there broke par. They averaged 79.3 swings on the exposed coastal holes, while scores at the other two courses hovered four strokes lower. Temperatures fell into the forties. The wind whistled twenty-five miles an hour and gusted to forty. Players donned mittens between shots. All three golf courses flooded. The Associated Press described the conditions as "some of the nastiest weather since Bing Crosby moved his clambake to the Monterey Peninsula in 1947," which was saying something. Jack Lemmon, one of the regular clambake amateurs in the field, said the ghost of Crosby was having a good laugh. "It was old Crosby weather," the actor Clint Eastwood, a fixture at the tournament since the 1960s, said Saturday night.

"I could think of better things to do on a day like this," said twenty-seven-year-old David Duval, who had won two of his three starts in '99 and who seemed to be in every wager about who would win what tournament. Duval was two shots from the lead Saturday on Pebble until he made two doubles and shot 76.

Payne played careful, crafty, and measured golf at Spyglass. He signed for a 73. He made three unlikely birdies on the most difficult holes, all with approaches with long irons. His last came at the eighteenth. He dropped a five-iron to a foot from 185 yards and, with the birdie, took the lead by a stroke. The wind had less velocity in the forest, but it swirled. Payne told reporters after his round about the fifth hole. In practice rounds, he'd hit a three-iron there. On Saturday, it was a straight-downwind seven. The elements favored the creative, intuitive player like Payne—the one who could see shots, feel them, and will them into existence. Payne had made his Mizunos sing.

"I'm pretty whipped," he said.

Payne finished at minus ten, a shot ahead of Frank Lickliter II. In keeping with tradition, the entire field would play Pebble on Sunday for the final round if the weather held. Lickliter was from Ohio. He'd played college golf in the snow. He said he was ready to play Sunday in hail if he had to. But tour weather officials were concerned. The forecasts were grim. If they did get to play, contestants would have to throttle down and ease their way around the course.

"The temptation is to swing harder, I suppose, especially when you're in the wind," Lickliter said after his third-round 71. "That's when you get in trouble." The fourth-year tour pro considered a final pairing with Payne. "For someone as silky as Payne, it doesn't matter what the wind is doing," he said.

Wind wasn't the problem on Sunday. The problem was, again, the rain. The final round began as planned, but by the time Payne and Lickliter were eating breakfast, the sirens had wailed. Play was suspended at 9:30 a.m. The players sought shelter in a big room behind the pro shop. Payne was there when they filed in.

"Let it rain," he said to Peter Jacobsen.

Then he thought about it. "No," he said. "I'm playing great. I want to play."

Tournament director Arvin Ginn summoned players and reporters. He said the puddled Pebble Beach course had become unplayable. He said officials considered a Monday finish, but forecasters expected the rain to remain. Crosby weather had sunk another clambake.

"For the tournament's sake, for the players, for everyone involved, it would be useless to try for seventy-two holes," Ginn said. "It seemed impossible."

Tour media official Lee Patterson brought Lickliter and Payne to the media room. Lickliter was crushed. He'd wanted to see how his stamina and shot-making would hold up against Payne and the elements.

"I feel like I'm kind of a mudder," he said, "and I think the rain and the wind would have probably been to my advantage today."

"Do you feel cheated?" a reporter asked.

"I don't feel cheated," Lickliter said. "I'm just disappointed."

Payne understood disappointment. With the exception of '91 and '95, the entire '90s had been a disappointment. But here he was, eight months after he'd left Olympic with new hope for salvaging the decade, preparing to answer questions about his tenth career win.

"Just a couple of thoughts off the top of your head, and then we'll start questions," Patterson said.

Payne thought about what he wanted to see in the newspapers the next day. He thought about the larger forces influencing his life now that he was forty-two. He was relieved. He also felt a faint tug of regret. He wanted to show himself that he still could win a tournament, and in a strange way, he hadn't done that. Fifty-four holes wasn't seventy-two. Three rounds wasn't four.

He gathered himself.

"First of all, I would like to thank God for the opportunity that I had this week," he said. "And with my golf career, I've been pretty fortunate. And, you know, if you stay out here long enough, what goes around comes around. And I'm not going to lie to you. It feels pretty good."

He spoke of vindication: In 1995, he'd won because, if he was being honest with himself, Scott Hoch let him. He recalled the near-misses at Pebble Beach over the years, how one revolution of the ball—his or someone else's—might've meant another victory or two on a course that brought out his best. He said he missed his family. He'd been on the road for three weeks.

He also knew he had many more months of golf left. It was only February. His runner-up finish at the U.S. Open last year had earned him an invitation to the Masters, whose devilish greens exposed his greatest weakness: the putter. But now he had the SeeMore. He had his Mizunos. He was eager to compete with the men he'd sparred for seventeen years, but he also wanted the chance to head to the back nine with a tournament on the line with a Duval, Mickelson, Woods, or any of the other young and rising players who hit the ball farther than he ever could but didn't have his fingers, feet, or feel.

"Where do you think you are now, compared to when you were winning PGAs and U.S. Opens?" a reporter asked him.

Payne cited his age and, as he had at Olympic, his gathering wisdom.

"I'm more mature," he said. "I grew so much last year at the U.S. Open. I grew in how I deal with all of you. I was actually pleasant, wasn't I?"

He told the reporters that he accepted them now. He remembered his second-place finishes at Pebble, when he avoided the media so he wouldn't have to bear the implied criticism in their questions about why he'd failed. He admitted that he'd actually hid from them in his car.

"I wasn't mature then," Payne said. "I was immature. I've grown up a lot. I know how important it is, what you do for a living. I know that's your job. So why shouldn't I give you that time? I've learned to accept that." He began to speak *about* the media *to* the media. "You have got to give them what they are due, so they shouldn't be critical if you don't. If you don't give them anything to be critical of, then they shouldn't write critical things."

It was a disjointed and bumbling confession, but it confirmed the new side of Payne that cooperated with the media, as he had at Olympic. Little was written for the Sunday editions of the newspapers that Payne deemed critical. The reporters waxed about the rain. Payne banked $504,000 and knew he would be in the Masters again in 2000. He and his black bag full of Mizunos left for home.

Azinger had tied for tenth. Jacobsen shared thirty-second, and O'Meara, the Pebble Beach virtuoso who'd won the pro-am five times before, tied for fifty-third. Neither Lehman nor Sutton played that week, but both players of Payne's generation were on a path that season to a remarkable conclusion, their final rally: the last stand of the American shot-makers.

Before he set out again for the tournament in Los Angeles, Payne saw a familiar figure on the practice range at Isleworth. It was Tom Meeks, the USGA official who'd set up the eighteenth green in the second round of the U.S. Open and, two days later, given him the bad time. Payne approached. Meeks looked up.

"You and I have got to talk," Payne said.

Meeks agreed. He wanted to have that talk, too, and had since June. They played nine holes a couple of days later. Meeks told Payne how he'd looked for him at Sahalee. He explained his regret as he'd done with Lehman, emphasizing how the timing of the slow-play warning and the tremendous scope of the moment had bothered him a great deal, but a rule was a rule, and he was simply protecting the field and honoring a decree. Payne accepted that. They shook hands.

A few days later, Payne left for California as content as he'd been in years.

It wasn't just the win at Pebble that mattered. It wasn't just the amends he'd made over those nine holes with Tom Meeks.

This was bigger. He was a step closer to making the Ryder Cup team that fall in Brookline, Massachusetts.

Part Three

PINEHURST

Seventy-second hole, Pinehurst No. 2, Pinehurst, North Carolina,
June 20, 1999

CHAPTER NINE

Tiger Woods had never been a threat Saturday at Pebble Beach. A week later and eight hours down the coast, he shot 62-65 on the weekend at Torrey Pines in San Diego, the tournament Payne skipped, to fetch his eighth tournament victory in his third season on the tour.

Woods in 1999 was the most compelling and charismatic individual in golf, an amalgam of vision, instinct, will, and ferocious kinetic potential. He was twenty-three years old. It seemed he'd been famous forever. He'd won the first of his three U.S. Junior titles (and six USGA amateur championships, counting his three U.S. Amateurs) in 1991, when the newspapers still called him Eldrick and drivers with steel heads were turning wooden-headed clubs into attic relics, but he liked to maneuver the ball when he was young, liked to see if he could bend it around a tree or hold it against a going breeze or punch a ball under a howling headwind. He had the soul of a shot-maker but no mandate to be one, not with what club manufacturers were producing in the 1990s. Woods valued feel. He was not a native feel player, though, not like Payne and Lehman and O'Meara and Sutton. He never had to take aim at a narrow curl of fairway, buffeted by crosswinds and bunkered on both sides, with a tiny wooden driver and a trophy at stake. He only did that in practice rounds for the Masters.

His colossal win at the 1997 Masters had led to enormous television contracts for the 1999 PGA Tour season. Rights fees to broadcast professional golf would double to $400 million under the new contracts, boosting average tournament purses from $1.7 million in 1997 to $3 million in 1999. The new season was the dawn of an era when players like Payne could earn more money than they had ever imagined while playing for more viewers than ever before. The six networks involved in the deal would carry 413 hours of golf, up from 353 in 1997. They knew audiences would flock to their televisions when Tiger Woods was in the field.

Even with just one win in 1998, Woods remained an imperative fans of golf craved: a blend of brio, refinement, and violence, all the more appealing because he was a minority from the middle class in an American sport historically maligned for classism and racism. Woods brought new audiences to golf. They fawned over him as they had over Long John Daly in 1991. But unlike Daly, Woods carried himself with clear purpose, seemed to contend every week, and won as often as he should.

His rise paralleled the ascent of ball, club, and shaft technology that made three-hundred-yard drives not just possible but expected (no less, however, thrilling to watch). In '99, while Woods was winning the eight tournaments he would eventually capture that year, he averaged 293 yards a drive, the third longest on tour and 30 yards deeper than the aging players like Payne. Woods ranked inside the top five in scoring, greens in regulation, and birdies per round. He was eleventh in scrambling and a top twenty-five putter. There always had been players who drove the ball a long way. Most of them were novelties, sideshows with a singular talent, but Woods in '99 was one of those rare cases: the long-ball power player who also scored. Jack Nicklaus had been one, too. The comparisons were inevitable.

Woods tied for second at Riviera the week after he won at Torrey Pines. Payne missed the cut. Payne finished second in Coral Springs, Florida, where another bomber, Vijay Singh, prevailed at TPC Heron Bay. Two weeks later, David Duval won this third tournament of the season at the Players Championship, and a week after that, he won his fourth at TPC Sugarloaf near Atlanta.

The 1999 season was beginning to feel like a bridge. On one side stood Payne, Lehman, O'Meara, Sutton, and the other players in their forties who'd learned to play winning golf with the old clubs and refined sense of feel. They'd adopted the new equipment, the balls and drivers especially, in a choice that represented acceptance of change and survival on the modern tour. But they still wanted to make each shot from their feet through their fingertips. They didn't know, or desire, any other way.

On the other side were Duval, Woods, Phil Mickelson, and other players in their twenties who'd benefited the most from advancements that made golf easier through forgiveness, length, and stability. They came to golf when golf was becoming simplified and more complicated at the same time.

In 1981, thirteen years after Karsten Solheim machined his first Anser putter in Arizona, a young, self-promoting club designer named Gary Adams had introduced a cast stainless-steel driver in his home-town of McHenry, Illinois. It was a lively and nearly indestructible club with the new brand name of TaylorMade stamped on the sole. Adams gave models to George Archer, Al Geiberger, Johnny Miller, and Dave Stockton, "and all have reported 20–30 yards more distance," staff writer John Seaburn wrote for the October 18 edition the *Akron Beacon Journal*. Retailers sold the TaylorMade No. 1 for eighty dollars. It was a lot of money. Most players, rutted in tradition, smugly rejected such an abomination. It became known as the Pittsburgh Persimmon, especially after Ron Streck missed just two fairways with one in a final-round 62 at the Houston Open, the first PGA Tour tournament won with a driver not sawed and sanded from a tree.

In 1982, PING had released its Eye2 irons, with square grooves on the face to increase spin, more mass on the perimeter to correct mishits, and an offset shaft to help average players swing through impact with their hands in front of the ball. Other manufacturers created their own versions of the perimeter-weighted iron, many of them cast instead of forged for greater durability and lower production costs.

Callaway rolled out its metal Big Bertha driver in 1991. It was the first driver tour professionals and amateurs embraced with equal enthu-siasm, with a shaft that penetrated through the clubhead for reduced twisting and torque through the swing. Four years later, the company unveiled the Great Big Bertha, constructed of titanium, which was lighter than steel, allowing for larger size and a thinner face that sprang like a trampoline. The Maxfli, Titleist, and Spalding brands introduced urethane-covered balls that offered unprecedented durability, distance with the driver, and a quiet, soft interaction with the green. No one played balata or persimmon anymore. Golf courses throughout the world now echoed with the tings of alloy meeting elastomer.

A new company called Adams created an odd-looking fairway metal in 1994 and named its series Tight Lies. The shallow face of the clubs could launch the ball, and launch it high, from anywhere: dirt, sand, mud, even caliche. TaylorMade referenced the shape of turn-of-the-century hickory-shafted woods to inspire the venerable Rescue, the first hybrid and the birth of a new category of golf club. The company offered the Rescue, which played with the ease of an iron and the distance of a wood, in 1999, at the same time Acushnet was developing a dynamic new ball to release early in the coming year. The company would call it the Titleist Pro V1. Professionals would make it the most successful ball on their tours. Consumers would make it the best-selling golf ball of all time.

Players now had more choices than ever before when it came to selecting fourteen clubs and a sleeve for their ball pockets. But the matter of moving from the tee to the hole, the essence of golf since the Scottish shepherds discovered the vexing intrigue of primitive golf on their pastures along the sea, was becoming a much easier task.

The bridge between the centuries was built with graphite, titanium, and urethane. It was the new industrial revolution for the ancient game.

Mark O'Meara turned forty-two in January, three months before he returned to the '99 Masters as the defending champion. He'd beaten Duval and Fred Couples the year before with a birdie putt on the seventy-second hole. Three months later, he'd won the British Open at Royal Birkdale and become the oldest player in history to win two majors in the same season.

They were the fifteenth and sixteen victories in a career with origins at Mission Viejo Country Club in Southern California, where a thirteen-year-old O'Meara, new to the neighborhood after moving from Illinois, got his first job picking balls on the practice range and taught himself to flight shots with his mother's clubs. He played college golf at Long Beach State. He won the 1979 California and U.S. amateurs, turned professional a year later, and left Orange County in 1989 after winning his first two Pebble Beach Pro-Ams and two other tournaments. He purchased a house on a lake in Bay Hill and moved to Orlando, where he met the showman in the flat cap and the plus fours who lived on the twelfth hole.

Like Payne, O'Meara took his share of lonely walks. Those walks were part of the math in an individual sport like golf, in which there is one winner, leaving 150-odd losers. O'Meara had finished in the top five in all four of the majors before 1998. His Masters title vacated a curse.

"People won't say, 'How come you haven't won a major championship?'" he said after he won.

O'Meara returned to Augusta in '99 to the pageantry due the defending champion and the tired, expected questions about whether he could do it again. He'd tied for third at the Honda, a stroke behind Payne, who took second alone. He'd placed sixth at the Players Championship two weeks before the Masters. But little else about the state of his game suggested O'Meara would be a threat. Even with his modern equipment—he played the newest TaylorMade metal driver with the so-called Bubble shaft—he averaged a meager 267 yards from the tee, and he missed every third fairway. Both concerned him. Augusta National was longer and tighter. Partly in a reaction to the way Woods had dismantled the course in 1997, the club introduced rough for the '99 Masters, added trees to smother inaccurate drives, and lengthened two holes, including the par-five second, which now spanned 575 yards.

"I can't reach it in two," O'Meara said after a practice round. "Some of the longer hitters can still get there, but it won't be that easy."

The changes to Augusta National were the most substantial since 1981, when the club replaced the Bermuda on its greens with bent grass. Payne didn't let the new rough, trees, or 6,985-yard length spook him. He was just pleased to receive an invitation again. He hadn't played the Masters since 1996, and while he'd missed the cut that year, at least he'd been there.

Payne believed that a condition of true greatness in golf was earning a place in all four majors—every year, without exception. He routinely qualified for the U.S. and British Opens and the PGA Championship. But Augusta National selected its limited Masters field through stricter requirements. Payne had missed the tournament three times, and the failure to earn an invitation embarrassed and irritated him, even though it was his least-favorite major.

Augusta exposed his chronic weakness: putting. Even with the help from his wife and her circle drill to improve his stroke and concentration, Payne never became an elite putter, and the torrid slopes of the greens at the Masters mocked him each April. He'd finished in the top ten just twice. His bother with the most important scoring club in his bag crippled his chances before he even made his first swing. Payne hoped his SeeMore putter would make some kind of difference in '99. But hope was different from belief on the agnostic greens of Augusta.

Payne and ninety-five other players started the sixty-third Masters on Thursday, April 9. He shot 73, one over par and four behind the leaders, in a round interrupted for ninety minutes by lightning. He'd not played himself into contention, but not out of it, either. The surprise coleader was Masters rookie Brandel Chamblee, the thirty-six-year-old former All-American at Texas, who shot 69 with a club in his bag that looked like a cross between a rubber mallet and a spark plug wrench.

It was called a Zoom. Chamblee said his carry distance with it was about 220 yards, as straight as a two-iron and with the height of a four-metal. An early version of the driving iron, it was made by PRGR, a company in Japan that dabbled in boutique technologies, such as carbon clubheads, longer driver shafts, early versions of bent hosels and lower centers of gravity on its drivers, and different golf balls designed for different swing speeds. It was the Zoom that Chamblee used to eagle the thirteenth, the winding par-five, from 216 yards to five feet from the hole.

"It's ugly the first time you see it," Chamblee said after his round. "But when you hit it, it gets much prettier."

Payne returned Friday for a second-round 75 to make the cut on the number, another pale concession in the pesky major that always seemed out of reach. A 77-75 weekend doomed him to tie for fifty-second, four spots out of last. He was done with his Sunday round by the time the last groups on the course got to the new 575-yard second hole. Payne was discouraged but not deflated. One more year of circle drills would help. He knew he could count on Tracey for those. So would one more year with the SeeMore.

The tournament belonged to José María Olazábal, the Masters champion of 1984, the wily and resourceful Spaniard who'd beaten Payne in their Ryder Cup singles match in 1989. Olazábal led Scott McCarron by one after a 70-66 start. He was a good story in a tournament that seemed to inspire such scripts.

Olazábal had missed eighteen months of golf, including the 1995 Ryder Cup, with a mysterious foot ailment that sometimes prevented him from leaving his bed. Now here he was, walking the steep slopes of Augusta National with the lead. Behind him, Lee Janzen, the U.S. Open foil of Payne's, sneaked into third with bewitched Greg Norman, now forty-four, who'd committed one of the gravest lapses in championship golf three years before by yielding a six-shot lead to Nick Faldo in the final round at Augusta.

His mien that afternoon in '96 had no bearing on his play in 1999. Norman shot tidy rounds of 71-68 to finish the first half of the Masters at minus five, three behind Olazábal. Clever columnists couldn't help themselves. "She is doing it to him again, this Scarlett O'Hara of a golf course," Skip Bayless wrote for the Saturday sports section of the

Chicago Tribune. "She is batting her azalea eyelashes at poor Greg Norman, leading him on, setting him up to break his heart again."

His readers knew his signature hysteria when they saw it, but this time, Bayless was onto something. Norman teased legend and lore with a third-round 71 to move a stroke closer to Olazábal, who shot a 73. The final pairing on Sunday would feature two international players: the charismatic and tragic Australian, the poised and sympathetic Spaniard. The Spaniard shot 71 to win by two and beat the Australian, his heart indeed broken again, by three.

"Somehow I just feel at peace when I am here," Olazábal said.

Olazábal shot an eight-under-par 280 on a new-look Augusta National that Tom Lehman called "a chamber of horrors." He did so with a titanium driver, a titanium fairway three-metal, and the Titleist Tour Professional, the ball that Payne also used. Jack McCallum, the reporter on-site for *Sports Illustrated* magazine, wanted his readers to remember that even though Olazábal was a relatively young man of thirty-nine, he moved through a golf course with his fingertips and his feet. "For the tournament is, after all, about shotmaking," McCallum wrote, "and few golfers design shots like Olazábal, a man with the hands of a seamstress and the heart of a warrior." McCallum recognized which side of the bridge his story subject stood on.

Davis Love III finished second, just as he had in riveting 1995, when a grieving Ben Crenshaw won four days after he flew home to Austin for the funeral for Harvey Penick, his lifelong teacher and muse. There was David Duval, who assembled four steady but unremarkable rounds to share sixth with Phil Mickelson. Woods tied for eighteenth. He never broke 70. Lehman and O'Meara shared thirty-first. With his tie for fifty-second, Payne beat only one other player.

Payne set out for Hilton Head and the MCI Classic, a tournament he'd won twice on one of the courses that seemed to produce his finest golf. He had no concerns beyond how to decode the greens at Augusta, but there was plenty of time to work on that. The season was nearly half over now. His victory at Pebble Beach assured him of a Masters invitation in 2000. He was exempt for the U.S. Open at Pinehurst. Physically, emotionally, and spiritually, Payne entered his tenth tournament of the season with a tranquility he'd rarely felt before.

The '90s were indeed special now. He was home more, cooking pancakes for Aaron and Chelsea before they went off to school at First Academy, fetching them in the afternoons, eager to hear what they'd learned about the Bible and the story of Jesus Christ and the disciples. He was going to Sunday school on his off weeks at First Baptist Church. He'd quit drinking as much or as often. He indulged on Sundays, Mondays, and Tuesdays, but Wednesday nights were when he left the beer in the refrigerator and the margaritas unmixed. His abstinence lasted through the four nights before he played golf.

He was thankful that Tracey had pushed so hard on him in the past. He was grateful to still be playing golf, and she was the biggest reason he was doing it, that he had not given up on himself. He was no longer awash in doubt down on the dock. He was happy with the big matters in his life, like his family and his friends, and also the little ones, like swinging those old Mizuno irons again, and rolling balls with the See-More putter that his caddie had handed him in California.

Payne shot 68-64 at Harbour Town and led by one midway through.

"What is it about this golf course that kind of suits you?" a reporter asked that Friday after his round.

"It's not a ball beater's course," Payne said. "Distance isn't everything."

But in some respects, distance *was* everything in the late spring months of 1999. Players craved it. Length was the elixir that influenced the new way tour professionals, especially the younger ones, pictured their attack on a golf course. A decade earlier, the longest drivers on the PGA Tour barely touched 280 yards. Now, a 280-yard drive ranked twenty-first, and players such as John Daly and Tiger Woods routinely averaged 300. If shots found the rough, so be it. A pitching wedge from long grass carried more appeal than a longer iron from the fairway. Pride factored. So did ego. To hit the ball farther than a fellow competitor might make no concrete sense on the scorecard, but it did make a man feel better about himself. Superior, even.

But some golf courses the PGA Tour played repelled distance for the sake of distance. Harbour Town was one of those places, which is why Payne led the tournament after two rounds and other shot-makers—John Cook, John Huston, Fred Funk, Scott Hoch, Larry Mize—were his nearest chasers. The 6,912-yard course, ringed with live oaks and pines, squeezed the sight lines from the tees. Players didn't just aim for the fairways. They aimed for sides of the fairways, and even sides of sides.

"You've got to think yourself around this golf course a lot," Payne said in his Friday press conference.

He widened his lead early Saturday, which got windier as the afternoon wore on. He hadn't thought much about luck since the Pebble Beach Pro-Am. But then he watched his wayward six-iron shot at No. 7, one of the Harbour Town's strong par-three holes, glance off a tree. His ball could've gone anywhere. It stopped four feet from the hole. He made the birdie that could've been a bogey.

Payne led by four. It was too early to wonder if this might be the week he would win a four-round tournament. His focus did crack, though, and through a series of bad bogeys on the back nine, he lost his lead. He told reporters after the third round that he was not pleased with his 72.

Then one of them asked about the role of chance.

"How often do things happen like what happened to you on seven today that we don't hear about?"

"It happens," Payne said. "If you play golf long enough, you get the good breaks, you get the bad breaks. That ball," he continued, "could have just as easily kicked and gone somewhere else. So, like I said, you have to take advantage when you get a break like that, and I did. I stepped up, knocked in the putt. That is good for me. That is reassuring that I am taking advantage of breaks when I get them. That's how you win golf tournaments."

The Atlantic breezes swirled Sunday on the coast of South Carolina. Payne missed a midrange putt to win outright on the eighteenth hole. It was a fine round of 70, but Jeff Sluman and little-known Glen Day had scored better, and now he was involved in a three-way playoff. Day won the tournament on the first hole of sudden death.

"Professional golf is a game of tremendous highs and tremendous lows," Day told the press.

Payne knew exactly how Day felt. But he was adjusting well now to the emotional swings of tournament golf. He'd missed his chance to win in seventy-two holes. It wasn't the wind's fault, a divot's fault, the fault of the speed of the greens. It wasn't luck. It wasn't a conspiracy of fate. It wasn't even one roll of the ball. It was the fact that someone else played better.

"It was a beautiful day," Payne said. "And you've got a great champion in Glen."

He packed up his Mizunos and the SeeMore putter and took a week off from golf. More pancakes. More questions about the Bible for his kids. He played the Houston Open in May but never contended. He missed the cut in New Orleans. He skipped the Texas tournaments in Irving and Fort Worth, part of three weeks at home before the Memorial, the FedEx in Memphis, and the U.S. Open. He was trying to build into the national championship at Pinehurst.

He played one good round in Dublin, a 65 on Friday, but that was it. He tied for twenty-fourth. No one was catching Tiger Woods that week anyway. Vijay Singh and David Duval tried, but Woods won by two, his ninth career title and his second of the last season of the century. Everyone was trying to build into the U.S. Open. Woods. Duval. Singh. Phil Mickelson, who tied for eleventh at the Memorial, was playing well. So was Paul Azinger, who would tie for sixth in Memphis the week after Dublin. The resurgent Hal Sutton had six top tens leading into the FedEx St. Jude Classic, where he would join Azinger in sixth place at TPC Southwind. Tom Lehman, who was collecting runner-up finishes in '99 like they rained from clouds, would nearly win in Memphis, going 63-68-68-68 to share second.

Payne, meanwhile, missed the cut by four in Tennessee. There were no post-round interviews, no questions about breaks or shot-making or length.

He felt restless for the U.S. Open. He and his caddie, Mike Hicks, decided to leave Memphis early for North Carolina. Payne asked his teacher, Chuck Cook, to meet them there for an early reconnaissance round Saturday on Pinehurst No. 2, which he'd last seen when the Tour Championship was there in 1991. It was June now. Payne still needed to make the Ryder Cup team. He still needed to prove to himself that he could win a tournament in four rounds. He wanted to vanquish the memory of the Masters and win another major.

Three remained. The '90s were running out.

"David Duval may be the new No. 1, but all eyes are on [Tiger] Woods," Doug Ferguson, the golf writer for the Associated Press, wrote in his U.S. Open preview.

"David Duval was asked to name some of the favorites," the *Montgomery Advertiser* told its readers in its preview. "He paused for a long time, then rattled off a long list of players that included Tiger Woods, Justin Leonard, Davis Love III, and Greg Norman."

"Woods is the player to beat every time he tees it up, and he's way overdue for a seventh USGA title," Del Lemon of the *Austin American-Statesman* wrote in his.

Rees Jones, the architect commissioned to restore the greens on No. 2 before the U.S. Open, had given a number of interviews before the championship. He noted the value of a creative and unconventional short game at the Donald Ross jewel on the sandy loam of the Pinehurst Resort in the North Carolina sandhills. The closely mown areas around the crowned greens of No. 2 would present players with many recovery options, from putters to lob wedges to bump-and-run seven-irons, even fairway metals from the fringe. Most of all, Jones said, the field would have to accept humility and limits. He predicted the winner would be "somebody with mental fortitude who has been around a while." He mentioned no names.

"It's really going to take a magician rather than a mechanic to win here," he said.

CHAPTER TEN

Payne walked No. 2 the Saturday he arrived from Memphis. He went out again Sunday for a practice round. He and Chuck Cook mapped the course, making notes in the pages of a yardage book with an orange cover, checking areas around the greens that represented safe harbor—the so-called good miss—from round-killing double bogeys. Cook marked the worst places in blue ink.

Payne's teacher knew the courses of Pinehurst well, especially No. 2. Years before, when he was on the staff at the Golf Digest School with Davis Love Jr. and other notable instructors, Cook played the Ross classic so often he could tell Payne before he hit a practice shot what it would do when it landed. He insisted Payne watch and listen to him. Payne thought the blue marks in the yardage book were brilliant.

Payne took the SeeMore and nine other clubs, six irons and three wedges, to his practice round Sunday, testing all of them from the tightly mown greenside slopes that made Pinehurst distinctive among the other parkland courses the USGA used for its national championship. Payne knew his faults. He ranked 123rd in greens in regulation and 137th in driving accuracy. If he were going to be the magician No. 2 would anoint, he'd have to do it with the little feel shots close to the hole, pulling par out of thin air.

In the canon of golden age golf courses, most authorities in course architecture considered Pinehurst No. 2 a magnum opus. Its designer, Pinehurst head golf professional and Scottish-born rose aficionado Donald J. Ross, sketched its holes through the namesake trees of central North Carolina, a region of subtle draws and hollows and, to the delight of Ross, the finest possible soil for shaping and growing a golf course. The fertile sandy loam, easy to manipulate, allowed Ross to create mounds, ridges, and swales throughout the routing. Ross knew those features would drain well and present resort guests with a range of ways to score (or fail to). Construction began in 1901. It ended six years later. The original sand greens, shaped roughly in the form of upside-down saucers, were sprigged with grass in 1934. Ross lived in a cottage near the confluence of the third and fifth holes. He labored on No. 2 for more than forty years. His fondness for the No. 2—one of four hundred courses he designed until his death in 1948, his signature endowment to the game—grew with every nip, tuck, and caress.

It was a championship course from the start. Tour professionals played the North & South Open Championship on No. 2 before the PGA Championship arrived in 1936 as the first major. "The mounding makes possible an infinite variety of nasty short shots that no other form of hazard can call for," read the championship program. "Competitors whose second shots have wandered a bit will be disturbed by these innocent appearing slopes and by the shot they will have to invent to recover." The defending champion, Johnny Revolta, played it and said, "The greens are as true as sunrise, but they call for careful study, a keen eye, and a perfect stroke to a greater extent than any other greens I have putted." Denny Shute met Jimmy Thomsen in the thirty-six-hole final, at a time when the PGA still employed the match-play format to determine the winner of its championship. Thomsen outdrove Shute by fifty yards. Shute focused on fairways and greens. He beat Thomsen on the thirty-fourth hole with accuracy, guile, and the patience of man who recognized a golf course that rewarded restraint.

Affection grew through the years for Pinehurst No. 2. The Ryder Cup matches were played there in 1951. The USGA set up No. 2 at a startling 7,051 yards for the 1962 U.S. Amateur, making it the longest course to date in the history of USGA championships. (A twenty-year-old Oklahoman named Labron Harris Jr. won with a deft short game, even having the audacity to putt out of greenside bunkers. Only one player older than thirty advanced to the quarterfinals, suggesting the advantage of youth on a long golf course. Frank Hannigan, covering the championship for *Golf Journal,* overheard someone call it "the slaughter of the ancients.")

Both the Western and Southern golf associations contested championships there in the '60s and '70s. The Tour Championship came in 1991 and '92, when Paul Azinger won it for his eighth career title. The USGA brought its U.S. Senior Open to No. 2 in 1994. And five years after that, on the Sunday before the 1999 U.S. Open, Payne walked the course with his coach and his caddie, marking spots in the yardage book with the orange cover and trying to make some magic with nine clubs. Payne was beginning to appreciate what Ross himself observed shortly before he died: "The golfer with one shot in his bag will get nowhere in the future."

As more players in the field of 156 arrived to see No. 2, some of them for the first time, the themes of the championship began to take shape. By Tuesday, everyone was debating the tightly mown mounds around the greens, the shorter rough in general, and the generosity of the fairways specifically, which were five to seven yards wider than typical U.S. Open courses. The USGA wanted players to have opportunities to score, or at least have more choices if they missed fairways. Pinehurst reminded some players of Augusta National. It was beginning to feel like a place for hope and potential instead of fear and limits.

"I can't think of anything I don't like," Corey Pavin, who'd won the '95 championship at Shinnecock, said after his practice round.

By now, Pavin and everyone else who played serious golf carried the clubs and balls of the new era. Balata was obsolete, a code word for the past. Persimmon was just a hardwood tree harvested for pool cues. Tour players still preferred steel shafts in their irons, but more than 90 percent of them now played lighter graphite shafts in their drivers, accelerating swing speeds in the pursuit of extra yards, even if it meant a wedge from the rough.

Seven of ten tour players in '99 still used a wound ball, most of them the Titleist Professional model, with its durable but soft urethane cover. Thirty percent of the tour now played a solid-core ball, more than ever before. No one used woods made of actual wood anymore. Davis Love III and Justin Leonard were among the last tour players to swing a wood driver in competition. Leonard switched to titanium in the summer of 1997 and promptly won the British Open at Royal Troon. Love made the move after the U.S. Open that year at Congressional and never gave it another thought. He dominated the PGA Championship two months later at Winged Foot with a Titleist 975D in his bag and a rainbow overhead at the end. Leonard was the runner-up.

It was fair to wonder if a long hitter like Love, whose 283-yard average drive in 1999 ranked seventeenth on the tour, enjoyed some kind of edge at welcoming, arms-wide-out Pinehurst. The USGA presented No. 2 at 7,175 yards to a par of 70. It was the third-longest course in U.S. Open history, a fact that concerned Pavin and Payne and other shot-makers who didn't hit golf balls as far as Woods or Singh or Mickelson or Love. Golfers rarely spoke of U.S. Open conditions as an invitation to unleash a driver at every opportunity. But the Open hadn't been to Pinehurst before now.

"[It] tempts you to make a shot you shouldn't be attempting," Lee Janzen said. "If you squirt left or right, you can end up in the pine trees or miss the chipping areas. If the rough was deeper, and you hack it on the fairway and hit a wedge on the green, you'd see more pars and bogeys. This way, you'll see maybe some great birdies, and also maybe some doubles."

"I think you'll see some bigger numbers for it," added Love.

Payne completed another practice round Tuesday in a light rain and building winds. Dick Coop had traveled from Chapel Hill to Pinehurst to walk some of the holes with his client in the plus fours. He wanted to make sure Payne was remembering his pre-shot routine and picking his intermediate target. Coop liked what he saw.

Payne and the rest of the players were getting a sharper sense for how shots spilled from the edges of the perniciously domed greens, the emerging crucible of the ninety-ninth U.S. Open. Woods saw his approach carom from the sides and crash twenty yards away, sometimes into pine straw, like a flushed dove. "Very severe," he said. Mark O'Meara said he thought imagination and creativity would prevail over power golf, and "I think that's wonderful." Jack Nicklaus saw a golf course early in the week that struck him as open to birdies and equitable. Colin Montgomerie, who typically played well in the U.S. Open and had finished second in 1997, said he wasn't even looking at the flagsticks on No. 2. He said he aimed at the middle of the green on every approach, "because if you start attacking this type of course, you're in trouble."

Payne had one complaint: the 489-yard par-four sixteenth hole, a converted par-five. He thought the green was built to hold short, higher iron shots.

He found Tom Meeks of the USGA. Friendly now since their amend-making day at Isleworth, they exchanged small talk.

Then Payne explained his criticism of the sixteenth hole.

"That green wasn't designed to accept a shot with a long iron," he told Meeks.

"I'll make a deal with you," Meeks replied. "We'll move the tee back a little and play it as a par-five—*if* you promise me you won't go for the green in two."

Payne stared at him.

"Why would you even try, if the green isn't designed to hold a long-iron shot?" Meeks said coyly.

Payne wheeled.

"You're impossible," he said and walked away.

On his fourth day at Pinehurst, Payne was now certain that no player in the field, including himself, would be on many of the greens in regulation numbers, most assuredly No. 16. So he practiced a lot of middle-range putts with the SeeMore. He kept toying with the recovery shots with all sorts of clubs from the tight grass, a performer running his lines before the big show. Cook and Coop and Hicks, the men who knew his mind and swing like no one else, began to feel that something special might happen.

"There's not just one way to play a golf shot out there," Payne told reporters Tuesday. It was an echo of Ross himself.

Payne would spend a lot of time with reporters that week. The stage would be his again.

A bright anticipation hummed in the days before the championship. The village of seven thousand residents, many of them in some form of retirement and infatuated with golf, welcomed forty thousand visitors for the week. Together they wondered how one of the deepest fields in history would cope with the sandy draws and hollows of old No. 2.

Ten previous U.S. Open winners were there, including Watson and Nicklaus, now fifty-nine, competing in his forty-second national championship. There were winners of the Masters (Fred Couples, Ben Crenshaw, Nick Faldo, O'Meara, Woods), the British Open (Tom Lehman, Greg Norman, Nick Price), and the PGA Championship (Love, Singh, Sutton, Paul Azinger). There were players who had not won a major (but would). There were players who thought they would win another major (but wouldn't), and there were players who thought they would win at least one in their career (and should have, but were wrong). All twelve members of the forthcoming U.S. Ryder Cup team to be assembled in August were in the field at Pinehurst. Half of the future European team was in North Carolina, too. The U.S. Open that summer wasn't just a collection of the best players in 1999. It was a convocation of some of the finest golfers of the century.

Many people expected David Duval, the top-ranked player in the world, to prevail in his nineteenth start in a major. He'd already won four tournaments in '99, and he'd tied for third in his last one, the Memorial. Duval was a fine driver and putter, straight enough off the tee, and the best iron player in golf. No one hit more greens in regulation. Second-shot precision was an enormous advantage at Pinehurst.

But Duval was a statistically mediocre scrambler. His swing and timing needed to be at their impeccable and unified best.

Others favored Woods. He'd won twice already, including in his last start, when he'd beaten Duval and Singh in Ohio. But he also remained an incomplete project. Woods and his teacher, Butch Harmon, were at the end of a project that began in 1997, when Woods revamped his mechanics for more consistency and control, especially when he was fighting his swing. He noted Tuesday that he'd won the Memorial in spite of himself.

"I wasn't playing that well, but I managed my game," Woods said.

Phil Mickelson was preparing for his twentieth start in a major, and after he'd tied for sixth in the Masters that spring and seen the relatively broad fairways and light rough at Pinehurst, his aspirations were soaring. Mickelson devastated the ball with his Yonex driver: an average of more than 285 yards that year. He also did so wildly, missing more than a quarter of his fairways, which was a recurring fault that often kept him from competing for four rounds in the national championship. But he knew how to scramble, and when he sniffed victory, he knew how to win. He possessed thirteen PGA Tour trophies by the time he arrived at Pinehurst, fresh off ties for eleventh in Fort Worth and Dublin. He liked the No. 2 the moment he encountered it.

In many ways, the venue and the occasion were perfect for Mickelson, a short-game magician who awed players and spectators alike with a waiflike softness when his hands held a wedge. The long-driving lefty from Southern California seemed to hold the ball on a string with lofted clubs, and there was no better practitioner when circumstances called for a wedge. He saw at Pinehurst a stage of his own, and himself as the showman.

Mickelson turned twenty-nine on the day before the first round. His wife, Amy, was pregnant with their first child. The baby girl was due June 30, but there were signs she might be born earlier, so Mickelson had a pager in his golf bag and an airplane on a runway nearby in case he needed to vacate in a hurry. He'd told family, friends, reporters, and his caddie, Jim Mackay, that he would leave at a moment's notice if he were summoned.

It was another layer of intrigue for Mickelson as a candidate to win his first major at Pinehurst. Everyone was waiting for a coronation that seemed as certain as daybreak through the longleafs. He was the face of amateur golf in the early '90s, when he'd won three NCAA titles at Arizona State, the 1990 U.S. Amateur, and the 1991 Northern Telecom Open in Tucson, Arizona, as a junior in college. He'd turned professional in '92 and won two PGA Tour tournaments in '93. A share of sixth place at the 1993 PGA Championship foretold a career of scrapes with success in the four biggest tournaments in golf. But Mickelson, like Payne before the back nine at Kemper Lakes, couldn't seem to realize the expectations so many in the game had placed on him.

He'd had chances. At Shinnecock in '95, Mickelson reached the sixty-eighth hole of the U.S. Open a shot out of the lead. He double-bogeyed the seventieth and tied for fourth. Three summers later, he tied for tenth at Olympic after a third-round 74 negated an otherwise fine score of 70 in the fourth. Mickelson tended to play the U.S. Open too boldly, ramming putts too far past the hole and missing the return, spraying drives into awful lies. His swing coach accused him of carelessly wasting shots, especially in early rounds, and then losing interest. Mickelson committed in 1996 to a new kind of discipline. He put more time into practice, often hitting three hundred balls in solitude after a tournament round in an effort to groove a consistent swing that Hogan would've admired. He toughened up. He won four times that season. Curtis Strange, the two-time U.S. Open champion, told *Sports Illustrated* writer Jaime Diaz, "When you think of Phil, you think of a guy who is going to win a lot of tournaments. What Phil has got is a sixth sense, a touch, an instinct, a feel, a way to win."

Like Woods, Mickelson straddled the eras, transcended generations, stood with a foot on each side of the bridge. But he wilted in the majors like Payne used to do. Pinehurst presented an opportunity Mickelson knew as soon as he saw what the USGA had done with the fairways, the rough, and the closely cropped grass around the greens. Back in California, meanwhile, his wife followed her doctor's orders to rest in bed. She kept the pager number near.

There were other players in excellent form as Wednesday came to an end in North Carolina. Singh, less than a year removed from his PGA Championship at Sahalee, was playing high-quality golf. So was Montgomerie, twice a winner on the European Tour. Hal Sutton had four top tens in his last five starts. The presentation at No. 2, an ode from the USGA to the spirit of Donald Ross and his vision for sandhills golf, gave a variety of players the opportunity to rise. As the final day of preparation wound down at Pinehurst, Duval and Woods were the cautious favorites. But every top player in the field had some kind of chance.

"Right now, I'd probably say there's thirty guys that have the ability to win this golf tournament," Greg Norman said Wednesday after his last practice round.

"What it boils down to is who is the most patient and who is the most focused and who makes the most putts for par and who hangs in there," Love said after his.

On the day before the first round, Payne was done with long practice. He was ready. He hit a small pile of balls, putted for thirty minutes, left to see a movie with Hicks, and spent the balance of the evening with Tracey. He cooked spaghetti for dinner. He slept well.

CHAPTER ELEVEN

Payne got to No. 2 on Thursday an hour before his 11:50 a.m. tee time, after a shower had doused the course overnight. He rolled some short putts on the practice green, limbered with a few pitches and chips, and walked to the range with his caddie. He ended his session piercing draw shots with his three-metal. Cook wanted Payne to finish his warm-up with the first shot he faced on the course.

The first hole was a gentle, welcoming, and straightaway par-four of 404 yards that Donald Ross created to, in his words, "give the player a chance to warm up a bit." Payne made an unhurried par. He carried the yardage book with the orange cover in his back pocket, which was unusual, because Hicks always carried the book. But Payne wanted it close at this tournament. A lot of work had been put into it. It was the chart that he would use to navigate the draws and hollows. He made par on the second hole, too.

Payne came to the third, a short par-four with a slight bend to the right, and asked Hicks for his three-iron. His ball bounced down the fairway and settled in a sand-filled divot. It was an unlikely result so early in a tournament, the kind of distressing low-odds surprise that used to wound Payne, back when he was a weaker man who did a lot of blaming.

This time, he took a pitching wedge, planted his left foot, and pinched a shot to fifteen feet. He made the putt for birdie. He'd turned bad luck into good.

He shot 68 that Thursday, including another stroke from a sandy divot on the thirteenth, where he converted an up-and-down par from one of the spots around a green that wasn't shaded in blue ink. He finished a shot behind Duval, Mickelson, and two other players. He shared fifth place with Woods and four others. Sutton, Singh, and a dozen more contestants shot 69 in an opening round ripe for scoring and rising hopes for more of them among the thousands of spectators. Payne made just one bogey. It came at the last hole.

Players had little trouble adjusting to a wetter, heavier Pinehurst No. 2. The damp greens absorbed shots better, and the golf course gave up twenty-three scores under par. But the effectively longer length created by the rain victimized older competitors like Nicklaus, who shot eight-over 78, his highest first-round U.S. Open score in years.

"Guys are playing eight- and nine-irons and I'm playing two- and three-irons," he said.

No one took a lot of risks that early. The first round of a U.S. Open, even after a rain, was neither the time nor the place for low-percentage plays. Duval said he was proud that his score was a reflection of conservative shot-making, timely putts, and the absence of misfortune. He felt his iron play was as sound as it ever had been at an Open. His misses into greens were minor. He and the other players figured the softer course was only going to get more and more difficult, given the forecast for continued sun and gathering heat for the next two days. Mickelson said he expected "a long weekend" if the greens dried and began repelling shots.

Payne felt good about his round. He'd missed a six-footer for birdie on the par-three seventeenth, but as he certified his scorecard and thought through his shots, he appreciated that he'd played prudent, thoughtful golf that, most important to him, avoided the ticklish collection areas he and Chuck Cook had marked in blue. His ability to see and hit targets reminded him of his first two rounds at Olympic. He said he thought the winning score would be under par, but not by very much.

Payne was glad he had that yardage book. It gave him a reference for every shot he faced. It gave him room for freedom but just enough structure to keep him focused on execution and goals. As he described his four birdies and single bogey to the press, he remembered how rarely he'd missed a target that afternoon with his Mizunos. He wasn't aiming at greens. He was aiming at quadrants. And more often than not, that's where his shots went.

"I thought very well out there and did what I wanted to do," he said. "I came in here and designed a game plan of how I wanted to play the golf course, and it starts with getting the ball in the fairway. Other than that, there's pins that you can shoot at, and then there's pins you better not shoot at. You need to know where those are."

Payne played early Friday, in the thin light of daybreak and the long shadows of the pines. A breeze rose, and the ground began to dry. Out came the sun.

He missed the first two fairways and the first three greens in regulation. He saved par on each hole with a good roll from the SeeMore. Hicks didn't have to remind him that par was a good score. Payne didn't have to remind himself to be patient and stay calm. This was the kind of golf that brought out the best in him. Make par. Make another. At the fourth, another par-four, he pounded his drive to sand-wedge distance and floated the approach to two feet. Birdie.

Wind and heat complicated cut day at Pinehurst, especially for the afternoon wave of players, and the course that surrendered all those low scores in the first round now was scoring more than two strokes higher. Mark O'Meara made six bogeys in the first nine holes. Greg Norman hit two greens in regulation in the entire round. The normally steady Ernie Els, who'd won the U.S. Open in 1994 and '97, committed two doubles and disappeared.

O'Meara, Norman, Els: All of them would miss the cut, along with Fred Couples, Nick Faldo, and Nicklaus, who'd post his worst two-round score in relation to par since his debut in the U.S. Open in 1957. José María Olazábal, the Masters champion, wouldn't even get the chance to play Friday. He'd punched a wall in his hotel room after his opening 75, broken his hand, and withdrawn.

Out on the course, Payne trudged ahead.

He made another birdie at the seventh to get to minus four for the championship, then bogeyed the eighth and ninth. He sensed his swing come apart slightly and suddenly, one stitch tearing loose in a hem, until he made an eleven-foot putt for par on No. 12 and, for reasons he couldn't articulate, he felt like himself again over the ball. The SeeMore kept saving him. He holed a series of midrange putts that kept him in position. He birdied the fifteenth and finished with pars on three hard holes that continued, as the wind and the heat and the day wore on, to get harder.

Payne was in with 69. It tied for the lowest score of the second round, a stroke under par on a difficult day in North Carolina. Mickelson and Duval tied him for the aggregate lead at three-under 137. Woods finished two behind, with Sutton and Singh. Mike Hicks had pulled only one club for Payne through two rounds. He was carrying a golf bag for a man in control of his mind and movement. All Payne wanted from his caddie was the yardage and the wind. Every swing looked the same. Every shot hit its spot. Every stride seemed to point the player and caddie toward a destination they didn't dare mention but sensed.

He's on autopilot, Hicks thought.

The theme of the day was resilience. Pinehurst turned vicious in stout winds under a relentless sun. Approaches that held near the flagstick in the first round bounced away in the second. The edges of the greens yellowed. The safe harbors vanished. The quadrants shrank. Payne was glad he'd played in the morning, when the dew coating the greens had given him a buffer, but players in the afternoon protested some of the holes on knobs close to the sinister Donald Ross falloffs.

Payne tried to dwell on the variables he could control, like his attitude about those expected adversities that made the national championship the most grueling test in golf.

"The people that are complaining about the pins, they haven't played in enough U.S. Opens," he said after his round.

He and the other leaders knew what the third round held in store.

The forecast for Saturday promised more sun and more heat. That meant an even faster No. 2.

"I think that that's going to require patience," said Mickelson. "The goal is to make pars as you stand on each tee."

"You're going to see players start backing up," said Duval. "I think I'm suited for it because I'm patient. I feel like I'm efficient at what this tournament demands."

"You have to keep grinding it out," said Woods.

Nothing would get easier on a weekend of grinding. That was one of the inescapable absolutes that charmed Payne as he shared the lead in the sixteenth U.S. Open of his career. He liked what Nicklaus said about the national championship: As soon as a player carped about obstacles, that player was defeated, done. Payne thought about the many times he'd looked to blame his shortcomings on misfortune he could neither control nor change: a poor lie in unfair rough, a missed putt on an imperfect green, a turn of the ball.

Chance. Destiny. Luck.

Payne now tried to work on owning mistakes and accepting consequences, looking inside instead of out, like acknowledging when a player such as Lee Janzen simply outplayed him. His time with Dick Coop helped him do that. So did the grounding and steadying presence of Tracey and her belief in him, without condition. He thought about the little putting game they used to play. He thought about the way she snapped him back into the realities of his life when he moped through golf tournaments because he refused to practice enough. Tracey seemed to know what he needed, every time. In an odd and unintentional way, so did Paul Azinger, who now was cancer-free and playing good tournament golf again. Their visits and fishing trips years earlier when he was sick had inspired Payne to think in ways he never had about the meanings of bravery, courage, and faith. He soon started to contemplate the ideas of higher influence and surrender.

His children had no idea how much they'd changed him. They were too young to understand. It went beyond fatherhood. When he was home, which had been much more often, Payne couldn't wait to pick them up from school and hear about what they were learning. He didn't study the parables of the Bible. He didn't know much about the gospels of Jesus Christ. But he listened to Aaron and Chelsea. He identified with the messages of commitment and salvation and forgiveness and the power of sincere prayer. The men's fellowship group at First Baptist talked about those things, too. All of it gave him a new way of looking at himself and his past. It mattered less who he used to be or how he used to be. What mattered was who he was now and who he could become.

Shortly before Payne left for Pinehurst, his son had given him a gift. A reporter noticed it after the second round.

"I was looking at the band on your arm," the reporter said, noting the "difficult times" and "highs and lows" in his career. "WWJD?" the reporter said.

"That helps," Payne said.

"Can you tell me how your relationship with God has helped you?" the reporter asked.

Payne considered the band. Aaron had gotten it at school. It could mean anything to anyone, those letters, as long as it meant something.

"If you don't have your peace with God, then you better make it," Payne said. "I've made my peace."

"Inner sobriety," he called it.

Payne was happy to explain what he felt his faith was doing for him. He wished the media would devote more time and copy to the subject, instead of reminding him and the rest of the world about his failures and misgivings. So did his wife, his friends, and the parishioners back at First Baptist in Orlando. They saw these moments, when Payne talked about what God meant to him, as public proclamations of an evolving selflessness and surrender. They wanted the media's stories about Payne to show a fresh side of a changing man who was trying to move beyond the burdens, both significant and miniscule, from his past. They wanted the good news, and they wanted it shared.

But the next question in the second-round press conference outside the draws and hollows of Pinehurst No. 2 had nothing to do with a dwelling spirit or a quest for grace.

"Payne," a reporter said. "How long did it take you to get over last year?"

Stewart had a lot of time Saturday to think about what happened at Olympic in 1998. He *was* over it. In fact, he'd said in his answer to the question, he hadn't even watched a tape of the broadcast, adding, "I know what I did." He'd accepted the loss and another lonely walk. But he also believed in closure, and his performance on the hills of the Lake Course through three and a half rounds told him he just might have another U.S. Open Championship in his future. Now here he was, after two rounds on a toughening golf course, with a share of the lead again.

"Unfinished business," he called it.

Melanie Hauser found Payne before he left the property. He agreed to talk. A longtime golf reporter and a regular presence at the majors, Hauser had known Payne since he'd played at SMU. She'd written about his winning the Morris Williams in Austin. She'd covered his PGA Tour career as a golf reporter for Texas newspapers. Hauser had been one of the first journalists to notice the early hints of change in Payne, back when she'd filed that piece from the '95 Masters about whirlybirds and trash cans, the one that acknowledged that there were times when Payne "didn't even recognize himself" in the early '90s.

"He looked like that cocky kid from Southern Methodist," Hauser wrote in her golf column for the *Houston Post*, "but underneath it all he was a mess."

Now, here in Carolina, Hauser saw a stronger, fuller, bigger Payne Stewart. She mentioned in her story for the next day his involvement at First Baptist and the school his children attended. She described a man who still craved attention but seemed more judicious around people. Payne told her that he'd learned to "accept what's out there," that "if you complain that doesn't change a thing."

Hauser wrote that evening about a man who'd mellowed with age, trials, and a million mistakes.

"Reminders of that brash, cocky kid that played No. 1 at SMU lingered perhaps a bit too long," she wrote. "But try to find them now."

Payne felt ready that night for the labors ahead. He was playing Saturday afternoon with Duval, one of the new and young stars, the top-ranked player in the world. Payne wanted to summon everything he knew about contending in a major and present it full-bore to Duval, to Mickelson and Woods, these machines of golf with no wrinkles around their eyes and no heartbreak in their history, who'd never witnessed the beauty and truth of a balata ball, soaring from a driver of solid wood on the seventy-second hole of a national championship: a shot harnessed from the fingertips to the feet, a shot seen and then made.

He slept well again on Friday night.

Payne wore a flat cap and plus fours in Carolina blue for a Saturday scented of rain. Tracey stayed in their rental to watch the round on TV. Payne made his first bogey on the second hole with a drive into the rough and a missed green. He made his first birdie on the third, a par-four of 335 yards, with a nine-iron to two feet. The greens quickened, approaching the Stimpmeter reading of eleven to twelve that the USGA wanted. The grounds crew, a hundred men strong, mowed the course twice.

Scores rose. Payne and Duval spoke very little, which elevated the tension as the two players tried only to survive. Duval fought every part of his game early. He bogeyed the third when his approach landed just short of Payne's pitch mark and, unlike Payne's, dribbled all the way to the front of the green. His second shot at the fourth hit a scoreboard. He took a drop from a sprinkler at the fifth. It came to rest in an even worse lie. He made double. He bogeyed the par-three sixth from a bunker.

Payne couldn't tell how the string of bad shots and bad luck affected the twenty-seven-year-old All-American from Georgia Tech. Duval wore wraparound sunglasses and no expression as he hit one discouraging shot after another. But the mounting strokes clearly wore on him. At the seventh, as Duval settled into his stance, Payne rummaged noisily through his bag for a cereal bar. Duval backed off and stared.

Payne made bogeys at the eighth and ninth with missed putts of twelve and four feet to make the turn at plus two. Duval shot 40. In the group ahead, Woods lost two shots to par with a bogey on the first hole and a double on the second. Only Mickelson, who coasted through the front side at even, held strong against the hardening dales and hollows of No. 2. He led the championship by two until Payne made his third straight bogey at the tenth hole from a cross bunker in the fairway. Mickelson's lead stretched to three. And the rain began to fall.

Payne refused let himself drift to Olympic or any of the other majors he'd lost on the weekend. This Saturday at Pinehurst wasn't about the past. Ever the veteran, he reminded himself that there were twenty-seven holes left. He lectured himself to work only on making pars for the rest of the way in. He knew Duval, Mickelson, and Woods could be tempted by impatience and their inexperience to try too hard to win the tournament in the third round. Professional golfers, especially of their immense talents and skills, tended to get restless when they weren't making birdies. Payne didn't care if he made another birdie all afternoon.

He and his SeeMore putter made a ten-footer for par on the eleventh. He missed only one green in regulation from there and took a satisfying string of pars to the eighteenth tee. He drove to the center of the fairway and waited as Mickelson and Woods completed their rounds. A generous cheer rose from the bleachers when Mickelson dropped a six-foot putt for birdie. It was an expression of approval and appreciation for the young man whose wife lay on the other side of the country with a daughter soon to arrive.

As much as the Ross greens, the lighter rough, and the youth-filled leaderboard had influenced the plot of this national championship, equal intrigue involved the possibility that Amy Mickelson would go into labor while her husband was playing golf. Reporters had asked Mickelson about it after every round. His answer had remained the same. He said he would leave Pinehurst the moment Amy paged him. He said it didn't matter where he stood. Spectators applauded him. Columnists praised him. "It says here that Phil Mickelson has made exactly the right decision," Bill Lyon of the *Philadelphia Inquirer* would write for the Sunday editions. "Imagine him walking off the course, the security guards clearing a path, the fans clapping, the players stopping to wish him good luck, the cameras getting shots of him jumping in his car," Mark Woods of the *Palm Beach Post* would request of his readers in Florida. "At that moment, Mickelson would become more famous, more beloved than if he won the title." Other journalists asked other players what they would do in the same situation. Their answers ranged. They were aware of how their words would be construed: at home, in the locker room, in the galleries at No. 2, among strangers reading them in the Sunday papers. Most said they would do what Mickelson said he would do. Some said it depended on how many holes they had left to play.

"That's a real tough call," Payne had answered. "Especially if you're leading."

He was tied for that lead as he stood in the eighteenth fairway and waited for the applause for Mickelson to dissolve. He found his intermediate target.

"Get your spot," Hicks said quietly. "Nice and slow."

Payne bored a seven-iron to fifteen feet under the hole. He knew he couldn't win the tournament right now. But did appreciate the value of a single stroke in a U.S. Open. It would be one shot to bank for the demanding final round. It would be one shot Duval, Mickelson, or Woods would have to make up on a punishing golf course. No one had to tell Payne the leaderboard was clogged at the top as he marked his ball on the eighteenth green. He'd figured the championship would be settled by one swing, maybe two. A single stroke today would grant that much more freedom tomorrow. He replaced his ball.

Payne studied the line. He leveled the SeeMore. He pulled it back.

"Green-light putt," NBC broadcaster Johnny Miller said.

The stroke sent the ball on a keeling left-to-right path. It brushed the left edge of the hole and tumbled in for birdie. Payne punched the air twice. It was a gesture of triumph and relief. He was the only player in the entire field under par through fifty-four holes. He had a one-shot lead with a round to go.

Three days of USGA scrutiny had firmed the greens, grown the once-docile rough, and turned No. 2 into a savage. The average score was 75.97. Only Steve Stricker broke par, and only then by a shot. Approaches that landed on greens rarely remained there, which was also true of some recovery shots that failed to crest the hardening slopes and returned to the feet of the men who'd played them. The sixty-eight players in the field managed just 80 birdies against 367 bogeys. Tom Lehman finished at ten over par, missing the final pairing for the first time in five years. "If we hadn't got this cloud cover, if the sun had stayed out and the wind kept blowing, it would have been the highest-scoring day in history," he said. No one had won a U.S. Open with an over-par score since 1978, when Andy North played Cherry Hills Country Club in Englewood, Colorado, at plus one. Now that looked probable, with the Sunday forecast for more wind and light rain. In relation to par alone, the '99 championship had presented the most exacting three rounds of U.S. Open golf in twenty-one years.

"I've been asked many times what's the hardest course I've ever played. Now I have the answer," said Janzen, the defending champion, who shot six-over 76.

"Whoever backs up the least amount will win," said Duval.

The four players in the last two pairings played the third round at twelve strokes over par. Duval fell the furthest on an afternoon of plentiful falls. He'd been five over through eight holes. His eventual 75 tied him for fifth with Stricker and Vijay Singh at plus two, three shots behind Payne. Woods shot two-over 72 for a share of third with Tim Herron. Mickelson lost his three-shot lead at the turn with four late bogeys. His birdie on eighteen sealed his 73. He was even for the championship, one out of the lead, and would play Sunday with Payne in the last pairing.

Mickelson said after his round that his short game had saved him from vanishing altogether. He said he was tense early in the round, steering his shots instead of swinging freely. He called his driving "sloppy." He called his iron play "poor." He was asked again about Amy, his wife. He said again that he was ready to leave. He said he could barely wait for Sunday to come.

"Tomorrow is something I have looked forward to ever since I played amateur and junior golf," Mickelson said.

Woods was in his highest position after three rounds in the major championships since his runaway victory in the '97 Masters, and living rooms from Ponte Vedra Beach to Carmel-by-the-Sea erupted in debate about how soon Woods would break Jack Nicklaus's record of eighteen majors. But skeptics had begun to wonder if the outlandish predictions about Woods were too much, too soon. Woods had placed third at the '98 British Open at Royal Birkdale, but it took a final-round 66 to do it. He had only two other top tens in the eight other majors of his career through the Masters of 1999. There was less talk now of breaking records. Then Woods went 68-71-72 at Pinehurst.

After his round, Woods spoke like a veteran of the virtues of patience and perseverance. A reporter suggested that he looked loose on the course.

"I love playing in the most intense pressure," Woods said. "How can you not? This is what we play for. This is why we play hard."

"Could you talk about today's pin positions and if you've given any thought to can they make them even tougher for tomorrow?" another reporter asked.

"They already did," Woods answered. "I saw the dots out there for tomorrow. Oh, lordy. They're going to be tough. Some of the pins are in corners, near slopes."

Payne waited for his press briefing so the Golf Channel network could broadcast it live. He stood behind the anchor during the delay, waving as a football fan would in the backdrop of an ESPN pre-game show at Alabama-Auburn. "While we're young," he chirped. Even the pros could recite the best lines from *Caddyshack*.

When the interview finally did begin, Payne reminded the press, and himself, of the prudence of playing for par. He described No. 2 as fair, much more so than Olympic, and repeated his desire to earn a spot on the Ryder Cup team, a prospect that looked much more likely now, even if he were to finish second, as he used to so often do. He recalled the 1991 U.S. Open at Hazeltine. He said he could look back on that and see how it changed his perspective for the worse. He'd signed that lucrative equipment contract because he thought he could win with any-thing in his bag. He'd traveled far too much in the second half of the year, accepting invitations to compete all over the world, exhausting himself physically and mentally. He'd simply tried too hard to prove himself, time and time again.

"I put this added pressure on myself that I had to perform differ-ently and better at the U.S. Open, and I didn't realize that I was already there," he said.

Now he did.

He admitted to reporters that he expected a fitful night and long morning, the spoils of a U.S. Open leader playing late on Sunday after-noon. He said he was nervous. He said he was prepared. He said he could control his own golf but not that of others. He confronted the pressure instead of denying it, as many less experienced players tended to do.

"Like I told myself today," Payne said, "you've won the champion-ship before. You deserve to be out there performing the way you are. And the other people that are not with me, that haven't won the United States Open, there's a different pressure on them."

And there was this: As he did after the second round, Payne felt a richer level of anticipation, being chased as he was by those younger players who had learned the game through a might and ferocity that seemed unfamiliar, even inelegant, to him. He was anxious again to see how his intuition and feel matched with their carry yardages and swing speeds.

"I'd like to think that my knowledge and my maturity and my understanding will all benefit," he said.

"Good luck," the moderator of the press conference said.

It was nearing dark when Payne finished. It was just like it was at Olympic in '98. He had just enough daylight to practice some short putts, minding his wife's advice to keep his head still during the stroke. On his way back to Tracey and the restless night he expected, he stopped to do a quick television interview.

"I wanted this opportunity," Payne said. He looked squarely at the camera.

"And now I've got go to out and deal with it."

CHAPTER TWELVE

Payne arrived an hour before what he assumed was nothing more than the final U.S. Open round of the twentieth century and his next, but not last, chance to win one. His walk to his three o'clock starting time conjured the same steps taken by other men who, through the course of their own final rounds in their own national championships, achieved a station of consequence and permanence in the lore of golf. Legacies hinged on those walks, just as Payne's did on that gloomy, overcast Sunday. These were the U.S. Opens people would remember and celebrate as long as golf mattered. This is what Payne Stewart approached when he finished his last swing on the range, another drawing three-metal, a rehearsal of his first shot, and wheeled to face Pinehurst No. 2 for the last time in 1999.

Though it was far from North Carolina, Francis Ouimet had made that walk in 1913. He actually made it twice. The twenty-year-old amateur and former caddie tied the great English professionals Harry Vardon and Ted Ray at The Country Club in Brookline, Massachusetts, in a rainy thirty-six-hole final round of the nineteenth U.S. Open. Ten thousand spectators, the biggest crowd in the young history of golf in the States, slopped through the 6,245-yard course, a classic specimen of parkland design credited to its first head professional, Willie Campbell of Musselburgh, Scotland. Ouimet shot 72 in the playoff Saturday to beat Vardon by five shots and Ray by six to become the first amateur to win the national championship. Golf arrived on the front pages of American newspapers for the first time. The *New York Times* devoted eleven different stories to the feat. President Taft issued a statement of congratulations. The popularity of golf blossomed in America. Francis Ouimet was the reason why.

Bobby Jones made that walk in 1930. It was less than a year after the stock market crash, and the country was mired in the early months of the Great Depression. America looked to Jones, the great amateur from Atlanta, for inspiration and hope, which he provided by winning the British Open and the British Amateur to complete the first two stages of what then was known as the Grand Slam. He arrived in Edina, Minnesota, that summer for the third leg: the thirty-fourth U.S. Open at Interlachen Country Club. The pressure consumed Jones. It had been building for years. Competitive golf had become a debilitating, suffocating task for the twenty-eight-year-old career amateur, with a rising sense of urgency and pressure that began to take too much of a toll on his well-being. He nonetheless beat Macdonald Smith by two. Eighteen thousand people watched—another record for spectators. Jones later won the U.S. Amateur at Merion. The *Times* called his completed slam "the most triumphant journey that any man ever traveled in sport." Jones promptly retired to build his own monument to the game on an old, rolling fruit orchard in Augusta, Georgia.

Ben Hogan took those steps in 1950—gingerly, though, because it was a year after he'd nearly died in a head-on collision with a Greyhound bus on a foggy highway in West Texas. His legs wrapped in bandages, wincing with every step, Hogan shot what he needed to shoot—a gritty 74—to get into a playoff at Merion Golf Club on the Main Line of greater Philadelphia. He bettered his score by five and won going away over George Fazio and Lloyd Mangrum. It nearly broke him. Hogan nearly fell down once. He struggled to bend over. The photograph of his follow-through after his long-iron shot on eighteen became one of the most iconic images in golf. "It will be said of Hogan that he was made of the stuff that refused to acknowledge defeat," John W. Cummings wrote in his June 13, 1950, column for the *Philadelphia Inquirer*.

"Virtually every account of the Hogan victory which we have perused will include the word 'comeback.' Indeed it was a comeback for Ben, a return, you might say, from the brink of the grave."

Arnold Palmer knew the walk. In the fourth round of the 1960 U.S. Open, he lashed his drive to the green of the par-four first hole of Cherry Hills, finished a few hours later with a stunning 65, and whipped his red visor into the Colorado air. It was the biggest comeback in the history of the tournament. Palmer started the final round seven strokes behind. It was a drama involving the biggest names. He survived rallies from Hogan and Nicklaus, who lost chances late to win. The great Hogan would never win again. Nicklaus was only twenty years old and had plenty of winning ahead. Palmer, meanwhile, "assumed the giddy platform of the world's greatest player," Dan Jenkins wrote for readers of the *Fort Worth Press*. It was the first and last national championship for the King. Thirty-nine years later at Pinehurst, Nicklaus had been asked before the '99 U.S. Open about that Saturday near Denver. He mentioned Hogan.

"We both, in many ways, gave it away," Nicklaus said.

Palmer had other opportunities. One came in 1962, when Nicklaus made the walk for the first time. The tour rookie out of Ohio State shot a final-round 69 at malicious Oakmont in suburban Pittsburgh to force a playoff with Palmer, and beat him by three as ten thousand spectators, most of them rooting for their hero from Latrobe, walked along. The spectacle was a glimpse into the future as it was back then. Nicklaus hammered drives ten to thirty yards past Palmer on every long hole. He struck bolder, crisper iron shots. He putted like a savant. "Jack is a hell of a player, and he has all it takes to become a great golfer," Palmer said in defeat. "He has lots of patience and he has the know-how. Of course, time will tell." Time did tell. Nicklaus went on to win seventy-three titles on the PGA Tour, from 1962 through 1986. His last one came at that epic, unforgettable Masters. He started the final round four strokes out of the lead. He shot six-under 30 on the back nine to win by one. "Nicklaus is unquestionably the best fourth-round golfer there has ever been," Herbert Warren Wind, the esteemed golf correspondent for the *New Yorker* magazine, wrote in retrospect. The men who walk the walk into golf history have to earn their place in it, often in the fourth and final round. Tom Watson did it in 1982 at Pebble Beach. He held off a charging—who else?—Nicklaus. Ten years later, again at Pebble, Tom Kite made the walk through a biting wind and flecks of rain. He played in the harshest conditions of the afternoon. He closed with an even-par 72. No one touched the craftsman from Austin in the bluster and havoc of that Sunday. Watson and Kite never won another U.S. Open.

Now here came Payne, approaching his.

He and Mickelson left the range with their caddies on a misty, sixty-eight-degree Sunday afternoon in the sandhills. They processed behind the eighteenth green to the first hole and acknowledged the spectators standing and sitting in the bleachers. Roger Maltbie, the NBC on-course commentator assigned to the last pairing, watched Payne closely. He tried to judge the level of turmoil inside the man wearing the navy plus fours and flat cap and rain shell with no sleeves, which Payne had cut away with scissors so he could swing with abandon. But Maltbie saw nothing to suggest any turmoil at all.

Payne took his stance on the left side of the first tee so he could better draw the ball, his favored and safest shape. He banged his three-metal to seven-iron distance. He watched from the fairway as Woods made his birdie putt. Cheers bounced through the pines. His own approach covered the flag on its path through the fog and stopped fifteen feet from the hole. More cheers. Payne saw the line. All he had to do was strike the putt firmly enough to roll through the water coating the green. As he made his stroke, Johnny Miller told NBC viewers to expect a turn to the right at the end.

"Looks good," Miller said, a moment before Payne's ball turned right and dove into the hole. Cheers again. His one-shot lead grew to two.

All morning long, as he was waiting to leave for the course, Payne had tried to think only about giving himself a chance. He tried not to remember the back nine at Baltusrol in '93. He tried not to brood about

Olympic. He certainly didn't want to start contemplating the role of luck, because luck was something he couldn't manipulate, so he thought instead about acceptance, a personal state of grace. He'd decided before his first swing that he would accept what Pinehurst would give to him or take from him. Whatever happened would be his alone to own.

Payne accepted the birdie on the first hole, but not as a symbol of anything beyond his wise choice on the tee to hit the three-metal, the solid seven-iron to the green, and a sure putt. His countenance on the second tee, a 447-yard par-four, betrayed no emotion. He drove his ball well to the fairway. He chose his three-iron from his bag and picked the intermediate target on his line. He made the pullback motion. He took his cut.

The shot sailed right. Payne knew immediately that it was a bad miss. For the first time all week, he'd hit into one of those green-side spots shaded in blue in his yardage book. He thought about acceptance on the walk to his ball. His first chip crested the edge of the green and rolled back. His second left him with a six-footer for bogey. Acceptance again.

He made the putt.

Payne birdied the next hole with a nine-iron to two feet. It was his last birdie on the front nine. He and Mickelson came to the tenth tee at one under par in their rounds.

For the next ninety minutes, the players with the real prospect of winning made no substantial ground on their goal. Woods was even for the day when he missed a short par putt on eleven. Duval never factored. Singh had made seven straight pars before birdies on the eighth and tenth, but even his final-round 69, the best score among the last ten players on the course, wasn't enough.

By the time Payne and Mickelson came to the long sixteenth, it was becoming clear to anyone watching that one of them would win. Payne had made two bogeys since the turn, with one birdie, which meant he was at even par for the championship. Mickelson was floating through his round, one birdie against no bogeys, a ship with a full mainsail on calm seas. He felt like he was in absolute control of the tournament. He led Payne by one and Woods and Singh by two with three holes to play, and when Payne missed another green at sixteen, he looked to be right. Woods bogeyed the hole ahead.

Reporters started typing their coronation stories about a man who won the U.S. Open, a long-awaited first major, while awaiting a page from his pregnant wife. Outside, the mist stopped falling. Then it started again. Tracey watched the tournament on the television in the rental cottage. She started to get her things together for the short trip to the course. Spectators lined the finishing holes. They were ten deep in spots. Inside, Colin Montgomerie, who had completed his round and would tie for fifteenth, was asked about the difficulty of No. 2, especially the stretch Payne and Mickelson were preparing to play.

"Lady luck plays a huge role here," he said.

"There's a long way to go in this golf tournament," Hicks had told Payne on the twelfth hole. He'd said those same words a year earlier on the back nine at Olympic, but it would mean something different in '99. Payne holed a twenty-five-foot par putt that wandered through two opposing downhill breaks on the sixteenth green. Mickelson had eight feet to keep his lead.

"Biggest putt of his life," Johnny Miller said.

He missed.

The dales and hollows hummed with the commotion of forty thousand people bracing for a finish they suspected they would never forget. Payne and Mickelson were tied at even par with two holes to play. No one spoke on the seventeenth tee. Payne rifled his six-iron, that familiar Mizuno, to four feet. An enormous roar vented from the gathering below. Mickelson dropped a high fade with his seven-iron to six feet. The cheers from the green volleyed back to the tee in waves. The two players marched to the green in silence, marked their golf balls, and tried their best to ignore the weight of what they were about to do.

Mickelson pulled his putt, and the ball drifted right of the hole. Par.

Payne aimed the SeeMore at the center of the hole, which is exactly where his ball rolled.

Birdie.

In twenty minutes, Payne had gone from a stroke behind one player to a stroke ahead of everyone. He never doubted his decision to hit driver on the eighteenth hole, and he liked the look of the rising shot until he and Hicks walked up the hill and saw where the ball lay. It was in the right rough, damp and deep, the worst lie they'd encountered in seventy-one holes. It was bad luck at a bad time, especially with Mickelson in the fairway with a good angle to the hole and a midiron in his hand. NBC trained its cameras on Payne's face. Bells rang faintly at a church in the distant village. Ron Crow, the walking scorer with Payne, heard the throaty welcome of the gallery and thought, *The ground is vibrating*. Payne consulted his orange-covered yardage book. Pinehurst gave. Pinehurst took. Acceptance came.

He decided to give himself a chance.

The indelible final scene at the 1999 U.S. Open earned its place in the lore of golf for actions taken and options dismissed. The USGA had wanted to present players with options from the shorter rough on No. 2, but Payne convinced himself he had only one. He calculated the yardage to the cross bunkers short of the green. He slashed an eight-iron shot to seventy-eight yards in the fairway, two paces short of the bunkers, "the most boring play in sports," as he'd called it at the PGA Championship at Shoal Creek in 1990.

It won him the U.S. Open.

By the time Payne stroked the winning putt—fifteen feet, scampering up the slope, bending right, slowing, and gone—Tracey had arrived from the cottage. She saw him punch the air and kick out his leg. She heard him howl. She watched him lift Hicks from the ground and hug him so tightly she could see the veins on his forearms. She wondered what he told Mickelson when he took the face of the runner-up in his hands. (*This isn't the important thing*, Payne had told the runner-up. *The important thing is that you're going to be a father.*) It was too loud to hear. It was too loud to think. She saw him kiss his ball.

Hal Sutton, who'd finished with a share of seventh, watched the celebration on a television in the locker room. *Maturity won the tournament,* he thought.

Johnny Miller told viewers, "You don't expect that out of anybody, especially a guy that's forty-two."

The men in charge of mowing the course thought about the curious role of timing. They'd cut the greens hours later than usual in an effort to keep the green speeds high in the persistent mist. It occurred to Paul Jett, the superintendent, that the later mowing schedule might've allowed the one revolution of the ball that had made Payne the champion.

John Garrity, a reporter for *Sports Illustrated,* dialed the number for Bee Stewart in Springfield. He asked Payne's delirious mother for her thoughts.

"Payne talks more with God now," she told him. "He's a different man."

The different man loped down the brick steps to the Pinehurst bag room to sign his scorecard. He saw a face he recognized. It was Tom O'Toole. Neither man brought up the scene in the parking lot at the 1979 Missouri state amateur, when Payne had insulted Jim Holtgrieve on the night before the final match at Wolf Creek Golf Links, or his conduct throughout the final match itself. Payne and O'Toole shared a quick, tight embrace.

O'Toole leaned in and whispered, "Your dad would have been really proud of you today."

Payne replied, "Thanks, Tommy."

O'Toole noticed that Payne was crying. He never saw him again.

Payne found Tom Meeks of the USGA, took him by the shoulders, and led him through a door.

"You set up one hell of a golf course," Payne told him. It was the last time they spoke.

Then Payne entered the caddie room and slumped in a chair.

"Give me a minute," Payne said. He rubbed his eyes.

Payne signed his scorecard for an even-par 70. His four-round total of 279 had beaten Mickelson by one, Woods and Singh by two, and the rest of the field by no fewer than five. He'd proven that neither age nor lack of length mattered in this national championship. His average driving distance of 255 yards ranked fiftieth in the weekend field of sixty-eight. But the numbers that mattered—putting, fairways, greens in regulation—told the story of his eleventh title on tour. He was eighth in every category, a winning formula at any golf tournament. No one could ignore his skill with the SeeMore through the final three holes. He'd taken only one putt on each of the last three greens.

Payne and his wife returned to course for the presentation of the trophy. Buzz Taylor, the president of the USGA, introduced him as the champion. Payne doffed his navy flat cap and held the silver cup so he could take a long look at it again before he raised it above his head.

"All yours," Taylor said.

In his speech, Payne said his faith was his source of conviction and belief in himself on the golf course. He blinked back tears as he spoke.

"Thank you, Lord," Payne said.

NBC anchor Dan Hicks reminded Payne of the close loss at Olympic.

"The scars were still there," Hicks said.

"I don't know what to say to that," Payne said.

"You said that experience made you tougher," Hicks said.

"Well, I couldn't ever give up out there," Payne said.

He mentioned Mickelson and his persistence. He sounded relieved that no playoff would happen in the morning.

Payne looked at Mickelson. "You'll win yours," he said.

Hicks asked about the putt to win.

"What was going through your mind when you knew you had to make it?" Hicks said.

Payne rubbed his brow.

"I just said, 'Give yourself a chance,'" he said. "And it went in."

* * *

Payne waited for Woods and Mickelson to finish their post-round inter-views. He asked a USGA official, Ron Read, if he could buy champagne for the reporters, just as Tony Lema had all those years earlier. Read found a manager at Pinehurst and asked for two hundred bottles. The manager told him it was impossible. There would be no party in the press tent at Pinehurst.

Woods took questions first. His tie for third represented his best finish in a U.S. Open. He sounded unimpressed with his feat. He talked about the mechanics of his swing, his tendency to pull iron shots, the short putt he missed at eleven, the moisture on the course, his grow-ing confidence in major championships, and his fondness for the way Pinehurst tested every skill, from the putter to the driver to the player's ability to think through the many ways to score. He reflected on chances he had given himself and not redeemed.

He also reflected on the winner and the way he'd won. Woods appreciated a good comeback story, and while he didn't consider Payne a close friend, he certainly admired the patience and guile it took for him to survive that Sunday, especially after his collapse over the last nine holes at Olympic.

"What were your thoughts as Payne played the eighteenth?" Woods was asked.

"It's great to see him come back after last year," he said.

"Did you see Payne make the last putt?"

"I was hoping he was going to make it. I prayed to God he made it, for him to battle back from last year, as well as all the other times he's been close."

Mickelson entered the room next. As he described his even-par 70, it occurred to him and everyone listening that he had played a much more complete round of golf than Payne had, but that when everything mattered, he hadn't risen to the task. The bogey on sixteen stung. The missed birdie putt on seventeen hurt more. His putt on the eighteenth green of twenty-two feet was just too far away.

It had come down to grit, not consistency, and not coasting through a road with steady pars. It had come down to the work of a magician. Payne missed a green badly on the sixteenth and hit a poor chip, but he made that long par putt with two breaks down the hill. Payne flared his drive on the eighteenth and caught his toughest lie of the tournament. But he chose wisely. The safe play to the fairway, short of the cross bunkers, was the decision of an accepting man who, through so many trials and errors in his past, understood odds and had learned, at last, to resist hubris.

"Payne Stewart made two exceptional putts," Mickelson said. "And I think those putts showed a lot of character."

He was asked about the exchange on the eighteenth green, when Payne put his hands on Mickelson's cheeks and said, *This isn't the important thing.*

Mickelson said he was genuinely touched. Here was the winner of the U.S. Open, someone begrudged for so long as aloof and self-absorbed, expressing compassion in the aftermath of one of the greatest finishes in the history of golf. Mickelson knew Payne's reputation. But he also knew dignity and mercy.

"Payne is a very thoughtful individual," he told the press, "and I have a lot of respect for him, on and off the course."

When Payne arrived, still wearing the rain shell with the cutaway sleeves, he apologized for the lack of champagne and insisted he'd tried to procure it. Reporters laughed. Payne fiddled with the cord of the microphone. He let out a big, deep sigh and tried hard to exude the image of a deferential champion. Someone asked him to describe his emotions.

"If I did that, I wouldn't be able to speak," he said.

The thirty-one-minute press conference covered the range of topics now familiar to anyone paying attention to Payne Stewart since the summer of 1998. He returned to the themes of faith, patience, and giving himself a chance. He'd proved he could still win a four-round tournament and that he could win another major, this one against a generation of power players with youth and technology on their side. He mentioned the Ryder Cup. His spot on the team was secure.

"Today means 300 points," he said, "and that gets me to 917."

A smug smile.

"Thank you very much."

Payne said he planned to take off a lot of time after his last start in November. He wasn't sure he really knew the meaning of his accomplishment. That was the problem in 1991, when his insecurities led him to do too much and try too hard. He said he wasn't going to let the new championship define him as it had eight years before. He said he was more prepared now to manage the celebrity, the expectations, and the demands. He said he felt whole. It had nothing to do with golf. The '90s had been everything he'd hoped for. He was a lucky man who knew it, and he would be a fine defending champion a year from now, in the first national championship of the new millennium, at Pebble Beach.

"There used to be a void in my life," Payne told one of the reporters. "The peace I have now is so wonderful. I don't understand how I lived so long without it."

When the questions ended, Rich Lerner, a broadcaster for the Golf Channel, persuaded Tracey to do an interview. She typically didn't like the attention. But she saw the value in it now. She was eager to tell people about the peace she saw in her husband, not just through four rounds at Pinehurst but at home, in church, and on quiet nights with his children, when he reminded himself that the purpose of his life was about more than making a big putt at the right time. She no longer knew him as the man who'd hoped for Mike Reid to lose the PGA. He wasn't the man who refused to properly shake Tom Kite's hand. He wasn't that man on television in Dallas, sulking about another loss, holding his wife's hand in silence, walking another lonely walk.

"How is the Payne Stewart that you know today different than the Payne Stewart you met more than twenty years ago?" Lerner asked.

"I think he's a lot more mature now," Tracey said. "I think he's become a better person, tried to be a better person."

Later that night, Melanie Hauser opened a new file and stared at the screen. The longtime golf writer had known Payne since he was in college. She had written about him at his best and at his worst. She wanted to harness it all, the man-in-full picture, for her account of his win at Pinehurst.

She wrote her first line. "You had to wonder what was going through his mind as he stared at those final fifteen feet."

Hauser then described the round, reported his past, noted the place he'd secured on the Ryder Cup team, quoted Tracey ("He's got a lot more courage than he's ever had"), and returned, at the end of her story, to the moment before he put the SeeMore on the ball on the seventy-second hole.

"He let it go. He trusted. He believed."

Payne was a long way from Pinehurst by the time those words were written. He and his caddie were barreling through the night, Payne sipping Bud Lights, with a police escort up front, lights whirling. They were going to Mebane, where Hicks lived, to play the next morning with Fred Couples, Paul Azinger, and Hal Sutton in a charity outing at Mill Creek Golf Club. They arrived at midnight. They drank Cristal and moonshine from the trophy. It was around four o'clock when Hicks, sitting on his kitchen counter, took stock of the moment: the U.S. Open, the drive to Mebane, the personal and professional redemption of the shot-maker nodding off at his dining room table, the taste of the Cristal, the promise of more majors.

Right here, right now: This was as good as it got for a caddie on the PGA Tour. A warm wave of pride and gratitude washed over Hicks. He was a lucky man and knew it. Payne had been hard to work with at times, but he had been a generous and thoughtful employer. Payne paid Hicks a handsome monthly salary. He was one of few players to do that. He realized Hicks had a family to support at home. Payne wanted to make sure Hicks was secure.

As the night wore on, Hicks remembered a special day a long time ago, a day that stuck with him, especially when times weren't very good. He and Payne were between tournaments at Payne's eighty-acre farm outside of Springfield. Hicks had told Payne that his wife was pregnant with their first child. Payne had told him to take some time off, maybe even consider a new career that would allow him to watch his baby grow. But Hicks was a caddie through and through. It was his life's work. He had thanked Payne and meant it, but he told him he wasn't going anywhere. And now here he was, woozy from the booze, hours since his greatest moment as a tour caddie, with a U.S. Open trophy in his kitchen and new dreams of more.

"Payne," Hicks said finally. "It's time to go to bed."

Payne said, "You're not going to bed until I tell you to go to bed."

No one—not even the man who had been with him through so much—was telling Payne Stewart when this day in 1999 was going to come to an end.

Part Four

BROOKLINE

Singles concession, The Country Club, Brookline, Massachusetts, September 26, 1999

CHAPTER THIRTEEN

The ninety-ninth U.S. Open had earned its place in the lore and legend of American golf by the time dawn broke on Monday, June 21. Over and over, sports highlight shows broadcast the winning putt, the kick of the leg, the punch of the fist, the embraces with Tracey and Hicks and Mickelson. Newspapers carried photographs of the champion in his navy flat cap, the silver trophy close to his chest, the WWJD band around his wrist, wearing a tight smile of satisfaction and pride.

Praise rained from journalists who'd watched Payne on the golf course since he'd buckled thirteen summers earlier under the hard stare of Raymond Floyd at Shinnecock. They had seen him at his worst. They now saw a man who was more sympathetic and relatable. They wrote stories about the U.S. Open at Pinehurst that touched the timeless themes of sports: Here was a victor who'd confronted his frailties—age, hubris, immaturity, impulsiveness, a kind of recklessness in conversation, a brittle fortitude in the presence of pressure—and if he'd not conquered them, he'd managed them. Here was a refined, reconstituted Payne Stewart. Here was a Payne golf deserved.

Frank Luksa, a columnist for the *Dallas Morning News,* wrote, "The '99 U.S. Open will be remembered for its first appearance in North Carolina and the drama that lingered until the last shot. It also shall be recalled as an event won with marvelous shots by a most worthy champion."

On assignment for *Sports Illustrated,* Jaime Diaz, who had reported on Payne for years, wrote, "What he gained is something as tangible as—and even more valuable than—his underrated talent. Simply, peace.

Through defeat he matured into a better person than the self-absorbed winner who high-fived a shattered Mike Reid after Reid handed Stewart the '89 PGA. At Pinehurst, Stewart possessed the glazed countenance ironically reminiscent of the Raymond Floyd stare that unnerved a callow Stewart in the 1986 U.S. Open at Shinnecock Hills. Serenity was at the heart of his amazing resiliency at No. 2, and it was the lubricant that kept his swing and putting stroke so smooth. Finally, it was his advantage over the young lions."

"Stewart, who was a teen-ager when Woods and Mickelson were born, won by doing whatever it took to survive," Christine Brennan wrote in her Monday column for *USA Today*. "He wasn't afraid to be boring when he had to be. He wasn't afraid to lag a putt up to the hole, take his par and move on. Yet he also was up to every challenge the kids threw at him Sunday."

"Stewart became the first golfer to win the Open with two different personalities," John Garrity wrote for *SI*.

It was almost like Payne had vanished, sent to serve a sentence of remediation, and then emerged in the dales and hollows of the Carolina sandhills with a markedly different sense of who he was. The maturity and ability to reflect that Payne had revealed the previous summer in San Francisco felt permanent now, like he'd had a long talk with himself while he was away and made some decisions. But it was never that simple, and it was never that clean. After winning the 1991 U.S. Open, Payne had lost his identity, both personal and professional. He'd tried vainly to rise to ideals that were impossible to achieve. He'd seduced himself into believing he should contend at every major, almost as if it were an entitlement after winning two. He'd allowed his celebrity and stardom to overwhelm him. He'd succumbed to the unbearable weight of his own success, and by the time he'd realized it, there was little else to do but start anew.

That process took longer than anyone appreciated. It took many shapes. Payne had to learn to live again with losing, as he had before the Bay Hill tournament in 1987, back when he had the reputation of a player who was content with not winning. He'd never admitted it publicly, but his only tour win between the 1991 U.S. Open and the 1999 Pebble Beach Pro-Am—the Houston Open in 1995—was more about the failure of Scott Hoch to keep a presumably safe lead than it was about the play of the man who'd beaten him. Payne had leaned on Tracey a lot through those hard seasons of meager earnings and missed cuts and trespassing doubt. He now tried to remind himself of her often-unrequited faith in him. She'd never wavered. She'd never allowed him to surrender. Without her stern and uncompromising discipline, Payne might've never come to the twelfth fairway with the lead in the fourth round at the 1998 U.S. Open and found his ball in a sand-covered divot. He certainly wouldn't have had the grace to deal with it as a part of golf, that aggravating and blessed game of touch, feel, fleeting confidence, of luck good and bad. Without Tracey, Payne might've never slept on a one-shot lead at Pebble Beach as the storms rolled in to drench the peninsula. He might've never believed in himself enough to color a yardage book at Pinehurst.

Tracey. Payne knew there were times when he annoyed and frustrated his wife of seventeen uneven years. He knew he'd hurt her. His childish lust for fun, his meandering commitment to practice, his impulsive proclivity to live in and for the moment when he should've been thinking ahead: Those flaws could threaten a marriage, but Tracey accepted them and gave her husband another chance, time and again. *What patience*, Payne thought. *What loyalty*. In weaker moments, he wondered if he deserved her. He was grateful for this evolving perspective, for seeing a picture that was bigger and richer. *Better now than never*, he concluded. In the glow of his triumphs on the golf course, a forty-two-year-old Payne imagined what lay ahead for his career and his family, and he defined Tracey's categorical fidelity in another way: as deliverance.

The slump gave Payne some depth and dimension. It humbled him in quiet ways that no one understood on that Sunday in June when a golf ball turned one more time and an aging showman from Hickory Hills

Country Club, the son of a salesman in southern Missouri, sobbed on the neck of his wife on a domed Ross green at Pinehurst. So did those afternoons on the fishing boat in Bradenton, casting for snook and skipjack and draining cans of light beer with an ailing Paul Azinger, from which Payne drove I-4 back to Orlando with questions about mercy and salvation, and what it means to live, and how. It seemed like every complication in his life had become scaffolding. Payne accepted that he was an unfinished project, framed on a sturdier foundation, nearing the stage of hanging good walls around clean windows and doors that could open and close well. Work was being done. He liked how it looked in the blueprint.

He also thought about his gathering interest in the messages of faith that his children were studying at school and that he was hearing at the men's group at First Baptist back in Orlando. Payne never understood the Bible or Christianity with the depth of Azinger or Tom Lehman or other players on the tour did. He never sought to. He maintained a level of belief in the unseen, but his was more superficial, a CliffsNotes version, just enough to give him a sense of what mattered without having to do the hard work of complete sacrifice and devotion. Still, the fact that Payne now professed his faith in public—in interviews that he knew a lot of people would read and hear—represented another shift in his identity as he saw it. The old Payne Stewart seemed to believe in one thing: himself. The new Payne Stewart appeared to recognize that other forces were just as important, if not more so. People close to him noticed. At Pinehurst, Dick Coop, the psychologist who'd helped Payne improve his attention and mitigate destructive habits, saw a more self-actualized man win.

"An athlete is used to proving himself by what he does on the field, and Payne was no different," Coop told a magazine writer at the U.S. Open. "But that approach ultimately makes the result too important, and the resulting pressure gets in the way. It's better to prove yourself by what you are in life. Then the understanding that you remain a good person, no matter the outcome on the playing field, allows you to release the pressure and more easily have a good outcome."

The doctor used the language of his discipline to express a simple and universal truth.

Payne was playing better golf because he felt better about himself.

Payne took a long break from the tour after Pinehurst. He drove the U.S. Open trophy to the Edwin Watts store in Orlando, where he had bought the plain black golf bag, and placed the artifact on the counter for shoppers to admire and photograph. He played a round at The Country Club in Brookline to get an essential first impression of the Ryder Cup course he would see in late September. He liked the way it moved through space, like a slow-rolling river with oxbows and channels, deep and green. It was a golden age routing to the core, long enough to be relevant in 1999 but not so long that it eliminated shorter drivers of the ball. It seemed to Payne to be just the kind of place for finesse and feel.

He kept his swing fluid and fresh on the ranges at his home courses. He played a few money games at Isleworth, rolled putts with the See-More, and practiced the bump-and-run recovery shots that he'd been exposed to in Asia nearly two decades earlier. Those shots had won him a second U.S. Open. Payne knew he would need them again in July for the British Open at Carnoustie.

He sometimes let himself think he should've won a British Open by now. Links golf suited his nature. It took imagination and feel and vision. It took temerity, especially playing from those deep pot bunkers, or heather or gorse, or in a gale. Links golf required the ability to picture the flight of shots before they flew, and in that way, it appealed to golfers of an older vintage, who learned the game the way Payne had. He had come close so many times: second-place finishes in 1985 and 1990, and top tens from 1987 through 1989. Now, with his confidence restored, he prepared to go to Europe with a resolve that felt like iron.

Payne knew guile would be essential at Carnoustie. He was at peace with his equipment, those familiar Mizuno irons and the trustworthy SeeMore, and the discipline he'd applied in preparing for Pinehurst would serve him well in Scotland, he reasoned. He accepted that his lack of driving distance would result in longer shots into the fierce par-four holes at one of the most taxing golf courses in the world. He would not let the allure of the long drive romance him into becoming someone he was not. He was no John Daly. He was no Phil Mickelson. He was no Tiger Woods. Payne was who he was: an aging shot-maker, a relic of the sepia-toned era defined by persimmon and balata, fighting to survive.

He joined a group of friends traveling to Ireland the week before the British Open. Woods was part of it, and so were Mark O'Meara, David Duval, and Lee Janzen. The men fished. They played Waterville Golf Links and Old Head with low shots that hugged the turf. They strolled the streets of Waterville, a town on the coast of the Atlantic Ocean in one of the southern lips of the country, and popped in and out of pubs, chasing whiskey shots with barbs and stories before they had to get down to business on the other side of the Irish Sea. Some of the wives went with them, but Tracey stayed behind with Chelsea and Aaron in Florida. That way, Payne could practice as much as he wanted for rugged and ruthless Carnoustie.

The group arrived in Scotland and encountered a golf course so hostile the players doubted its par of 71 was reasonable. Peter Alliss, the respected golf broadcaster for the BBC, called Carnoustie the Mount Everest of golf. Five-time British Open champion Peter Thompson speculated that a score of 300—*sixteen shots over par*—could win.

Founded in 1842, the rumpled links on the North Sea coast of Scotland had been lengthened from 7,065 yards, when Gary Player won there in 1968, to 7,361. Fourteen pot bunkers and ten back tees had been added since Tom Watson earned the first of his own five British Open titles at Carnoustie in 1975, the last time the championship had been played there. It was a different golf course in 1999. The final four holes were punishing: a 250-yard par-three at the sixteenth and three par-fours of more than 450 yards. The eighteenth crossed the Barry Burn, a rock-lined ditch connected to the sea, and out-of-bounds markers surrounded the green. It was a 487-yard ribbon of risk.

Carnoustie greenkeeper John Philp explained before the championship that the changes to the course maintained its integrity as golf evolved.

"Modern players fly the ball so far that courses are becoming obsolete," he said before the first round, a familiar defense in the age of graphite, titanium, and urethane. "I wanted to preserve all the traditional challenges of Carnoustie," Philp explained. "This course has an aura, a reputation. Why take that away?"

Payne assessed the links in his practice rounds and saw opportunity. He knew the thigh-high rough, narrow fairways, forecasts for cold wind, and sheer length of the longest course in British Open history would eliminate a lot of players, if only because their doubts about the fairness of Carnoustie would compromise their ability to manage their emotions. He embraced his new identity on the tour as a player of latent wisdom and perspective. A topic that week concerned players such as Justin Rose and Zane Scotland, who were in their teens. Payne wished he could have an hour with them alone. He wanted to share with them the strains and risks of playing professional golf. He thought they should wait.

He thought about his years in college at SMU in Dallas. Payne cherished his memories of freedom and fellowship with Earl Stewart, Lamar Haynes, Mark Hanrahan, and Charlie Adams. He'd kept up with those friends, especially Adams and Haynes, who still lived in Dallas. He wanted Justin Rose, Zane Scotland, and all young players considering a run at tournament golf to be as lucky as he was: to grow and try and fail and bond in a safer environment like college.

"Look at me," Payne said on the Wednesday before the British Open began. "I'm forty-two, and I'm just now maturing. It has taken me a long time."

He had a story to tell. He saw value in his life in a way he hadn't before. He was an example. He could teach it.

* * *

Conditions and scores on the opening day of the 128th British Open surprised no one in the field. A stiff breeze scraped Carnoustie, flinging golf balls into insurmountable lies in the hay. Only one player, Rod Pampling of Australia, shot a round of even par. A third of the field failed to break 80. Payne made two bad swings in his round of eight-over-par 79.

"I mean, 79?" he said after he finished. "I'm sitting here thinking that's not a bad score."

His friend Mark O'Meara, the defending champion, shot 83.

"I'm a professional golfer," O'Meara said. "I'm not looking forward to shooting in the eighties, but I got the score I deserved today."

O'Meara missed the cut. Payne did not. Through three rounds, he'd become so annoyed with the height of the rough—it reached the cuff of his plus fours in places—that he complained publicly about it. "If they do this at St Andrews [site of the British Open in 2000], it's not going to be any fun at all," Payne said Saturday afternoon. He was nowhere near the lead by then.

That was the solitary station of a little-known Frenchman, ranked 152nd in the world, who led by five strokes with uncannily fine driving and putting, especially Friday and Saturday. He looked like Woods had at the 1997 Masters, like Nicklaus had on the back nine in 1986: unstoppable, in control, and destined. The ABC production team met Sunday morning to plan its coverage and wondered how many Americans would watch what looked to be a runaway victory by a stranger with a French accent.

Jean Van de Velde, thirty-three years old, was a dark-haired, handsome, and self-deprecating European Tour player from Mont-de-Marsan who'd won precisely one tournament in ten seasons. He did not exude the confidence of a champion-in-the-making in his interactions with the international golf media assembled at Carnoustie. He seemed vaguely uneasy with the lead. After his third-round 70, a brilliant round of golf under the circumstances, Van de Velde said he planned to prepare for the biggest moment in his life with a mission that evening to procure a fine meal and a glass of red wine. He looked oddly, endearingly troubled. Haunted, even.

"Five shot[s] is not enough," Van de Velde said Saturday after his round. "I wish I had fifteen."

The Scotsman Paul Lawrie and Justin Leonard of Texas, who finished ahead of Van de Velde at six-over 290, were glad he didn't. So was the ABC production team, which had front-loaded commercials during the broadcast so there would be few interruptions in the final hour, which turned about to be a most riveting, mesmerizing, and anguishing span of television as Van de Velde and his pale young caddie, Christophe Angiolini, marched toward the final hole in the dim light of that July afternoon.

Payne had shot 74 (for an eventual share of thirtieth place) by the time fate began dismantling the fragile Frenchman. He didn't see Van de Velde, who had a three-shot lead, remove the driver from his bag as everyone paying attention—spectators, broadcasters, players, journalists, viewers back in the states—privately scolded the choice. Payne said he understood the impulse. He knew the seduction of hubris and ego better than most. But he also thought it was the wrong play, and he said later that if he'd pulled the driver from his bag in that situation, Hicks would've told him to put it back and take a smooth swing with a long iron. The risk was too severe, as Van de Velde discovered when his tee shot peeled right and the gallery groaned. The ball missed Barry Burn, however, and the leader now merely had to scrape a safe and dry passage in five more swings through approximately two hundred yards of Scotland.

"The greatest prize in golf is waiting to be plucked," Peter Alliss told his BBC audience.

Van de Velde settled over the ball for his second shot: also bold, also doomed, also a contributing error in judgment in what later would become known as the Collapse at Carnoustie. The ABC broadcasters, including Curtis Strange, noticed that Van de Velde was holding a long iron and aiming directly at the flagstick. He would have to carry the burn, which bisected the hole near the green, but the lie was good and the decision was quick. He was pushing luck to its outer limits, a balloon about to pop. Strange and the rest of the announcers narrated the remaining thirty minutes of golf history in tones that alternated between astonishment and the funereal.

The second shot clanged off a bleacher, leaving a powdery welt on the blue metal handrail.

Van de Velde's ball then struck a rock on the burn, bounced high in the air, and landed in the long rough that annoyed Payne so much.

A sense of dread settled over the tableau.

"Is this real, Mike?" Strange asked Mike Tirico on the ABC broadcast.

"No," Tirico replied.

Van de Velde wedged his third shot from the tangle of rough. It splashed into Barry Burn.

No one knew what to do or say or feel.

"The more I think about it, this is one of the most stupid things I've seen in my life," Strange said finally.

Van de Velde removed his shoes and appeared to consider a shot from the shallow water, swelling in the rising tide of the distant North Sea. Photographers nearly tumbled into the creek. Onlookers bellowed. Rain began to dapple the grounds. Van de Velde smiled as he stood in the burn in his bare feet. Part of him seemed to be enjoying the spectacle. Part of him seemed powerless, a marionette handled by a sinister puppeteer. After a few moments of quiet deliberation, Van de Velde crouched to fetch his ball and pitched it to his caddie: three shots in, four out, now dropping with a penalty for his fifth. Ian Baker-Finch keyed his microphone so he could speak directly with the ABC production truck.

"This is making me physically ill," he said.

Two swings later—one from the wet rough, one from a greenside bunker—Van de Velde stared at a seven-foot putt to qualify for a four-hole playoff with Lawrie and Leonard, themselves as surprised as anyone at the arresting circumstances on the eighteenth green. Van de Velde inhaled. His mind raced. *I haven't lost yet,* he thought. He addressed his ball.

"You root against no one. You root for no one," Tirico told his viewers. "But you've got to hope this goes in."

It did. When the ball tumbled into the hole, Van de Velde took a swipe at the air with his right hand and howled. He would not factor a bit in the playoff, which Lawrie would win, but that would matter little in the legacy and lore of golf in 1999. The season was becoming sprinkled with pixie dust, especially the majors: Olazábal at the Masters, winning after not being able to walk. Payne at the U.S. Open, winning after not being able to win. Winning after losing so much.

"It's a game," Van de Velde said after the ordeal at Carnoustie had ended, once and for all. "The thing is, I never stopped trying."

He later would describe the 1999 British Open as one week of his life. "Not my whole life," he would say.

He would add, "A lot of people are going to remember this."

To be remembered. Somewhere, Payne Stewart knew exactly what Van de Velde meant and why it mattered.

CHAPTER FOURTEEN

The finish in thirtieth at Carnoustie did nothing to dampen Payne's optimism for the remainder of 1999. He looked forward to another restorative break from golf, this one until the PGA Championship in August. He planned to start two more tournaments after that, the NEC Invitational and the Air Canada Championship, before the Ryder Cup, which loomed ahead like some great reward. He approached the rest of his year with a sense of emotional lightness and freedom from doubt, with a conviction that he was living for his family and his friends as well as for himself. All felt proportionate and balanced and right. Payne had nothing more to prove and every blessing to count. His season would be winding to a close after the tournament in Canada, breaching September. Then it would be on to Brookline.

He took the family to the Bahamas. He tossed a football to the kids and razzed them when they missed an easy catch. They boated. They swam. They watched Orlando Magic games on one of their many TVs. Payne grilled by the pool behind the mansion on the lake and invited Jon and Martha Brendle, who lived in the small house he owned next door, to bonfires in the dark. They drank the best champagne. They smoked the best cigars. They toasted good fortune and friendship and no regrets. Payne and Jon Brendle had been close for more than a decade, since Brendle was a young golf professional at one of the Disney courses in Orlando, the brother Payne never had. Now a traveling rules official for the PGA Tour, he and Payne saw a lot of each other on the grueling nomadic grind of professional golf, but their bond transcended the sport. Aaron and Chelsea, now ten and thirteen, had grown to regard Brendle and his wife as extensions of their family, a surrogate uncle and aunt.

Payne left for the PGA Championship in early August. The last major of 1999 brought a sparkling field to Medinah No. 3. It was the last opportunity for players who hadn't qualified for the Ryder Cup teams to impress the two captains: Ben Crenshaw, the nineteen-time PGA Tour winner from Texas, and Mark James, an Englishman with eighteen career titles on the European Tour. Both of them had two captain's picks to round out their teams of twelve.

The PGA of America gave the 148 contestants the longest golf course in the history of major championships. Spanning 7,401 yards among 4,161 trees in a northwest suburb of Chicago, the course seemed to play longer still after rain fell Thursday and Friday. Payne shot 75-71 to make the cut by two. But he made no move on Saturday; a forgettable 75 left him at five over par, without a whisker of hope. Thirteen other players entered the final round at minus four or better, among them a nineteen-year-old Spaniard named Sergio García and, to the surprise of no one who'd watched him that season, Tiger Woods.

Michael Wilbon, a columnist for the *Washington Post,* wrote that Sunday at Medinah was going to be "battle of the ages, a war between the generations." The four players in the last two pairings, which included Stewart Cink and Mike Weir, averaged 24.2 years old, but the tension that week had less to do with age than it did with attitude. A controversy over player pay at the Ryder Cup had cleaved the team before it was even completed. The September issue of *Golf Digest* had reported that the matches would generate $63 million in gross revenue. The PGA, which ran the event, expected a profit of $17 million–$23 million, and The Country Club in Brookline would clear about $6 million, according to the magazine. Players on the American team would earn a stipend of $5,000 for the week. Now some of them wanted more.

Mark O'Meara had long advocated for paying players at a more equitable market value. When the *Golf Digest* report had become public (it also noted that NBC was paying $13 million in television rights fees and that the sixty corporate tents at The Country Club were being sold for $25,000–$500,000 each), Woods, Mickelson, Janzen, and Duval had joined O'Meara, the second-oldest team member next to Payne, in agitating for an increase in what players would get. Duval had tendered the idea of a boycott, according to the magazine. He'd also denied the suggestion when asked about it at Medinah.

"I never intended to say, nor did I ever say that I believe, David Duval should get paid to play in the Ryder Cup," Duval had said earlier in the week. "I simply said that, as a player who's on it, I think we should get money to take back to our community. And if people see a problem with that, I'm sorry. Five Ryder Cups ago, eight, ten Ryder Cups ago, there wasn't money to do that. Now there is."

When asked about the equity of the $5,000 stipend, Duval issued a quick and terse reply: "And we're not being used?"

Everyone had taken a side. Woods had insisted the players were being treated unfairly, and he'd likened the matches to "pros on parade." He'd said, "They take us to a bunch of functions that raise money, yet everybody is compensated except us." He and the others in favor of higher compensation had said they wanted only to give more to charities, but some of their peers—Payne, Justin Leonard, Tom Lehman, and Davis Love III—had said that playing for their country was compensation enough. So did Crenshaw, the American captain, who'd attended a gathering on Tuesday with his players, tour commissioner Tim Finchem, and Jim Awtrey, the CEO of the PGA of America. The men met on the second floor of the Medinah clubhouse and agreed to quell the controversy, for the sake of harmony and public perception. No one who attended revealed the details of the meeting.

"We talked enough to know that everyone's on the same page," O'Meara had said.

Now, on the eve of the final round of the PGA Championship, O'Meara, like his fellow shot-maker Payne, was nowhere near the top of the leaderboard. No actual war was being waged in the suburbs of Chicago on that Sunday in August 1999. There was no battle per se. But something significant was about to happen at Medinah No. 3, and the veteran sensed it like an old farmer can feel the approach of locusts.

Woods and Weir, tied at eleven under par, played in the last group, right behind Cink and García, who started the final round at minus nine. The sun warmed Medinah to eighty degrees. Tens of thousands of spectators lined the holes of No. 3. Woods birdied four of his first eleven and built a five-stroke lead, while Weir was on his way to an 80; Cink, a 73. But Woods faltered late. García stayed close, and when the wispy teenage prodigy from Castellon holed his birdie putt on the par-three thirteenth, he stared mischievously, even provocatively, at the tee up the hill, where Woods stood, waiting, watching.

García wanted Woods to know that he would have to earn the PGA, that nothing was his for free. Forty minutes later, Woods led by one when García opened the face of his six-iron on the sixteenth hole and addressed his ball, which was snuggled against the trunk of a tree, with nothing to lose but a chance to win a major championship. García figured he would have more of those, and so he shut his eyes and took a blind lash that endeared him to everyone who ever aspired to get a golf ball airborne. García sprinted up the fairway to trace his shot. He looked like a boy chasing an ice cream truck. His boyish leap and midair kick reminded everyone who witnessed it that golf was indeed a game. That it was play.

García lost the tournament by a stroke. Woods ground out an even-par 72 to capture his second major and first PGA Championship. He led the field in distance from the tee: 310.3 yards a drive, more than the veterans like Payne or O'Meara or Lehman or Sutton could ever muster with their best swings. And Woods made a powerful statement. He was ready to emerge. He was locked.

"I'm learning how to play the game," he said after his round. "I've learned more shots. I've learned to manage myself around the golf course better, and it's just going to get better." O'Meara, who'd become friends with Woods back in Orlando, where they were neighbors and informal practice-round partners at Isleworth, told reporters, "Tiger has become his own man. He has taken greater control of his career, and he's to the point where he feels extremely comfortable in all aspects of his life. I'm not sure that was always the case."

García won $378,000. He secured his spot on the Ryder Cup team for Europe and earned an exemption on the PGA Tour for 2000. His miserable play at Carnoustie, where he'd shot 89-83 and bawled on the shoulder of his mother, seemed to be an anomaly now, like it had never happened. He was irrepressible in his post-round interview. He acted like he'd won.

"It was joy," García said. "It was pressure. It was, I will tell you, the best day of my life."

Then he said he wanted to play Woods at the Ryder Cup.

Crenshaw, meanwhile, had watched García and Woods with absolute awe. *It was a peek into the future of golf*, he thought, *and it was mesmerizing.* He'd seen García's shot at the sixteenth and considered it one of the greatest efforts, and demonstrations of passion, that he'd ever witnessed. Crenshaw admired the young Spaniard's charisma and grace. It reminded him of Ballesteros. It reminded him of how and why he fell in love with golf as a boy in Texas, when his father handed him a cut-down club and sent him to Harvey Penick at the Austin Country Club. Most of all, García represented...a spirit in abstraction. Crenshaw, himself a feel player of forty-seven summers, wanted that kind of buoyancy and effervescence on his own Ryder Cup squad. "Magic," he called the young Spaniard.

"He captured America," Crenshaw said.

The next day, Crenshaw was ready to disclose his captain's picks for the Ryder Cup team. He and his vice captains, Bill Rogers and Bruce Lietzke, had considered Fred Couples, Bob Estes, Lee Janzen, Tom Lehman, Steve Pate, Chris Perry, Steve Stricker, and even Hale Irwin, who was fifty-four years old when he'd opened the PGA Championship at minus five after two rounds, four shots behind the lead. But Irwin, the tenacious grinder from Missouri, had shot 78-75 on the weekend, and now he was out, leaving the seven other candidates vying for two open slots.

Crenshaw selected Lehman and Pate. He'd anguished over the choice. ("I really was worried about him," said his wife, Julie. "This was a very tough week.") His decision reflected a desire to load the team with cagey veterans who knew the peculiar pressure of playing on a Ryder Cup team. Lehman, now forty, had been on the 1995 and 1997 squads. Pate, thirty-eight, was on the 1991 team at Kiawah. Both players had performed well in 1999: Lehman had finished second four times in twenty-three starts; Pate had been a runner-up twice in twenty-eight, and he'd tied for eighth at the PGA. The captain noted that Pate "would walk through a wall if you asked him to." In Lehman ("I really wanted to be on this team," he said), Crenshaw saw "diligence and determination" and admired his "strength" and "character." The captain had been especially conflicted about Couples, a consummate feel player who hadn't missed a Ryder Cup appearance since his debut in 1989. But Crenshaw couldn't ignore 1999. Couples had played only sixteen times. His best finish was tenth. He had been five under par at one point Saturday at Medinah—until a double bogey and triple bogey cast him into a tie for twenty-sixth. "I had my chance," Couples would admit.

The teams were set. Europe had four-time Ryder Cup player Colin Montgomerie, five-time stalwart José María Olazábal, and seven rookies, including García and Van de Velde, who had fired the caddie who'd carried his bag at Carnoustie and would have a veteran working for him in Brookline. The US team included one rookie—Duval—and four players who'd been on the team once before. Payne and O'Meara were the elder members, each with four appearances on the team. No one knew how, or even if, the long-drive mandate of the modern power game in 1999 would factor into the matches at a golden age golf course like The Country Club.

"Routine drives of three hundred yards," Crenshaw mused. "Six-irons going two hundred yards. I can't believe in my lifetime that I'm seeing it. It's talent. It's youth. It's power. It's imagination. It's something that's changed a lot since I've been playing." Now, though, he was concerned only with unity, especially after the quarreling at Medinah over the stipend.

"My job as a captain is to bring these guys together and bring the cup back," he said. "That's all that matters."

And it mattered profoundly to him. The Americans had lost the last two matches. But more than that, Crenshaw felt an affinity to The Country Club that had stirred in him since he was fifteen years old, when his father gave him a copy of *The World of Golf*, by the esteemed golf writer Charles Price. In its pages, Crenshaw had lived the 1913 U.S. Open. He read about Francis Ouimet and his crucial putts on the seventeenth hole that helped him beat Harry Vardon and Ted Ray. He learned that The Country Club, one of the five clubs that had formed the United States Golf Association, featured a racetrack for horses and a steeplechase course before a golf course, which came in 1893 in the form of six crude holes shaped at a cost of fifty dollars. The course expanded to a regulation eighteen holes in 1899 under the supervision of Alexander "Nipper" Campbell, the club's head professional. Then, in 1923, the golden age architect William Flynn of Philadelphia—known for his work at Shinnecock and Merion—established the nine-hole Primrose Course, from which three holes would be borrowed for the 1999 Ryder Cup composite routing of 7,033 yards. The young Crenshaw was particularly intrigued by the legend of No. 17: a short par-four with a right-to-left turn in its fairway, with a tricky two-tiered green. Vardon had attempted a risky tee shot there in the U.S. Open playoff in 1913 and made bogey from a bunker. Ouimet had birdied it. The hole seemed to Crenshaw to hold secrets.

He qualified in the summer of 1968 for the U.S. Junior Amateur at The Country Club. It was his first trip beyond Texas. It was everything he'd imagined it to be. He gazed at the yellow clapboard buildings and tried to picture the mayhem of 1913. He found Ouimet's boyhood home on Clyde Street, so close to the seventeenth fairway that he could hear the crack of a shot from his open bedroom window upstairs. Then Crenshaw saw the course. He'd never pictured land like that, with golf holes that heaved and poured and rose through the property as if formed by lava. Crenshaw was so smitten with the bold granite outcroppings and bent grass fairways that he feared taking a divot. He lost in the quarterfinals. But the place seized him. "The Country Club was, for me, the Fountainhead," he would write (with Payne's friend and chronicler Melanie Hauser) many years later in his memoir, *A Feel for the Game*. When named Ryder Cup captain in 1997, Crenshaw felt anointed.

"My feelings are so tied to this place," he said.

He saw his return to Brookline as a pilgrimage to consecrated ground.

Two weeks after the PGA at Medinah, Payne tied for fifteenth at the World Golf Championships–NEC Invitational. He played well until Sunday, when he shot 75 and Woods followed a third-round 62 with a good-enough 71 to win his fifth tournament of a season that foretold the convulsive changes at hand for the PGA Tour.

In his last seven starts, a span that included three major championships, Woods was forty shots under par. He was on the green in regulation more than 70 percent of the time; his tee shots were in the fairway at about the same rate. There also was this: He was ravaging the golf ball with his titanium Titleist driver. His average drive traveled 301 yards. One of those covered 349 at the Motorola Western Open. It was golf writ large, brutal, and savage. Woods had won four of those tournaments. He'd finished inside the top seven in two others.

"Nobody plays like him," said Crenshaw, his Ryder Cup captain.

"I can still get better," Woods said.

The day after the NEC Invitational ended at venerable Firestone, Crenshaw and eight of his twelve Ryder Cup players decamped for their first formal practice round at The Country Club. Woods, O'Meara, and Lehman had commitments they couldn't break. Love was healing a sore neck.

Nothing could keep Payne from going.

He and his seven teammates spent the day motoring around the course. They hit shots, mapped strategies, and pointed out places to avoid, as Payne had done with Chuck Cook and Mike Hicks at Pinehurst No. 2. Crenshaw wanted them to pay particular attention to the blind shots and small greens that made The Country Club so iconic in his view. A photographer for the *Boston Globe* snapped a picture of Crenshaw and vice captains Bruce Lietzke and Bill Rogers, huddled around a cart with Jim Furyk, Justin Leonard, and Payne. No one was smiling.

Payne had pestered Leonard for weeks about preparing for the matches. The two of them, casual friends since their late night at the bar in Illinois after the 1998 U.S. Open, shared much in common in their styles of playing golf. Though fifteen years younger than Payne, Leonard carved his way around a course, hooding irons when he needed a low right-to-left draw, swiping an open face at his ball when the shot required a soft and soaring left-to-right cut. Leonard saw shots the way Payne saw shots. He felt them with his fingers and his feet as Payne did. He was a short-ball player born a generation too late.

"What are you doing to get ready?" Payne would ask Leonard as the matches approached.

The question resonated with the twenty-seven-year-old Texan, a U.S. Amateur champion from the University of Texas at Austin who'd won the British Open at Royal Troon three years after commencement. He'd been on that 1997 team that lost in Spain, the one that Payne had campaigned to join as a captain's pick, though Tom Kite had decided otherwise. Leonard wanted to shake the sting of that year. So, when his telephone rang and he saw that it was Payne calling, he made sure he always had an answer.

At the practice round, Crenshaw wanted Payne, Leonard, and the rest of the team to soak in the aura of The Country Club and become, to the extent they could, part of it. He worried privately about Love. A nerve in his neck had hampered his play at the PGA, and now he was in Alabama, seeing a doctor. Fellow Texan Bob Estes, who ranked eleventh in the Ryder Cup points list, would replace him if he couldn't play.

The captain hoped for the best. He wanted Love, a three-time member of the Ryder Cup team, in that locker room in Brookline. Crenshaw also needed Payne. The Ryder Cup inspired the Missouri showman like nothing else could, even more than the U.S. Open. Payne saw the matches as an expression of the deepest kind of patriotism, as a solemn duty to his country, as close as he could get to national service. He took great pride in being an American. His enthusiasm could irritate others, even his teammates, but they respected his passion, even when Payne blared Bruce Springsteen in the team hotel in the early hours of morning, his own peculiar form of reveille. The zeal Payne brought to the Ryder Cup infected the other players, whether they liked it or not. It couldn't be helped.

The practice round at Brookline lasted for hours. The team kept to itself on the course. The players and captains met with reporters when they returned to the clubhouse, where most of the questions addressed the practice round. Crenshaw waxed again about the spirit of The Country Club. Sutton said it was "dripping with history." Leonard called it "an old, classic course." Pate said, "The center of the green makes for a good target." The other players tried to deflect any suggestion of pressure to win for the first time since 1993.

Someone asked Payne to identify the emotional leader of the US team.

"You're looking at him," he said. "I don't know if you'd call me a motivator," Payne added, "but I am enthusiastic, and that enthusiasm will show."

Payne tied for fourth in the Air Canada Championship. He shot no round higher than 69 at Northview Golf & Country Club in Surrey, British Columbia, to complete a year to date of two wins, two seconds, five top tens, eleven top twenty-fives, and more than $2 million in earnings. It was his best season so far in a decade by almost every measure. It felt like his finest yet. Even with one start remaining after the Ryder Cup—the Walt Disney World Classic in Orlando, the second tournament Payne had won back in 1983, in his new hometown, the place where he'd met Jon Brendle and his friends in the men's group at church, where his children had been born, where he and Tracey had raised them, where he owned a mansion on a lake with a boat dock and a theater and a basketball court and a swimming pool, *where dreams come true*—Payne could picture no year in golf as meaningful as this one. The '90s had been awesome, as it turned out. He now appreciated even the lean years, those lonely walks between late 1991 and early 1998, which had taught him something fundamentally important. They taught him to care. Payne spent the two weeks before the Ryder Cup in Florida in a state of vivid gratitude: for Tracey and Aaron and Chelsea, for his parents and sisters, for his career in professional golf, for his SMU teammates in Dallas, for Mike Hicks, for his two years in Asia and India, for the Mizuno irons and the SeeMore putter, for Missouri, for Springfield, for the halcyon afternoons after school at Hickory Hills. The feel player was feeling a great deal.

He arrived in Boston in late September with a task at hand, but Payne also looked ahead. He planned another long rest between seasons. Then it would be on to his twentieth campaign on the PGA Tour. Twenty. Such a nice, round number. The platinum-anniversary year. Payne was ready, in body and mind, for 2000.

But now it was time for the Ryder Cup practice rounds at The Country Club. He and Tracey checked in at the Four Seasons in Boston. Payne reported to the course, and there he joined all his teammates, together in Massachusetts for the first time. There were Duval and Mickelson and Woods: the future. There were Lehman and O'Meara and Sutton: the shot-makers of his generation. Payne didn't see them, or himself, as the past. He considered everyone, all twelve players on his team, as the present. He felt that distinct spirit dwelling in him again, as it had in 1987, 1989, 1991, and 1993.

You're looking at him.

Payne went out to have a long look at the course again. He wasn't the custodian of golf history that his captain was, but he respected

Crenshaw's convictions about The Country Club, and he paid particular attention to the par-four seventeenth, which Crenshaw spoke of with reverence. Like the other holes, seventeen slithered through New England like a brook. But it lacked the convulsing topography of the earlier holes. There were no dramatic blooms of granite as there were elsewhere. It was only 370 yards. It favored a draw. It looked harmless.

But it wasn't harmless. Ripples in the fairway promised dodgy lies, and craggy bunkers dotted the inside of the dogleg like potholes. And then there was the green. It was tiny, with two distinct tiers, and every putt seemed to peel from the left to the right. Payne didn't know the story of Francis Ouimet—how he'd made birdie there in the final round, and then again in the playoff—but he could see how the seventeenth could be meaningful.

The ten thousand spectators who watched the playoff in 1913 never forgot it. The British press, there to chronicle Ray and Vardon, took umbrage with their conduct at the hole, noting that Ray even had to stop in the middle of his swing for their cheering to subside during the playoff. "The action of the gallery had little or no effect on the match," the *New York Tribune* explained in its September 20 editions, "but a number of golfers publicly stated their regret that cheering like that at boat races or football games should have occurred, although they realized and stated that it was impossible to check these spontaneous outbursts of enthusiasm when Ouimet made particularly good plays." There was something about the seventeenth that roused the spirits. Crenshaw was counting on that in 1999. There was something about this place in its entirety, and he was counting on that, too. Even Ouimet himself waxed about the grounds. "To me, the property around here is hallowed," he'd said in 1932 at a dinner honoring the fiftieth anniversary of the founding of the club. "The grass grows greener, the trees bloom better. There is even warmth in the rocks you see around here. And I don't know, gentlemen, but somehow or other the sun seems to shine brighter on The Country Club than any other place I have seen."

The program for the Ryder Cup informed readers about Ouimet's connection to Brookline. The 129-page magazine also carried stories, written by Peter Alliss, John Feinstein, E. M. Swift, and Frederick Waterman, about the history of the club, its origins in the racing of horses, the curious landforms and granite outcroppings, and the rules of match-play competition. It also featured a two-page essay by John Updike under the title "Need International Mean Nasty?" In it, Updike wondered if the Ryder Cup, and its allusion to patriotism, had become a bit too bombastic and hostile for its own good. "Golf has something to lose if it loses its cool, its air of disinterested courtesy," he wrote. "Not *un*interested, but not persuaded that winning is the whole point, either." But Updike didn't know what Payne already had said.

Back in August, before the PGA at Medinah, Payne had made a spontaneous, impolitic remark about the team from Europe: "On paper, they should be caddying for us." It sounded a lot like the old Payne Stewart, proving that as far as he'd come, he still had far to go. Payne hadn't meant to annoy or insult anyone. He rarely did, really, although he often succeeded in doing just that. Even now, at forty-two years old, he failed to grasp the carelessness of his words and their consequences.

But Mark James and his team remembered them, tucked like a note in their pockets for another day.

CHAPTER FIFTEEN

These would be the last Ryder Cup matches for the American shot-makers. They had won many times on the PGA Tour and abroad, and they would win still, but none of them would claim another major championship in their twilight years of tournament golf. It was Payne's fifth appearance on the team, as it was for Mark O'Meara. Hal Sutton was on the squad for the fourth time in his career. Tom Lehman, the captain's pick, was playing on this third. Now in their forties, the four of them hoped, as all athletes hope, for an unlikely renaissance, even as they accepted stiffening joints, fading endurance, waning flexibility, and the cold glare of truth that their sport now favored power over finesse. There would be no such revival for them.

The reckoning had arrived for Team Europe as well. For the first time since 1977, the team excluded Nick Faldo, the great Englishman who'd been on eleven Ryder Cup teams, a contestant in forty-six career matches—twenty-three of which he'd won, a record that would hold for two decades. Faldo had played in the historic 1979 matches at the Greenbrier in West Virginia. That was the first year the team included players from throughout Europe. Seve Ballesteros of Spain and Sandy Lyle of Scotland were rookies on that squad. Bernhard Langer of Germany qualified in 1981, and Ian Woosnam of Wales made his debut two years later. The balance of Ryder Cup power thus began to tilt. In 1985, with those five players in uniform, Team Europe beat Team USA for the first time since 1957.

Born within eleven months of each other in 1957 and 1958, those five towered over men's golf in Europe for twenty years. Like Payne, they were the golfing artists on the far side of the Atlantic, the creators on their continent, stylists of substance and flair who willed their way around a golf course with their fingertips, feet, and florid imaginations. Ballesteros, Faldo, Langer, Lyle, and Woosnam won sixteen majors between them and hundreds of tournaments around the world, from Monte Carlo to Munich. They were particularly magical together. Faldo built a Ryder Cup record of 23-19-4 through the 1997 matches. Ballesteros, whose panache and quiet swagger inspired Team Europe in eight appearances, went 20-12-5. Langer had played on nine teams, going 21-15-6, and Woosnam (14-12-5) had played on eight. Only Lyle had a losing record: 7-9-2 in five appearances on the team.

Their presence had lifted Team Europe into lasting relevance. They were five parts of a machine that, when assembled, ran better than engineered or imagined. They brought new loyalty to their sport. They unified all of Europe in a way it never had been: through and for golf. Proud spectators streamed to Ryder Cup venues in the '80s and '90s to rally behind Ballesteros, Faldo, Langer, Lyle, and Woosnam, and the players responded with spirited play that generated even more passion in their galleries. At least one of them had been on five winning teams since 1985. But the dynasty wouldn't last. It couldn't. Lyle played his last Ryder Cup match in 1987. Ballesteros made his final appearance in 1995. Faldo, Langer, and Woosnam completed their Ryder Cup careers two years earlier, on the 1997 team that won at Valderrama. Now, in 1999 in Massachusetts, it was over for the five titans of Europe, their era now a sentimental memory, their own last stand complete.

"Time goes by. It's getting to the end," Ballesteros said.

In the four days of practice rounds, the players and captains of both teams dodged questions about acrimony, pressure, tension, which team should be favored, and the issue of whether players should be paid more. Justin Leonard opened his press conference by requesting no more questions about compensation, explaining that his team wanted to concentrate on golf, not a topic that presumably had been settled a month earlier at Medinah. One was asked anyway. Leonard declined to answer. Mark James, the captain of Team Europe, defended his choice of rookie Andrew Coltart of Scotland as one of his picks when he might've selected Faldo or Langer for their mere presence, experience, and gravitas. But questions persisted. James refused to capitulate.

Crenshaw continued to wax about ethereal holiness of The Country Club. The US captain kept thinking about something Hal Sutton had said at the practice round after Firestone. Sutton—after Payne the second-oldest member on the American team—had suggested the team focus on "doing something right instead of doing something wrong." In Crenshaw's view, Sutton was telling his teammates to play with aggressive abandon: to play to win, *not* not to lose. Match play, a format in which each hole counted for a point and the sum number of strokes counted for nothing, demanded it.

"You can't tiptoe through this thing," Crenshaw said.

Everyone wondered how the crowds would behave. Boston was one of the great sports cities in America: loud, proud, and partisan. Bostonians considered their teams—the Bruins, the Celtics, the Patriots, and the Red Sox—a core part of their identity, and when their teams won or lost, so did they. (Boston sports fans would soon celebrate two decades of astonishing success, twelve professional championships in all, but in 1999, they knew only bitter sports heartbreak.) The players and captains were curious to see how that identity would factor at The Country Club. Golf wasn't typically a stage for hostility. But the Ryder Cup was different.

A more aggressive and combative tone had been brewing by the time the two teams arrived for the 1991 matches at Kiawah. With its five veterans in their primes, the Europeans had held the Ryder Cup for six years when the two sides assembled in South Carolina less than a year after the onset of the Gulf War. They had welcomed a promising and polarizing rookie: Colin Montgomerie, a new target for American spectators eager for another villain. Hale Irwin, a member of the US team that year, noticed a startling mood of confidence in Montgomerie and a European team preparing to defend the cup for the third time.

"Almost a swagger," Irwin said.

Team USA won that so-called War by the Shore. It was the first Ryder Cup broadcast in its entirety on television. An international audience saw a new iteration of a biennial event founded as a gesture of transatlantic goodwill. There was a military flyover. Some Americans wore camouflage hats. Ballesteros and Paul Azinger quarreled over perceived infractions of the rules of golf. Loud and bombastic spectators cheered the Europeans' poor shots. British broadcaster Ben Wright called the spectacle "the most exciting and infuriatingly antagonistic contest ever in the series."

Now at Brookline, eight years after the last time the US team had won the cup, Montgomerie was the top-ranked player in Europe and number three in the world. He was thirty-six years old, the face of Team Europe now that Faldo and the others were gone. He and José María Olazábal were the veterans of a young team with seven rookies who had no idea what to expect. Montgomerie and Olazábal reported that the Boston crowds had been respectful during their practice rounds. Their captain recalled the matches in 1995 at Oak Hill Country Club in New York, where he had competed on that winning European team. Mark James remembered a spirit of sportsmanship in a well-mannered gallery of disappointed but gracious American observers.

"I have no reason to suppose it will be different this time," James said Wednesday afternoon. "I hope I'm not proved wrong."

Outside, a misty rain coated the golf course. Speculation simmered about the pairings for the opening matches. Payne and Mark O'Meara came to the press building to answer questions that, at this point in the week, were beginning to seem old and tired. They again assured reporters they were loose and relaxed. They again tried to explain the unpredictable nature of match play. O'Meara mentioned the presence of a Ping-Pong table in the team hotel. That was Payne's idea, he said.

"Payne being Payne," O'Meara said. "He loves life."

To his left, Payne sipped Diet Pepsi and listened, a goofy smile pasted to his face. He clearly enjoyed the validation and fellowship that came with being back on the team. He felt like he belonged right there. He felt like a part of something important. He was living in the moment again, not dwelling on the past or, even more tempting, getting carried away by what the future seemed certain to hold after such a thrilling season. It wasn't easy, that last part. As he listened to O'Meara, he could've lost himself in looking forward to the remainder of the year: one more regular tournament in Florida, the Tour Championship in Houston, and two months at home with Tracey and the kids. But his imagination wouldn't have taken him very far. A question snapped his attention to the here and now. *Did his omission as a captain's pick in 1995 and '97*, a reporter wondered, *make him mad?*

Payne ignored the bait. He said he respected and understood why Lanny Wadkins and Tom Kite had chosen other players. It had hurt, had damaged his pride, but he had been honest with himself: He was playing lousy golf then, and his head was in the wrong place. He said what had frustrated him the most was his inability to do something as the US team lost the Ryder Cup twice in a row.

"I can do something this week," Payne said.

Céline Dion sang at the gala for the teams that night at Symphony Hall. Payne and his teammates wore tuxedos with black ties and picked at plates of lobster and lamb. They tried to project an air of calm composure, but inside they roiled, champing to get to the golf. The two captains spoke. They pleaded for civility. The words sounded noble but perfunctory. Everyone in the room—players, captains, spouses, officials—defaulted to the romantic notions of integrity and honor as the texture of golf, but there were times when one man just wanted to go out and destroy the other, and this was one of those times.

Both sides returned to The Country Club the next afternoon for the opening ceremonies. The captains revealed the pairings for the foursome matches on Friday, in a blind order chosen by each side without knowing who would play whom. In the third of four alternate-shot matches that morning, Payne and Davis Love III would play Miguel Ángel Jiménez of Spain and Pádraig Harrington of Ireland, two of

Team Europe's rookies. Crenshaw felt good about sending Payne in the first wave. He valued his experience and resolve in the tone-setting matches on the first morning of play. He knew he could count on Payne's pure desire alone.

"You've got to hand it to him," Crenshaw said of Payne. "Here's a player in the prime of his career."

"He *is* what the Ryder Cup's all about," said Love.

Payne could barely wait. He wanted to show Crenshaw he was smart to pair him with Love and send him out in the first session of the day. He wanted to redeem that trust. Payne thought about the note his captain had left him earlier in the week, during one of his practice rounds, after he had hit a shot onto one of the greens. Crenshaw scribbled five words on a scrap of paper and placed it under the ball in the bent grass.

"Keep doin' what you're doin'!!" the note read.

Payne gave it to his swing coach, Chuck Cook, for safekeeping. He told him not to lose it.

Phil Mickelson and David Duval partnered in the first match of the 1999 Ryder Cup. They lost to Montgomerie and Lawrie, a pairing of Scots. In the match many had wanted to see since Medinah, Tiger Woods and his partner, Tom Lehman, lost to Sergio García and his partner, Jesper Parnevik of Sweden. Love and Stewart won two of the first four holes in the third game, but they found themselves in trouble for much of the morning after that. Love emoted little. Payne wanted more out of his partner. He poked Love in the chest.

"If we're going to play together, I'm going to need a little more passion," Payne said.

Love told himself he would try. It wasn't his style, but playing alongside Payne seemed to bring out the frisky side in a lot of players. It made it easier to ride the emotion of the match, almost like surfing it. When Love plunked his approach shot on the seventeenth into a greenside bunker, he told Payne, "Get that anywhere on the green and I'll make it [the putt]."

Payne did. Love did.

Payne roared, "That's what I'm talking about!"

They halved the match for a tie. Payne and Love had earned a half point for the team, but it was of little consequence. Crenshaw rested Payne in the afternoon four-balls, a format in which both partners on a team play their own ball and record the best score of the two (in foursomes, or alternate shot, both players play one ball). The Europeans won three of those four-ball matches and halved one. The first day ended with a score of 6–2 in their favor and a number of tough questions about what had happened to a US team so bloated with talent. Woods and Duval, the two highest-ranked players in the world, won no points. Mickelson lost both of his matches. Hal Sutton won one of his, the morning foursome match with Jeff Maggert, but the Europeans tied or won the seven others. Rich Lerner, a broadcaster for the Golf Channel, opened his post-round segment gravely.

"This was a disastrous day for the United States," he told his viewers.

Crenshaw struggled that evening to explain the performance of his team. He said he saw plenty of good golf from tee to green, but too many missed putts to tie or even win holes. He acknowledged the gritty play of Sutton. He said Sutton and the rest of the team had met and decided that maybe they had tried too hard. It was all they could come up with.

"There's a very, very fine line between trying too hard and allowing yourself to play," Crenshaw said.

He paused. "We're searching."

Payne learned that he and Leonard were in the fourth match of the Saturday-morning session. There was still time. There was no panic. Payne liked that he was playing with the young Texan he'd encouraged since early summer to get his game and mind ready. Payne tried to forget about the lost match to Jiménez and Parnevik. It wasn't easy.

"We let them back in," Payne said. "I guess I'm supposed to be standing here thrilled to death with a halve."

The tone of his voice made clear he wasn't.

* * *

Payne and Leonard never led against García and Parnevik. They made their first birdie on the thirteenth hole, but by that time, they were three holes down, staring at a scorecard with five bogeys on it. The Europeans finished them on the sixteenth. The galleries grew restless. Payne had driven the ball poorly, putting Leonard into impossible spots. He'd also missed five putts of five feet or less, including one of three feet. Payne made a decision. After shaking hands with García and Parnevik, he marched over to Bruce Lietzke, one of the vice captains, who'd been watching the match. Lietzke thought he saw tears in Payne's eyes.

"I don't deserve to play in the afternoon," Payne told his vice captain.

The US team won two of the morning foursomes. Sutton and Maggert prevailed again, a triumph sealed by Maggert's long birdie putt on the seventeenth hole and his approach to a foot on the eighteenth. Now his legs ached. Sutton's shoulder was sore. At lunch, the two exhausted Americans saw Crenshaw approach.

"I need you guys to go," the captain said.

"I can't," Maggert said, an admission that hurt him to make. "I'm too tired," he said.

Crenshaw appreciated the honesty from Maggert. He'd been telling his players all week to be candid with him. But he also needed some kind of correction. The US team was down 8–4 after morning play, and Crenshaw could feel the direction of the matches slipping beyond his control. Maggert and Sutton were 2–1 together. On a team filled with ball-bombing youth, the two veterans had become its most reliable pieces. Crenshaw needed his best team to keep playing.

"I'll go," Sutton said.

The captain knew his forty-one-year-old shot-maker was suffering. He looked into Sutton's eyes and searched for salvation.

"I want to play with Payne," Sutton said.

Crenshaw paused. He knew Payne wasn't sharp, especially with his driver. Sutton knew it, too. Crenshaw told Sutton he had a feeling about

Justin Leonard. He called it a "hunch." He wanted Sutton and Leonard together in the afternoon four-balls, but as much as Sutton liked Leonard, he wanted that moment with Payne. Sutton had a hunch of his own.

"He might not be playing very good," he told Crenshaw, "but I'll tell you what he does do: He bleeds red, white, and blue."

Crenshaw needed holed putts, not patriotism. He paired Sutton with Leonard. He left out Payne, whose candor he respected just as much.

Sutton and Leonard halved that afternoon with Jiménez and Olazábal. Love and Duval halved their match, too. Mickelson and Lehman won; Woods lost with Steve Pate. The NBC broadcast crew fawned over Mickelson's "monster" three-hundred-yard drives and Sutton's tenacity. But Colin Montgomerie kept making putts. Sergio García kept gliding through The Country Club, shot after quality shot, goading the crowd with every halved or won point. As nightfall approached in Brookline, the US team scrambled to reconcile another session of missed fairways, missed putts, missed greens, and missed chances to turn these matches into something that would rally the now-desperate Boston galleries. The score was 10–6. No Ryder Cup team on either side had ever come back on singles Sunday from that much. No team had ever come back from more than two points behind.

"We've got twelve great players on this team," Sutton said. "We've shown a lot of fight this week, and we've got a lot of fight left."

The belligerence of the pro-American crowds had become the issue Team Europe captain Mark James had hoped it wouldn't. Spectators bellowed during his players' swings. They cheered and chanted after missed putts. Reporters likened the scene to the "boisterous bleachers" at nearby Fenway Park when the New York Yankees were in town. Some European players blamed their opponents for encouraging the outbursts. Montgomerie and Lawrie accused Sutton of lathering fans with ill-timed fist pumps in their morning match, which the Americans won.

"Their behavior was just ridiculous," Lawrie said. "I don't mind it when we've both played, but to do it before an opponent hits a shot, it's just not right. If it means that much to them, then all the best to them."

Countered Sutton, "I guarantee the crowd would be cheering for them over there. It's not going to hurt for them to do it here."

The captains' appeal for civility at the black-tie gala seemed like it never had happened. Montgomerie in particular absorbed volleys of spectator abuse in both Saturday sessions, just as he had in the second round of the 1998 U.S. Open at Olympic. Fans called him names. They swore at him. Montgomerie privately took it as a point of pride. *No one heckles an irrelevant player,* he thought, and his 2-1-1 record so far stood as proof enough of that. He showed as much on the sixth hole of his match with Maggert and Sutton, when a spectator shouted as he lined up a six-foot putt to halve the hole. Montgomerie backed away, took a breath, and rammed in the putt. He glared at the offender. He felt like he was finishing a fistfight.

"They have home advantage, and you know that's to be expected," Montgomerie said.

That evening, the thirty thousand spectators streamed from The Country Club in a simmering state of disbelief. Even the European fans were stunned. No one expected such a young Team Europe, unproven in the hot light of a Ryder Cup, to dominate an American team playing at home. But that's exactly what had happened. There was a sense that the remaining matches were nothing more than a formality. Now, as the sun set, the captains for the US team assembled around a table in the locker room as the dazed players showered and changed clothes. Crenshaw, Lietzke, and Rogers looked at the twelve names and tried to find an order for the singles matches on Sunday that would give them any reason for hope.

The players wandered over. Soon they circled the table.

Lehman asked to play first. The captains agreed. Lehman had led off singles in 1995 at Oak Hill and won, beating the great Ballesteros. He'd played later in the order in 1997, when he'd dismantled his opponent at Valderrama, Ignacio Garrido, on the twelfth hole of the match, but his case was strong: Lehman had proved his mettle in singles. He'd earned the right to lead.

"You're a strong man," Crenshaw told him in the locker room. "I know you can get the job done for us."

The captains put Sutton in the second slot. Sutton was weary and hurting, but he was playing the best golf of anyone on the team, and Crenshaw needed his reliability and toughness early. Mickelson and Love would go next, then Woods and Duval. The original pairings, designated long before Team Europe had built its seemingly invincible lead, had Woods playing late. But there was only one path now. Crenshaw had to send out his best players first. He needed to build a charge.

The captains put Payne tenth. Payne didn't object, but he wondered if his match would even matter. The Europeans needed only four points to keep the cup, and there were nine of those points available before his position in the order of the matches. Payne noticed that Leonard was in the group ahead of him. *At least he and Leonard might know the stakes before they hit their first shots*, he thought. Now, in the subdued team locker room, Payne studied Crenshaw. He had known his captain for years, played with him, beaten him, been beaten by him. They were of the same era. Crenshaw was a maker of shots, one of the best there had ever been. Payne felt a kinship with him as golf changed around them, beyond their control or wishes, and he tried to discern how being a captain had altered Crenshaw, if at all. Payne had long hoped that he would have his opportunity to become a captain of a Ryder Cup team. He could imagine no better way to serve the game and his country. He pictured himself around a table, shuffling names, trying to get things just right. He tried to imagine doing that now. He watched Crenshaw for clues about leadership and loyalty and faith at the precipice of extraordinary loss. Payne wanted that chance.

Crenshaw finished the pairings and took one last look. He submitted the names to the Ryder Cup officials and prepared himself to meet the press.

Payne and his teammates left for the hotel. They slipped past reporters gathered in the dark. They took the elevator to the sixth floor of the Four Seasons, where it occurred to them that they were in for a bit of a surprise when they would see the pairings for the team from Europe. Three rookies—Andrew Coltart, Jarmo Sandelin, and Jean Van de Velde—hadn't struck a single shot yet in competition. Their singles matches represented their Ryder Cup debut. No one on the US team thought that was a good idea. If they weren't so far behind, the Americans might've even taken pity on them.

CHAPTER SIXTEEN

The weary captain of the US squad gathered himself to answer questions that he hoped would be simple. No simple questions came. As Crenshaw sat in his yellow cable-knit sweater vest and wished to be anywhere else, PGA of America official Julius Mason read the singles pairings. Crenshaw betrayed no reaction, his affect flat and dark, but the pairings did buoy him slightly. The European team had loaded its best players in the back of the order. A path was there.

Crenshaw craved a cigarette. He uncapped a bottle of water. He wanted empathy. He wanted clarity most of all. He wanted someone to remember 1913. He kept thinking about the unlikeliest national championship of them all, when a wispy amateur from Boston, a former caddie at The Country Club, beat Vardon and Ray. *Ask me about that,* Crenshaw thought, even though he knew it was irrational. *Ask about destiny.*

Reporters instead battered Crenshaw about how and why the US team was losing by four points. The captain searched for words that came less easily than they had in the week previous. He bit his lip. He took twenty questions in a news conference that lasted twenty-seven listless, maddening, and wandering minutes. He summoned now-familiar themes: belief, confidence, evidence of good golf, a path. Crenshaw looked drained. It all demanded an accounting that an exhausted captain could not provide. He finally had had enough.

"I'm going to leave you all with one thought," Crenshaw said. "I'm a big believer in fate."

He wagged a finger. He almost seemed to wink.

"I have a good feeling about this," he said. "That's all I'm going to tell you."

Then he rose, marched out of the room, and drove in a haze to the Four Seasons to be with his team.

The players waited for Crenshaw in the team room on the sixth floor. They picked at boxes of P. F. Chang's and tried not to contemplate the odds. They watched a video spliced for the occasion by a film producer in Dallas. There on the screen was George C. Scott as Patton. There was Huey Lewis, the pop singer, making a joke about Europe. Frank Sinatra sang "Here's to the Winners" over highlights from each team member's substantial career, a sizzle reel before such a thing existed. The footage included performances from college cheerleaders: women from Centenary chanting for Hal Sutton, women from UCLA kicking for Steve Pate. There was Bill Cowher, the head coach of the Pittsburgh Steelers. There was Jay Leno, the comic. There was that scene from *Animal House* when the fraternity house was about to be shut down. "Was it over when the Germans bombed Pearl Harbor?" bellowed the lovably incompetent Bluto Blutarsky. The room rippled with laughs. Everyone began to feel better. Looser. Lighter. John Belushi made losing the Ryder Cup by four points more palatable. Then walked in the next president of the United States.

George W. Bush, the governor of Texas, greeted the team and produced a piece of paper from his pocket. He cleared his throat.

"I am besieged," Bush began.

The players listened to William Travis's refusal to surrender to Mexico in 1836. No one mistook Brookline for the Alamo. But as Bush read, Payne and his teammates accepted a certain parallel. The way Bush read the letter—his inflections, his pitch, his voice, like some central-casting West Texas cattleman—conjured a kind of can-do spirit that ignored logic and rationality. Bush read the letter all the way through.

"I am determined to sustain myself as long as possible," Bush recited. He finished with the line about victory or death.

He told the players that their country was behind them.

The players and wives stirred. The conviction of their fate-believing captain, the college cheerleaders and their chants, the scene from *Animal House*, the surprise appearance of the governor of Texas—all of it seemed to summon unity and dreamy hope. Crenshaw recognized the shift. He met the eyes of everyone there, wives included. He asked them for their honesty. He wanted each of them to reveal what the Ryder Cup had meant to them so far, with no regard for the score or potential outcome. Ashley Sutton spoke of the pride she felt for Hal. Robin Love conjured Harvey Penick, whose best-selling *Little Red Book* advised dead aim and sold millions of copies. Tracey Stewart told the younger players and their wives how happy she was to have met them and how thankful she was to have been a part of another Ryder Cup team. Then it was her husband's turn to speak.

In another time, Payne might have tried to rally his teammates with combative words and bluster. He might have made a remark he later would like to take back. But not tonight. Tonight, he thought about his dead father. He told Mark O'Meara that he envied him because O'Meara's father traveled the tour with him. Bill Stewart might've advised his son on his earlier conduct, when conduct was all people had by which to judge him. He might've helped his son make better choices. Payne regretted that the man who showed him how to make shots wasn't able to see his only son think through the possibilities from the right rough that summer at Pinehurst—on Father's Day, no less—and now he mourned the loss of him all over again. Payne wanted Bill Stewart to know that he'd wisely chosen a wedge on the final hole at the U.S. Open. That he'd stroked that last putt so purely. That he'd not lost perspective as he gingerly approached a hurting Phil Mickelson, wearing the pager that wasn't necessary after all. *This isn't the important thing.* Payne wanted to believe that his father somehow knew his son had recognized the important thing. Sitting nearby, O'Meara, Tom Lehman, and Hal Sutton—the last of their generation preparing for their last singles Sunday of their Ryder Cup careers—were moved by Payne in a way they never had been before or even thought possible.

Sutton studied the Missouri showman, now as vulnerable as he'd ever been. He noticed the wrinkles around the shot-maker's reddened eyes. He thought about all the tournaments through the seasons when they occupied lockers next to each other. So much time had passed. So much change. Sutton remembered the way the younger Payne signed hats and flags, a rococo autograph in sweeping bold strokes, as if he were trying to instill self-belief by leaving the biggest impression possible, with no room for another signature on the space. Sutton pictured the flamboyant ensembles Payne used to wear when he was searching for an identity that no one would forget. Payne wore muted tones now, fewer reds and yellows, more navy blues and grays, a touch of Hogan and Jones. Sutton admired the way Payne had grown into himself in 1999, how he'd become more of a man of honor and dignity and measured words. He realized that he'd grown closer to Payne as the hours passed in the Four Seasons. He'd grown closer to everyone.

Sutton had been a golfer for his entire adult life. He'd awoken each morning with the zero-sum goal of beating everyone else, no matter how he felt about them. He understood what made the culture of golf different from the union of teammates in other sports. Golfers guarded their entire selves. They protected their secrets. Hal thought about that a lot: *If I tell you my secret, you're going to use it to beat me.* But walls crumbled on the night before the singles matches at Brookline. Payne missed his father desperately. No one had appreciated how much that still weighed on him, because he never had revealed it, not until now. Sutton felt he knew Payne and the ten other men in the room at the level of the soul. It had nothing to do with golf. It had nothing to do with 10–6. The night had begun with fatalism. It ended with a bond that felt permanent. *There are no secrets anymore,* Sutton thought. He went to his room with a sense of gratitude, as if he'd already won as much as there was to win.

The players were in bed by midnight. None of them dreaded the morning to come. They actually welcomed it.

On Sunday morning, as the sun streamed through the old elms of Brookline, Crenshaw found Lehman in the locker room, which was quiet in a charged manner the captain couldn't interpret. He hoped the players were lost in constructive focus. Lehman lay in the rear of the room. A massage therapist stretched his back. Crenshaw put his hand on Lehman's chest and told him he believed in him.

"I can do the job," Lehman said.

His match would begin at 10:38 a.m. No one in the locker room could hear the thrum of thousands of people pouring through the gates of The Country Club with their flags and sunblock and questions about their side's resolve. Sutton arrived. He had questions of his own. His shoulder bothered him, a disability he kept to himself and his wife. He felt a special burden that morning because he'd played so well, winning Friday and Saturday morning with Maggert, halving his match with Leonard on Saturday afternoon. He knew the team depended on him to sustain his solid play. He hoped it were possible. He wondered if it were fair to expect him to. He opened his locker and got ready to dress.

In walked O'Meara. He also had doubts. Crenshaw hadn't played him at all on Friday, and when he'd competed Saturday, he and Furyk had lost. O'Meara had admitted at his press conference Wednesday with Payne that he was not at his best that week, that he was fighting his driver. He had to forget about that now. He was one of twelve points, of which his team and his country needed eight and a half. As he prepared for his 11:50 a.m. start with Pádraig Harrington, the young Irishman, O'Meara tried not to dwell on the fact that he'd played only sixteen holes. He laced his shoes.

Outside, under a crackling clear sky, Lehman reported to the first tee and shook the substantial right hand of Lee Westwood, the sturdy young Englishman. The spectators assembled around the first tee and sang the national anthem. There stood Lehman in his billowy khaki trousers, creased by pleats, wearing the busy burgundy shirt Crenshaw had chosen for the singles matches, a montage of sepia and gray-scale portraits, including one of the Ryder Cup trophy. There was the victorious US team in 1935. There was the 1937 team, the team in '47, the squad of '51, all of them triumphant. Lehman looked like a geometry exercise. He felt like a king. He checked the wind. He settled into his stance and took one last look down the bent grass fairway ahead.

He took aim.

Lehman was well into his round by the time Payne reported for his 12:26 p.m. match.

Lehman won the fourth and fifth holes. He beat Westwood on the ninth and tenth, too. He struck a thirty-foot putt on the fourteenth and knew it was true after two rolls of the ball. When it tumbled in, Lehman hopped and wheeled, skipping nearly all the way to the fifteenth tee. Stewart saw the score of the Lehman match on the leaderboard at the range. He and Mike Hicks said nothing to each other as Stewart dug divots and Hicks wiped the dirt and grass from the grooves of the old Mizuno irons.

Sutton rifled his approach on the first hole to twenty feet. He was already counting his one-up lead when Clarke feathered a chip from the greenside rough and watched his ball drop for a birdie. Sutton had lost the first hole in every match he'd played. He saw Lietzke on his walk to the second tee.

"This is perfect," Sutton told him.

He made a fifteen-foot putt on the second hole to even the match, roared to three up after six holes, and never thought about his shoulder again.

Sutton won, up four holes with two to play.

The triumph over Clarke had drained and emboldened him. Three days of pressure-packed golf had put on him a kind of stress he hadn't felt in years. He'd accepted the responsibility of leading this team, and his spirited play had endeared him to the younger players still learning what the Ryder Cup meant. Hal Sutton was the personification of that education.

As he left the sixteenth green, where he had completed his week with a team-best 3.5 points, Sutton stopped for an interview on NBC. He mentioned the emotional weight of the night in the team room at the hotel, when honesty and a rare vulnerability seemed to inhabit and soften his teammates. He thought again about what that experience had meant to him, how it had touched him. He swallowed hard.

"I've been fighting tears," Sutton said, struggling through his words. "This team's a family."

Mickelson, Love, and Woods raced to early leads against the European rookies now confronting, in real time and on real terms, their absence from the team matches on Friday and Saturday. Love won next, then Mickelson. "We've been saying all along that if we could win the first four matches we could get this thing to level," he told Jim Gray of NBC. Now it *was* level. Woods won on the sixteenth hole. When Duval closed the sixth match with Jesper Parnevik, five and four, the US team had earned the first six points in singles to go up 12–10. There was the path. It had been cleared with a machete.

"Holy shit," Jim Furyk said to his caddie in the eleventh match, behind Payne and Montgomerie. "We're right in this."

Furyk dispatched García with three holes to play. Pate beat Jiménez with one remaining. Fidgeting in his golf cart, Crenshaw now regretted nothing about his mentioning fate the night before. Around him, spectators sprinted between holes, their US flags snapping in their wakes, their throats hoarsening, as the bedlam at The Country Club riveted the nation. Seventeen million American televisions were tuned to the NBC broadcast, one of the highest shares in the history of televised golf.

"There are comebacks, and then there are unbelievable comebacks," Dick Enberg, stationed in the tower at the eighteenth hole, told his NBC viewers.

"I've never heard more noise on a golf course," added Johnny Miller.

"The gallery's just bulging," Enberg said.

Trouble loomed in the crucial ninth match. A deflated and demoralized Leonard withered as Olazábal built an intimidating lead for now-desperate Europe. The US team needed only a half-point to claim the Ryder Cup it had lost under Kite at Valderrama, and it had to come from Leonard, O'Meara, or Payne. O'Meara hadn't had the opportunity to prove himself. Stewart hadn't carried into the Ryder Cup the golf that had won at Pebble Beach and Pinehurst. Leonard had halved two matches and lost one so far, but his record that week had disguised his lackluster play, specifically his spotty putting. In fact, on Saturday, as Sutton carried Leonard in their four-ball match against the Spaniard team of Jiménez and Olazábal, Miller recalled for NBC viewers that Crenshaw had inserted Leonard that afternoon because the captain had "a feeling he [Leonard] would make a few putts," as the captain had intimated to Sutton and Maggert over lunch.

Miller smirked faintly in the booth. "I have a feeling he should've stayed home and sat on the couch," he said in a moment of bluntness he later would regret. "He's not doing any good out there."

Now the Americans needed him. On the course, Crenshaw keyed his radio and paged Davis Love, who'd won his point against Van de Velde. The captain wanted Love to report to the tenth hole, where Leonard was down four to Olazábal, and remind the twenty-seven-year-old Texan that everyone on the team believed in him. Love and Leonard's caddie, Bob Riefke, kept telling Leonard to wait for a chance to turn the match.

He waited. And his chance appeared.

Olazábal missed a short putt and lost the eleventh hole. Leonard won the twelfth and thirteenth to creep closer still. "You know what?" Love told him. "You're going to win it." Lehman arrived. He studied Leonard's face and liked what he saw. *He has gotten himself together,* Lehman thought as he watched Leonard settle over a thirty-five-foot putt on the fifteenth green that turned a yard or more, right to left. No one expected him to make it, but that's exactly what happened, and the teeming, tittering crowd around the match burst like a giant bag of red, white, and blue glitter.

In the match behind, Payne and Montgomerie observed the commotion with rising interest. They already had endured a raft of distractions beyond the pressure of the Ryder Cup, and now it appeared their match might be the one, if not Leonard's, that foretold the custody of the cup.

All they wanted to do was play good, fair golf. But the gallery wouldn't allow it. The trouble really had started years earlier. Montgomerie had never won on the PGA Tour since turning professional in 1987, but the portly Scotsman from Troon tapped something inside that produced his best golf at the Ryder Cup matches. He'd carried the European teams in 1991, '93, and '95. He exuded a cocky, smug, and often pouty countenance. Some American golf fans despised him for it, but Montgomerie reveled in the disdain. He was taunted often, and he often taunted back. Few fan-player interactions in golf had become as toxic.

There were times when it was too much. In the 1997 U.S. Open at Congressional, the one Tom Lehman lost late on the last day, Montgomerie studied a short putt on the seventy-first hole to keep him in the championship. He waited five minutes for the boisterous gallery to quiet. It didn't. Montgomerie missed the putt, scowled, had a good cry later, and went another year without a major. The Scot figured he'd get his redemption at the Ryder Cup, and later that year, at Valderrama, he'd cobbled three and a half points for the European team.

Now here it was, two years later. Nothing had changed.

From the beginning of the contentious Montgomerie-Stewart singles match, abuse rained from the ever-rowdy spectators at The Country Club. "Shank it, you fat pig!" someone yelled as Montgomerie settled over a shot early in the round. "Fatso!" someone shouted. "Tubby," someone called him. "Asshole!" "Tits!" Montgomerie ignored the hate and settled into a deliberate pace, rankling the impatient hecklers. Payne hit a lovely approach at the third, earning a concession. Montgomerie buried a long putt to halve the hole. The satisfaction that registered on his face widened the target on his broad back. He slowed his pace more.

"Get on with it!" someone shouted during his pre-shot routine at No. 6. "I've got tickets to the Patriots tonight!"

Montgomerie got on with it. He went three up through seven. Stewart took the eighth and ninth. Between the ninth green and the tenth tee, someone threw a beer, spraying Montgomerie's wife with foam. Payne had seen and heard enough. This wasn't the 1998 U.S. Open. "I'm sorry," he told Montgomerie and then pointed out the offender. Security ejected the culprit.

The defense of Montgomerie struck some as odd, especially in the heat of a Ryder Cup comeback. A younger, brasher Payne Stewart might not have objected to the verbal assault on singles Sunday. He might've seen humor in it, even encouraged it, and certainly would've considered it a competitive edge. But the Payne Stewart in the tenth match at the '99 Ryder Cup was the man who leaned in and told Montgomerie over the din, "Look, if there are any more problems, let me know. I'll let the referees know. We'll deal with it." This was the Payne who found himself in the left rough of the seventeenth hole, a short-iron shot from the hole, with Montgomerie in the fairway, the two of them tangled in a now-tied match with career Ryder Cup records in the balance, when Justin Leonard locked into his stance over a long putt on the green ahead and took one last look at his line.

Payne and Montgomerie squinted to watch.

Leonard knew his circumstances. He'd practiced that exact putt— up the slope, straight at first, bending right when it reached a ridge, gathering speed, racing as it reached the hole at the back of the green— a dozen times that week in practice rounds. Now it mattered. Leonard had squared his match with Olazábal, who had a simpler and shorter putt for birdie. All Leonard had to do was tie, at worst, the last two holes to win the cup for his team. He was thinking about making the putt for birdie, of course, but he was also thinking that it was not the kind of putt he could attack. It was too long for that, too slithering and too slippery, and just too meaningful. Leonard was thinking about not ramming his ball past the hole. It was far too late in the match for a nerve-splintering five-footer to halve after Olazábal, Leonard was sure, would make par.

Crenshaw watched with his daughter, Katherine. Through the trees and across the busy street was the old Ouimet house. Crenshaw thought he could feel a presence in the air. He wanted to feel it. If he were right, if fate were real, it would reveal itself here. And then Leonard struck his putt.

Sutton watched the ball leave Leonard's putter and thought, *My God. Hit the hole.*

Olazábal thought, *He's got a good line.*

A hundred yards distant, Stewart and Montgomerie thought, *Will this come down to me?*

Love thought nothing. He said nothing. He watched Leonard and his widening eyes.

Leonard thought, *That ball needs to slow down.*

It turned right on the ridge, as he knew it would, and collided with the hole. Crenshaw bent over, kissed the ground three times, looked at his daughter, and thought, *Run!* The ensuing mayhem came from a primal place. It was relief and disbelief and a sack of gunpowder. Leonard ran left, arms high. *The force of his wake sucked everybody else with him,* Love thought. Lehman galloped down the fairway toward Montgomerie and Payne, who were trying to process what they were witnessing. O'Meara, who had lost his match to Harrington, sprinted into the careening American players, caddies, captains, cocaptains, and wives who rushed the green with giddy abandon. They hugged, they leaped, they lost all awareness. It was like 1913, when spectators hoisted Ouimet on their shoulders and paraded him through the property like a prince on a throne.

Olazábal still had a putt to tie the hole. It was shorter than Leonard's, but now it seemed so much longer, with too many imperceptible twists and planes and gravitational influences. The Spaniard stepped away from the scrum. He tried to gather himself, to no avail. On the fairway, Payne, Montgomerie, and their caddies listened for the roar that affirmed either the halving of the hole by the European team or the most improbable clinch in the history of the cup.

The sound they heard was American delirium.

Jim Gray found Crenshaw. The captain could barely breathe. "I'm stunned," he said. He shook his head.

"It's up in the trees," Crenshaw said. "It's fate."

Payne and Montgomerie halved the seventeenth. Few noticed. Montgomerie slumped and marched ahead with no evident conviction, a player with no purpose. They made their way through the claustrophobic mass of humanity and teed their balls at the eighteenth as the last singles match still in play in a Ryder Cup that was over for all but these two men.

Both drove well. Payne's approach missed the green and finished in a bunker. He wanted the point—his career Ryder Cup record mattered to his prospects as a future captain, as it did to his pride—but he also began to reflect on the appeal of a concession, of giving Montgomerie his putt. *A tie would save Montgomerie from even more unearned belligerence*, Payne thought. He remembered that Friday at Olympic. He hadn't cared then. But he did now. Montgomerie had been through a lot in their singles match, after all. Payne looked up for a moment and scanned his surroundings: the primrose-yellow clapboard clubhouse, the old elms, the frothy gallery waiting to explode. So many American flags. So many fists in the air. He saw Mickelson with his arm around his wife, Amy. He found Lehman, O'Meara, and Sutton huddled with his teammates. He pictured Azinger and imagined the smile on his face. *What a moment*, Payne thought. *What a year. What a year it will be next season and the season after that.*

And then he made his choice.

Montgomerie had marked his ball on the green. He could see the crowd swelling, but not his sullen teammates. He could hear the slapping of backs, the chanting of drunkards, the whoops, and the howls.

He leaned on his putter and waited for Payne's splash from the bunker. Montgomerie gave a quick, half-hearted look at the line on his medium-length putt that might mean a point or a halve to a losing cause. He tried to summon enough pride of his own to make it matter.

Then he saw Payne pick up his coin.

It was over. Payne accepted the loss. Montgomerie bowed his head, rose, and applauded his opponent. They shook hands.

"That's enough for today, don't you think?" Payne said.

"I'd have to agree," Montgomerie replied.

A few steps away, Bill Rogers, the US vice captain, sat in his cart and absorbed the celebration. He considered the unexpected beauty of the gesture he had just seen.

Payne, Rogers thought. *The man for the moment.*

The repercussions and broader lessons of the 1999 Ryder Cup would be debated for years. Many on the European side, especially the team's captain, saw the spontaneous celebration on the seventeenth green as an assault on the decorum of golf and an insult to the spirit of the matches. "That behavior is not what anyone expects," Olazábal said. "It shouldn't have happened." No one disagreed.

The players for Team Europe took great care to not blame their loss on anything more than the American rally on singles Sunday. The media were not so accommodating. Commentators on both sides of the Atlantic Ocean criticized the US team—players, captains, caddies, wives—for their loss of control. They argued that the volatility of the circumstances undeniably affected Olazábal, who had to wait for the miscreants to vacate the green before he could compose himself to attempt his putt to tie. Leonard took full responsibility for inciting the outburst by running on the green. Crenshaw apologized on live television. Other players on the US team said they regretted their behavior but not the feeling behind it. Team Europe captain James never forgave the spectacle. His players forever wondered what might've happened if no one had stormed the green.

In the immediate aftermath of Payne's concession to Montgomerie, players for both teams tried to understand what had happened in the hours since Tom Lehman promised his captain that he could do the job. Crenshaw found Leonard in the locker room, showed him a photograph of Ouimet that hung on the paneled wall, and told him the story of the seventeenth hole. "The Country Club has been very, very kind to the Americans," Crenshaw explained. The captain walked outside with the cup, stood on an old stone wall, and held it high for the chanting spectators spread below. Lehman ripped off his shirt and tossed it into the crowd. His teammates shook bottles of champagne.

Gary Koch, who was on the broadcast team for NBC, found Payne. He leaned into his ear and asked about the concession.

"The crowd was really tough on Colin all day," Payne said. "We'd won the cup, and that's why I came. He didn't deserve to have to hit that putt."

"A true show of sportsmanship," Koch told Payne.

Later, Payne clambered through a second-floor window and joined his teammates on the balcony of the brick locker room. At the top of the portico, the gold hands of a black-faced clock registered 4:28 p.m. A photographer on the ground leveled a lens and snapped the shutter.

There was Payne, in the bright sunlight of a late September afternoon, dousing himself with Moët & Chandon and turning the bottle to the celebrants below, captured in a photograph of another moment of rapture in a season of resurrection. He felt a different kind of joy here, heightened in ways the pictures of his smiling with the trophy at Pebble Beach or punching the air at Pinehurst never quite addressed. A greater sense of triumph dwelled in him now. This was for country and team. It was for Duval and Woods and Mickelson—the new generation of strong players who smashed the golf ball. It was for Lehman and O'Meara and Sutton—his generation, with magic in their fingertips and feet. It also was for a gesture. Payne could live with himself, with his 0-2-1 record that week, because he'd made a choice for a greater cause: the dignity of Colin Montgomerie and the integrity of an ancient game.

The concession would assume its symbolism over time. No one yet knew how it would be remembered in exactly one month, when a Learjet left Orlando and kept rising toward a South Dakota prairie. None of the American players, captains, caddies, and wives even gave the concession much thought that evening as they cleared the team room at the Four Seasons of furniture so they could dance and sing after too many rounds of tequila shots and a throaty toast to providence.

The party hummed through the Massachusetts night. Payne wore pajama pants with chili peppers, and when he bit an unlit cigar and mounted a piano to sing "Born in the USA," one of the wives took his picture and promised to share it with everyone on the team so they could remember Payne being Payne. One by one, players and wives retired to their rooms. Payne spent the last, late hours with Sutton. When just the two of them remained, they relived the intimacy of the team meeting on Saturday night and hugged each other. They looked at one another with bloodshot eyes. They wondered if they had played their last Ryder Cup. They hoped they hadn't, but they would be two years older in 2001. Was it really almost the year 2000? Was it really the end of 1999? They talked about time, and they talked about becoming captains someday for their own Ryder Cup teams, and they talked about the honor to serve as vice captain for the other when that inevitable moment arrived. Payne offered to take Sutton fishing behind his house. Sutton invited Payne to his ranch to ride a horse.

"I've never ridden a horse," Stewart told his friend.

"We can take care of that," Sutton said.

It was very late when they decided that it was time to end one of the greatest days of their lives. They would see each other again soon, they said. They would fill a boat with fish. They would ride a gentle horse. They would always have the last Ryder Cup of the millennium and the belief that fate was real.

Part Five

CHAMPIONS

Bagpipes, Champions Golf Club, Houston, Texas,
October 28, 1999

CHAPTER SEVENTEEN

In the days after the Ryder Cup, Payne addressed a two-paragraph letter to John Cornish, an attorney in Boston who served as the general chairman of the matches. He thanked Cornish, a member at The Country Club, for the work he and other volunteers had done for the event, which Payne called "one of the most memorable weeks of my life." He asked if Cornish would share his gratitude with everyone who had helped. He placed it on a pile of envelopes to put in the mail.

Payne truly cared about the people who performed the quiet and uncelebrated duties that went into staging professional golf tournaments, but his letter also was another effort to mend bitterness over the way the Americans, players and spectators alike, had conducted themselves on Sunday in Brookline. The scathing adjudication of the tenor of the matches had only intensified since the closing ceremony. Mark James, the captain of the European team, warned that international players might boycott tournaments in the United States. He accused a spectator at The Country Club of spitting on his wife. Colin Montgomerie disclosed that his seventy-year-old father, the respected secretary at Royal Troon in Scotland, had felt so threatened by the boorishness in Boston that he'd fled the course early. An official with the Royal and Ancient Golf Club of St Andrews in Scotland called the atmosphere "a bear pit" and said he was "embarrassed for golf." Organizers in charge of the next Ryder Cup, scheduled for 2001 in England, announced plans for tighter security and far less tolerance for unbecoming behavior.

A British golf correspondent said he'd felt like "a spectator in Rome when the Christians were thrown to the lions." Another wrote, "The behavior of the American team, and not just on the seventeenth green, might have been juvenile, but it certainly wasn't surprising. This is a country which is so insular that most Americans still believe that the Second World War was won by John Wayne." Coverage in the US press avoided such insulting generalizations. But this much now was very clear: the more people discussed what *Sports Illustrated* called "the putt heard 'round the world," the more they found fault in what had happened as a result of it.

The relentless heckling of Montgomerie and other Europeans made it worse. Thomas Boswell of the *Washington Post* devoted much of his September 28 column to praise for Payne and his concession on the eighteenth. It was, after all, the final act of the thirty-third Ryder Cup—literally the last thing that happened in the last match. "The moment of sportsmanship exemplified the best in golf," Boswell wrote. "Unfortunately, it glittered in stark contrast to much else that transpired during one of the most exciting days the game has ever known." Boswell found in Payne a reason to aspire to the spirit of civility Mark James and Ben Crenshaw had tried to promote in the black-tie gala before the matches. "In the end, the American celebration will be remembered as just another piquant bit of Ryder Cup lore," Boswell concluded. "We got the cup back. But there's a tarnish on it."

Payne had a lot of time to think about that tarnish. He flew to Scotland the next week for the Alfred Dunhill Cup at the Old Course at St Andrews, a three-player team competition with his old friends Lehman and O'Meara. The long trans-Atlantic flight gave Payne another opportunity to reflect and wonder how the Americans would be received in a country that viewed golf as a birthright. They saw their appearance there as a chance to make amends. They hoped for a fair hearing and a fresh start.

Though weary from the Ryder Cup and ready for a long rest in Orlando with his wife and children, Payne was eager to compete again. He'd signed an equipment contract earlier that year with Golfsmith, a Texas company known primarily for selling components to club-makers.

Golfsmith had acquired Lynx Golf, which made a popular line of irons, and Payne had consulted with the company to design and market a new forged iron that he had yet to play. He took a bag of them to debut at the Dunhill. He left the old Mizunos at home.

The Dunhill Cup was the encore for the three aging American shot-makers. When they arrived at the Old Course, the gallery regarded them as what they were in the middle days of October 1999: setting suns, veterans on the far side of their primes with their major championships behind them, relics of golf more in the manner of Jones and Hogan and Nicklaus, not Duval and Mickelson and Woods. The crowds in St Andrews granted Payne and his teammates many of the courtesies the spectators in Boston had not. Aware throughout their first rounds of how their every step would be scrutinized, the Americans heard no ill will. In fact, they heard almost nothing at all. "Polite silence," the newspapers reported as the top-seeded US team beat New Zealand to advance to the second stage of the Dunhill.

"They were very appreciative of good golf and very warm," Lehman reported. "I'm not a monster. I'm not a rogue. I'm not a hooligan."

The warm reception continued. The good golf from the Americans did not. They lost to Italy and Sweden, two of the sixteen nations competing. Spain won. Swinging his new clubs from Golfsmith, Payne lost to every opponent he played and determined his prototype irons needed more work before he would use them again. Peter Kessler, a broadcaster for the Golf Channel, found Payne after his round, and the two of them sat on the ancient stone steps behind the eighteenth green. Kessler asked him to do a television show with him at the end of the season. Payne wasn't the only good story in golf—no one could get enough of the emergent stars like Woods and García—but his story resonated with people who appreciated journeys both professional and personal. Kessler took great pride in his ability to probe the humanity of the biggest names in golf. He wanted the world to hear Payne share his testimony. He thought it could be one of the more memorable and revealing interviews he would ever do.

"We'll both be in Orlando in November," Payne told Kessler, "so let's play golf, and I'll come do the show." He added, "It's not like we don't have all the time in the world."

Payne returned to the United States to finish a 1999 season that had exceeded his every hope. All he'd wanted to do was make the Ryder Cup team. Instead, he'd won again for the first time since 1995, and he'd beaten a crop of powerful young players at the U.S. Open with a yardage book full of cautionary notes, a newfangled putter, and that pullback motion of his. He'd finished second twice that summer. He'd earned more than $2 million. He had not a care in the world.

He and Tracey attended a banquet on Friday, October 15, at the Portofino Bay Hotel in Orlando. The First Orlando Foundation presented him with a glass sculpture of an eagle, an award that recognized his charitable giving. Payne and Tracey earlier had announced a $500,000 gift from their new foundation to enhance the lives of children in Orlando. He told the gathering that a group of his friends had donated an additional $700,000 to the cause.

When Payne rose to speak to the guests, he adjusted his checkered cummerbund and bow tie. "I think that we all have something in common," he said, "in that we all have dreams. And the thing about dreams is that sometimes you get to live them out. I've always dreamed about playing golf for a living. And here I am, living out my dream."

The next day, Payne flew to Austin, Texas, to speak to the Golf Clubmakers Association about his new affiliation with Golfsmith and the Lynx brand of irons. It was a casual affair; Payne wore khaki pants, a black blazer, and a red tie on a pale blue shirt with a white collar. More than 350 people listened as he gripped the lectern at the Renaissance Hotel and, without a script, bumbled through a few clumsy words about the irons and his association with the company.

He then paused. His mind drifted.

He began to remember.

Payne had been feeling nostalgic since the conclusion of the Ryder Cup. Until this year, he hadn't been inclined to talk about the past, but his success on the golf course and his satisfaction with his life now filled him with wistful appreciation for where he had been, where it all began.

He was loose and vibrant and warm at the dais as the banquet room in Austin fell silent. He described how, as an ornery boy learning golf in Missouri, he'd discovered his purpose through the game, how its artifacts felt like a talisman in his hands, how he used to sand the finish from the heads of persimmon drivers to admire the grain of the wood. He mentioned the loving home his parents had given him and his two older sisters. He said he learned his passion for competition from his father. He told a story about his first job after college in 1979, a position he'd held for two weeks at a men's clothing store in Springfield. He said his first paycheck for two weeks of work was worth $83.75. He said he stared at the figure on the check, remembering how he'd won $300 on side bets playing golf recently at Hickory Hills. He decided then and there to quit selling shirts.

"The golf course was where I belonged," he told the clubmakers.

Payne smiled often as he spoke. It was clear he was at ease. He was charming and buoyant, punctuating his stories with laugh lines and self-deprecation. He described his two years in Asia, where he studied players with inferior instruction and inferior equipment, scrappy men who beat him week after week on inferior golf courses. He said he'd wondered, "What do they know about this game that I don't?" He said he realized those players understood their limits. They knew who they were and who they were not. It would take Payne a long time to understand his limits, but now, in the tenth month of 1999, at the age of forty-two years, he did.

He recalled for the clubmakers how he'd met Tracey in Malaysia. He described his impression of her as she'd entered the room, how he'd noticed her hair and her eyes, how she'd seemed to glow. He told a story about one of their early dates, when he'd tried to use a number of American credit cards to pay for dinner and how each one had been rejected. He said he'd worried in that moment that Tracey wouldn't take him seriously. He said he'd thought he lost his chance with her. Now their eighteenth anniversary was two weeks away, on November 10. "She is the reason why I've been so successful," Payne said. His father, he added, eventually accepted her, and by the time he died, Bill Stewart recognized that Tracey wasn't a threat to his son's potential to become a great player of golf. She was its assurance.

"He understood that she was good for me," he said.

Payne had spoken for thirty minutes, all of it without notes, about his life and his work. He'd talked less about himself and more about the important people, like his parents and Tracey, who'd made his career possible. The banquet room felt like a reunion of old friends and family—intimate, trusting, connected, communal. The people there, many of them strangers, felt close to Payne, and he to them. He invited questions. A dozen hands rose.

A man in the audience asked about what Payne hoped to accomplish in 2000. Payne feigned surprise, pretending as if he'd never once given it a thought. He said he was confident he could win another major, and he thought about the next U.S. Open, which would be at Pebble Beach, one of those places where, no matter what condition his game was in, he always seemed to play his best golf. Payne knew his chances were fading. He praised the way Duval and Mickelson and Woods attacked the game in ways he never did or could. But he also believed in guile. He felt certain that, if it came down to him and someone half his age on the last hole at Pebble, he would rise.

"It's not always about power and strength," Payne told the gathering. He smiled again. He'd proved that.

The man on the dais had been taking inventory since the end of the Ryder Cup. He'd recently told friends that if he died now he'd be at peace.

"When you have such a special year, what do you do?" he said. "You really have to look deep down inside."

The room went quiet again. A wave of reflection swept the darkened space. Payne wasn't often the source of such introspection, but the approaching closure of the 1999 season, the occasion to remember and distill, summoned that emerging side of Payne. A man at a six-top table asked for advice. He wanted to know what Payne would tell a boy or girl who wanted to play professional golf. Payne said he would encourage balance. Work at it, he said. Commit to it. But don't get lost in it. Don't neglect the other things that matter, said the man who sometimes had, who added, "Enjoy life. Because it's short."

Back in Orlando, tour officials finished preparations to the Magnolia and Palm courses at Walt Disney World. It was time for the National Car Rental Classic, a popular tournament since its founding in 1971 given its proximity to Isleworth, Bay Hill, and the other neighborhoods where tour players lived. Payne and his fellow Orlando residents liked the Disney tournament. It required no hotel rooms, courtesy cars, restaurant reservations, or airports. The out-of-town players also enjoyed it; they brought their families, and their wives and children could go to Splash Mountain or Magic Kingdom while they played golf. Payne often invited the veterans to his mansion on the lake for a cookout on the patio and a walk to the dock.

"It's always nice to play here," he said on a practice-round day. "It's special."

It was never lost on Payne what Disney and the Classic had meant to his career. He'd earned his tour card at Disney. He'd won his second tournament there in 1983. He'd never missed a start in the Classic, where spectators embraced him as a neighbor and friend, one of theirs. Disney delivered dreams. Payne faced a stout field—Woods, Sutton, Lehman, his friend Paul Azinger, and others—but he had to wonder: Would it happen again? Could it? He put the Mizuno irons back in his golf bag with the SeeMore putter. He decided he would play the old forged irons through the Tour Championship the week after the Classic. He checked the weather forecast for the opening round Thursday. Rain.

But the weekend and the days beyond looked clear. Payne was relieved. He was flying Monday morning early. He'd been talking lately with Charlie Adams, his old friend and teammate from SMU, about a consulting role in a project in North Texas involving a golf course, and he'd arranged to lease a business jet with a couple of his agents to see the property that afternoon. He'd been thinking about design work as a natural epitaph to his playing career, as Jack Nicklaus and Arnold Palmer had done. Payne imagined borrowing his favorite features from golden age courses like the Olympic Club, Pebble Beach, and Pinehurst—maybe even a hint of The Country Club, with its curious angles, dramatic bunkering, and scruffy rough—and lending them to a place that would bear his name as the architect of record. He was sure he could create a routing with the kind of flair and style that recreational golfers would expect of a self-styled Missouri showman famous for his ubiquitous plus fours, flat cap, and gold-tipped shoes.

Payne reported Thursday for his first round at the Classic, which he played with Azinger. The forecast proved true. Rain delayed play, giving him time to fill. Mark McCumber, a ten-time winner on the tour and part-time broadcaster for ESPN, found Payne, who agreed to a quick interview. The subject turned to comments made after the Ryder Cup by Peter Alliss, the respected British golf analyst and ABC broadcaster, who'd told a European newspaper, "Americans are totally different to us. They might as well be Chinese."

Payne was tired of debating the conduct of the US team and its fans. It had been a month since the matches, after all. He'd hidden his frustration well, but he couldn't help himself now, not even in this season of personal and professional redemption, when his reputation and self-awareness had grown so much. Squinting his eyes and baring his teeth, Payne leaned into the microphone.

"I just want Peter Allis to know that all of us American golfers on the Ryder Cup team, we are Chinese, too," he said in a mock Asian accent. "Thank you very much."

The indignation was swift. Radio talk show hosts raked him. His hometown newspaper in Orlando called it a "major blunder." Other commentators framed the incident as something between a sense of

American superiority, stereotypical white-male-athlete privilege, and subtle racism. ESPN kept airing the clip, reminding its viewers that despite how long it had been since his last public misstep and how much he had evolved and matured, Payne Stewart was who he was, and there might be a part of him that would never grow up, like a modern-day Peter Pan without the innocence. *Payne being Payne,* as Mark O'Meara had said before the Ryder Cup. It was like 1990 all over again.

When play at Disney resumed, reporters banded together near the eighteenth green and waited for Payne to finish his first-round 71. He apologized, but he also didn't understand the controversy, and he wasn't entirely convinced he had anything to be sorry for. He was just trying to have a good time. He was just trying to be witty. He was just trying to annoy Peter Alliss. He'd managed to offend a lot of other people, though, and after another round of 71 on Friday and a missed cut, Payne strode briskly to his car. He had no interest in discussing it anymore.

"I said all I have to say yesterday," he told a couple of reporters.

Those would be his last public words.

Tiger Woods won the Classic by a shot over Ernie Els of South Africa. It was his sixth win of 1999 and the thirteenth of a career nearing full roar and bloom. Payne spent the weekend at home, where he avoided the press, small-talked with Tracey and her parents (they were visiting from Australia), cooked for Chelsea and Aaron (Aaron, who had a Little League football game Saturday, caught a touchdown pass that his father saw), checked NFL scores (the nearest team, the Tampa Bay Buccaneers, beat the Chicago Bears), wondered how Doc Rivers and his Orlando Magic might fare against Charlotte in the upcoming first game of the season (they would lose), and prepared for his trip to Texas. The year was almost over. Payne packed ten ensembles of shirts, plus fours, and flat caps for the Tour Championship and the new World Golf Championships tournament the following week in Spain, which would be his last official start of 1999. He practiced Sunday at Isleworth. That night, his next-door neighbor and close friend, tour rules official Jon Brendle, dialed Payne from his front yard and tried to coax him to go to a Kenny Wayne Shepherd show. Brendle saw Payne in his bedroom window as they spoke, a backlit silhouette of the showman in the dark. Payne usually would be quick to accept such an offer—the trinity of cold beer, loud music, and fellowship always sounded like the right way to spend a long and spirited evening on the town. But not on this one. Payne had to be at the Orlando airport for a flight scheduled to leave the ground by 9:30 in the morning.

Next time, the silhouette told Brendle. *Drink one for me.*

Payne retired early. His alarm woke him before 7:00. He prepared his golf bag: the Mizuno irons, the SeeMore putter, the titanium Titleist driver. He blew kisses to his family from the garage stairs. Tracey pulled away to take Aaron and Chelsea to school, passing boxes of the *Orlando Sentinel* bearing a large picture of a triumphant Woods above the fold on the front page. The newspaper reported also that the Yankees had taken a 2–0 lead in the World Series and that a gunman had killed someone at an Orlando shopping center. There was an article about plans Orlando was considering to prepare for the next big hurricane next to an article about hopes to grow the business footprint of the city. Another story promised a pleasant week ahead in Central Florida: IF YOU LIKE PERFECT WEATHER, the headline declared, STICK AROUND.

Payne promised Aaron and Chelsea he would see them in two weeks. He told them he would miss them, and he told them to be good for their mom. He watched without a second thought as his wife, thirteen-year-old daughter, and ten-year-old son disappeared down the road. The sky was so clear he could see all the way to space. He left for the airport, as he had so many times before, and passed a thousand strangers who, in a few hours, would be riveted to their televisions, watching to see what would happen to him.

CHAPTER EIGHTEEN

High above him that Monday morning, a retired air force major named Michael Kling guided into its descent a twenty-six-year-old Learjet 35.

His flight had begun fifteen miles away at Orlando Sanford International Airport, a former naval air station where Kling, the forty-two-year-old pilot in command, had ordered the aircraft to be removed from a hangar and filled a cooler, a snack basket for his passengers, and 5,300 pounds of jet fuel. Kling and his young copilot, Stephanie Bellegarrigue, twenty-seven, had been told they were picking up someone famous. They landed without incident at Orlando International at 8:10 a.m.

Kling was an able, experienced pilot. He had flown 4,280 hours in the cockpits of lumbering military planes such as the KC-135, a refueling tanker, and the E-3A, a surveillance aircraft, both derived from the Boeing 707 airliner. Kling had been hired a month earlier by SunJet Aviation, which operated ten airplanes, including four Learjet 35s; this particular one had accumulated 10,500 flight hours and 8,043 landings, and had a new interior and compact-disc system installed less than a year before. Kling had just notched his thirty-eighth hour flying Learjet 35s. "According to SunJet Aviation employees, the captain was an excellent pilot who transitioned into the Learjet without difficulty," a National Transportation Safety Board (NTSB) report would note months later. "They also indicated that he was knowledgeable about the airplane and that he was a confident pilot with good situational awareness." His first officer was twenty-seven years old with 1,751 hours of flight time, 251 of them for SunJet. Bellegarrigue was a former synchronized swimmer at Ohio State University who had left Columbus to study aviation at

Embry–Riddle Aeronautical University in Daytona Beach, Florida, and achieve her dream of a career in aviation. SunJet had hired her in February. "Pilots who had flown with the first officer before she was hired by SunJet Aviation indicated that she was a knowledgeable pilot with good aircraft handling skills," the NTSB report would explain. "One pilot stated that she was a serious pilot who had a 'meticulous' style in the cockpit and was not someone who abbreviated procedures or neglected checklists. SunJet Aviation pilots indicated that she was a confident pilot with excellent radio communication skills." Neither pilot took medication. Neither was in poor health. Both lived in greater Orlando and went to bed at around 10:00 p.m. the night before they met at Sanford and flew to Orlando International in the gray-trimmed Learjet 35 with the registration number N47BA on its tail.

It was a sleek luxury business jet favored by both pilots and passengers who could afford its accouterments. It was agile, reliable, and fast, and it could fly great distances at high altitudes, which made it popular among wealthy clients who wanted to travel comfortably above turbulence. Learjets operated by SunJet had carried the actor Matt Damon, the singer James Brown, the stock car driver Rusty Wallace, and Bob Dole, the senator from Kansas. Payne often flew 35s through a fractional-share contract, but he was one of the few professional golfers in 1999 willing and able to spend that kind of money on such opulence. He liked the speed of the 35 and its status symbol. A few feet longer than a school bus, it was the kind of aircraft that enthusiasts could recognize from afar, with its long nose and iconic fuel tanks on the tip of each wing. It could feel claustrophobic inside, though, and when Payne and the other passengers boarded shortly before 9:00 a.m., they had to bend at the waist as they made their way single file through the newly appointed cabin. The golf bag barely fit. The four men took their seats, whose backs opposed each other, and waited for Kling and Bellegarrigue to complete a pre-takeoff checklist to make sure the airplane was fit to fly. The flight instruments showed nothing amiss.

Payne sat with two of his representatives at Leader Enterprises, a sports agency in Orlando whose clients also included football coach Bill Parcells and baseball player Orel Hershiser. One of them, forty-six-year-old Robert Fraley, was a former quarterback for Bear Bryant at Alabama who'd studied tax law at the University of Florida. A creative and tireless negotiator who sometimes spent two hundred nights a year in hotels, Fraley had been responsible for Payne's lucrative contract in the 1980s with the NFL, and he'd secured for Hershiser a $7.9 million, three-year deal with the Dodgers in 1989, the biggest contract to date in the history of professional baseball. Fraley wanted to travel to Texas to help Payne examine the details of the potential agreement with the developers of the golf course. Van Ardan, the forty-five-year-old president of Leader, joined them on the flight. So did Bruce Borland, an Illinois-born golf-course architect who worked for Jack Nicklaus. Borland also had been contacted about the design of the course in Texas, and he'd booked a commercial flight to Dallas, but Payne invited him to take one of the extra seats on N47BA. Borland accepted. He didn't know Payne well. The flight would give them time to get acquainted, and Payne liked the idea, too. Payne already was close to Fraley and Ardan, longtime friends who were involved in the Christian community in Orlando. Payne respected them for their faith and the ethical way they conducted business. He had known them for years. Fraley was the godfather to Aaron and Chelsea. The three families socialized when the men were home. Their wives did when they weren't.

When Payne looked around the cramped cabin of the Learjet 35 that morning, he saw two men he considered nearly family, and another a new friend.

Kling aimed the slender nose of N47BA along the dotted line on runway 36 at Orlando International. He checked the ailerons, elevators, rudder, and flaps. He listened for clearance to go and, getting it, pushed the two throttles. The Learjet sprang. Payne felt the tires under him leave the pavement between 9:18 and 9:19 a.m. eastern standard time. Two minutes later, N47BA scraped through an altitude of ten thousand feet. Six minutes after that, the Lear reached twenty-three thousand feet, bearing northwest toward Cross City, Florida, where it was supposed to turn toward Dallas Love Field. At 9:27, controllers at the Jacksonville Air Route Traffic Control Center heard the voice of Bellegarrigue, the first officer.

"Good morning, Jax," she said.

Mike Hicks was glad to have the weekend with his family in North Carolina after the missed cut at Disney. Like Payne, he was weary after a long season of carrying golf clubs five or six days a week. But, just as Payne was, Hicks also was eager to compete in the Tour Championship, with its small field, early finishes each round, and purse of $5 million. Hicks traveled alone to Houston. He planned to arrive at Champions Golf Club early enough Monday morning to walk the course, chart yardages, and get a sense, with his feet and his eyes, for the shots he and Payne would face. It was time to get back to work. When he got to the club, volunteers were busy organizing the media tent, polishing the flatware in the dining room, arranging towels in the lockers, and unboxing the tournament programs. Payne was one of eight players pictured on the front cover of the program. The back bore these words: *This Sunday will never be the same. Well, at least for one pro.*

Hicks displayed his caddie credential to security. It was a lovely morning: sunny, temperatures in the low seventies, a feathering wind.

There were two golf courses at Champions, a serious, golf-only private club founded by Jackie Burke Jr. and Jimmy Demaret, monarchs in the Houston golf community. Half a century before, the two men, both of them former Masters champions who lived in Houston, went searching for property for a club and found five hundred acres coated with oak, pine, and sweet gum trees twenty miles northwest of the city. They hired golf course architect Ralph Plummer to design the Cypress Course, named for a creek on the flattish property, which often was damp given the ample rainfall in southeast Texas. Plummer was a safe selection for Demaret and Burke. The bulk of his work had been done in Texas. A former caddie and club professional in Galveston and Greenville, Plummer had worked on the construction of Colonial Country Club in Fort Worth and Memorial Park in Houston, and he later would design Dallas Athletic Club, Preston Trail, and Shady Oaks, some of the best Texas golf in existence, then and now. Plummer favored long, broad-shouldered courses with big greens and muscular par-four holes that rarely ran parallel, allowing for differing influences of wind, plentiful in Texas. Plummer routed his eighteen holes at Champions after Burke and Demaret hit hundreds of shots from the dirt and knew exactly what they wanted. The Cypress Course opened in 1959. It was hailed immediately as a competition-grade venue. By the time Hicks went out to walk it on the cool morning of October 25, 1999, it had been the site of the Ryder Cup matches in 1967, the U.S. Open in 1969, two Southern Amateurs, a Nabisco Championship, and a U.S. Amateur. Burke ran the club on the premise that it should test professional players, and in 1997, the Cypress Course had become the host course for its first Tour Championship. Hicks and Payne weren't in the field in 1997. That was one of the lean years. Those were the years of lonely walks. There were no lonely walks anymore.

In Dallas, Charlie Adams prepared to drive to Dallas Love Field, the busy city-owned airport just north of downtown.

Close to Payne since they were teammates at SMU, Adams thought about the last time he'd seen his old friend. It was at the Ryder Cup, when Payne was on the balcony at The Country Club, shaking bottles of champagne. Adams smiled at the memory. He and Lamar Haynes, the Mustang teammate from Louisiana, had traveled to Boston and walked with Payne as he played. They would never forget that afternoon, watching their friend at his best.

Now Adams and Payne had business to consider. Adams was the broker involved in the land development with the proposed golf course Payne and his agents were on their way to see. Adams and Payne had talked about it Sunday afternoon, in fact, while Payne was still at home in Florida. Borland, the architect with Nicklaus's firm, had contacted Adams about the trip, and it was Adams who suggested he fly with Payne. Adams called Payne to see if there was an extra seat on the Learjet. Payne was making green bean casserole when he answered. He told Adams there was plenty of room. He told Adams to have Borland meet him at the airport.

The developers of the project, which encompassed four hundred acres of lowland in a northern suburb called Frisco, had arranged for the men to take a helicopter tour of the property. Adams first wanted to treat Payne, Borland, and the two sports agents to lunch at one of his favorite Tex-Mex restaurants, where they could talk about some of the details, including the probability that the unnamed course would become the home of the SMU golf teams. They would eat, drink, reminisce, take the helicopter tour, and get Payne back to Dallas Love Field for the short leg to Houston. Adams glanced at the sky. It was clear. There was almost no wind. It would be a fine afternoon to fly.

Payne was due to land at 10:15. Adams checked his watch. He would get to Dallas Love Field early. He might even see his friend land.

The air traffic controllers watched the passage of N47BA on their screens in Jacksonville. Its path followed the flight plan the pilots had filed. There were no other aircraft in the vicinity. Weather conditions remained calm. After Bellegarrigue greeted them and the Learjet reached twenty-three thousand feet, the controllers directed her and Kling to continue their ascent.

"November Four Seven Bravo Alpha, Jax Center, climb and maintain flight level, three niner zero," said controller Lloyd Sloan.

Bellegarrigue acknowledged she'd understood the guidance to climb to thirty-nine thousand feet.

"Three Nine Zero, Bravo Alpha," she said. It was 9:27:18 a.m.

Sloan was responsible that morning for monitoring a sector of Central Florida airspace above twenty-seven thousand feet. He had been on duty since 7:00 a.m. He would soon hand responsibility for the Learjet to another controller in charge of a different sector of the airspace as the flight continued to Dallas Love Field. Sloan scanned his radar scope as the time approached 9:28 a.m. "Flat-out routine," he noted. He instructed Bellegarrigue to switch to a different radio frequency so the new controller could take over. She gave no response. At 9:31, Sloan noticed the plane had deviated slightly from its flight plan. The Learjet, locked on autopilot, was nine miles northeast of its mark and nearing Gainesville.

Sloan and the controller for the other sector exchanged four queries regarding the whereabouts of N47BA. Six minutes and twenty seconds passed. Sloan again directed Bellegarrigue to switch frequencies in order to communicate with the controller in the next sector.

"November Four Seven Bravo Alpha, contact Jax Center on 135.6," Sloan said at 9:33 a.m.

Silence.

"November Four Seven Bravo Alpha, contact Jax Center on 135.6," he repeated thirty seconds later.

Nothing.

"November Four Seven Bravo Alpha Jax?" Sloan repeated at 9:35.

He began to feel uneasy. Eight minutes had passed since the first officer's last words. A brief loss of communication between pilots and controllers was common enough to cause no initial alarm, but the duration of the silence now began to concern Sloan at the Jacksonville center. The Learjet passed through the thin air of thirty-nine thousand feet. It kept climbing. Sloan had a bad feeling. He heard one of his colleagues at the Jacksonville center, a traffic management coordinator named Sherry Callon, mention a similar situation from years earlier, when a jet lost cabin pressure and a condition called hypoxia, or a lack of blood-oxygen saturation, killed its occupants and their aircraft crashed. Hypoxia begins at about twelve thousand feet. At the altitude at which the Learjet carrying Payne was now flying, the time of useful consciousness in an unpressurized aircraft amounted to less than sixty seconds.

Inside N47BA, the pilots and passengers might have begun to feel disoriented and dizzy. They might have felt a tingling sensation in their fingertips and feet. They might have experienced headache. They might have felt drowsy, like they had just finished a hot meal after a long day. Or they might have felt utterly euphoric, brimming with self-assuredness, which is another symptom of hypoxia, the most ironic of them all, as an aural warning chimed inside the cockpit to inform the pilots they needed to put on their oxygen masks and return to a lower and safer altitude. There was no indication that Kling and Bellegarrigue attempted to perform either function, the only two that, at that stage in the flight, could have saved their lives. There was only silence as the time of useful consciousness expired and the Learjet kept rising and tracking north instead of west.

"We may have a problem," one of the supervisors said inside the Jacksonville center.

The center declared an emergency. Controllers asked commercial and private aircraft flying nearby to join the effort to contact N47BA. Pilots in an American Airlines flight seven miles away tried reaching Bellegarrigue and Kling on the radio. They heard nothing from them but detected their contrail, a white wisp of condensed water, like a line in the sky. A pilot for a Cubana de Aviación passenger jet tried communicating with the Learjet at 9:38, twenty minutes after it left Orlando.

"November Four Seven Bravo Alpha from Cuban, Jax is calling you. How do you read?" the Cubana pilot said.

"Did he answer you?" Sloan asked.

"No contact, sir," the pilot answered.

"Thank you," Sloan said. He added, "I think we've got a dead pilot up there."

No one spoke.

At 9:45, the mission coordinator at the Jacksonville center alerted higher FAA authorities and the Air Force Rescue Coordination Center. The Learjet had reached forty-three thousand feet with "altitude excursions" that indicated the aircraft was oscillating: bobbing gently up and down. Radar told controllers that N47BA was ascending at a rate of one hundred feet a minute. The Learjet was about to reach its ceiling, where it could climb no higher without stalling. It was touching the lower reaches of the stratosphere. It passed forty-four thousand feet. The Jacksonville center asked the air force to intervene.

Staff sergeant James Hicks, a controller at Eglin Air Force Base in western Florida, instructed one of his pilots to abandon air-to-air combat training over the Gulf of Mexico, refuel, and chase down N47BA. That pilot, Captain Chris Hamilton, turned his F-16 Fighting Falcon toward the coast.

Hamilton, thirty-two, was assigned to the Fortieth Flight Test Squadron at Eglin. He answered to the call sign Bullet One. Once it refueled, Bullet One began its pursuit, closing on N47BA at a hot five hundred miles an hour as the F-16 passed over Eufaula, Alabama, and entered the central time zone.

Hamilton said, "Say type of aircraft I'll be intercepting and the nature of the problem."

Hicks said, "Nature of the problem is unknown. Type of aircraft is Lear 35."

Bullet One caught N47BA about 46,400 feet over Memphis, Tennessee, and flew in formation alongside it, near enough that its pilot could study the windows of the cockpit and the cabin. Through the bubble canopy of his F-16, Hamilton tried to find evidence of a problem. It was now 10:00 a.m. in the central time zone and 11:00 a.m. in the eastern, an hour and forty-one minutes since N47BA departed Orlando International, an hour and thirty-three minutes since Bellegarrigue last confirmed the clearance to climb. Hamilton saw no ice on the Learjet. He noted that both engines were running, and the aircraft had electrical power, as indicated by the red rotating beacon on top of the jet. Hamilton studied the windows of the cockpit. They were opaque. He scanned the five passenger windows on the side of the aircraft. Dark. Hamilton saw no movement inside. He felt helpless. He heard a controller back in Florida mic his radio and tell N47BA to go to 100 percent oxygen in a last, desperate attempt to save the people inside. There was no reply. The staff sergeant at Eglin asked Hamilton to tell him what he was seeing.

Hamilton replied, "Looks like the cockpit is either frosted or basically condensed over. I can't see inside." He feared the worst.

The emerging crisis now involved the FAA, the air force, and the North American Aerospace Defense Command, known as NORAD. Navy captain Rick Mayne was the officer on duty on Monday, October 25, in the NORAD command center inside the Cheyenne Mountain Complex near Colorado Springs, Colorado. He tracked the green icon on his radar screen that represented N47BA on its northwesterly journey. It now was known to the agencies monitoring it as a "derelict" airplane.

NORAD and the FAA calculated how long the Learjet might stay aloft based on variables such as speed, fuel supply, and weather. The authorities notified the NTSB in Washington, DC, which maintained an on-call team of investigators, ready at a moment's notice to cross the Potomac River and board a flight at Reagan National Airport. Federal officials also contacted SunJet, whose employees tried to reach the pilots on their personal cell phones. SunJet confirmed the passenger manifest. A representative of the company called Leader Enterprises in Orlando.

"We've lost contact with the plane," the SunJet official told the office where Fraley and Ardan worked.

Television news channels interrupted their programming with the scant details of the situation over the Midwest. Experienced pilots knew what was supposed to have happened in the cockpit of an airplane with a faulty pressurization system. The pilots of N47BA should have consulted an emergency checklist when the aural alarm sounded, indicating the loss of cabin pressure. They should have put on their pressurized supplemental-oxygen masks and taken the Learjet down to a lower and more oxygen-rich altitude. But none of that happened. No one on the ground knew why. Neither pilot flying N47BA had informed the traffic controllers of an anomaly on the flight. They made no attempt to descend. And as the minutes passed into the first hour of the mystery, questions lingered. Had the airplane been hijacked? Had its skin been ruptured after colliding with something in the air? Had a seal come apart? Was anyone on N47BA alive?

Correspondents for CNN and NBC were told privately that the jet was carrying Payne. They first told their viewers that "a prominent person" was on the flight. They soon referred to that person as a "prominent golfer." Then, when they were certain that Tracey Stewart knew through official channels that her husband was aboard the airplane the world was watching, they revealed his name.

Charlie Adams arrived at Dallas Love Field and walked inside to wait. He watched for an airplane that did not appear. At 10:30, fifteen minutes after his friend and former SMU teammate was due to arrive to talk about the golf course, Adams found an airport employee and asked about the Learjet from Orlando. The employee said he knew nothing.

Adams left the terminal to go to his car and use his telephone. He overhead a pilot in the parking lot shout to another pilot about an "out-of-control Learjet over Missouri." Adams returned and found another airport employee, one who was aware of the situation involving N47BA. The employee took Adams to a quiet lounge reserved for pilots. The television was on in the lounge. Adams stood there, watching in silence. For a long time, he didn't know what to do.

Hicks was on the ninth hole of the Cypress Course when he got a call from North Carolina. He recognized the voice: a golf professional at his club in Mebane.

"Something's going on, Mike. They're showing it on TV right now."

* * *

Melanie Hauser, the newspaper reporter who had written about Payne since he was in college, parked at Champions and noticed the television-news vans. It occurred to her that it was unusual to see them this early in a tournament week. Hauser entered the media tent. She recognized the tour media employees from her many years of covering golf. They had just finished installing telephone lines and deciding where to put the coffeepots. A local reporter had just approached one of those media officials, Ana Leaird, and asked her, "What are you hearing about an airplane?"

Hauser saw a knot of reporters around one of the televisions in the media tent. She joined them and listened. When she discovered who was on the Learjet, she dialed Payne. No answer. She went outside and saw Jim Furyk and David Duval, alone on the practice range. They were talking instead of hitting balls. She steeled herself to approach them. She told herself she had a job to do.

Paul Azinger was in his car, driving from Orlando, where he had finished in a tie for seventeenth at the Disney Classic, to his home in Bradenton, near Tampa.

Ben Crenshaw also was driving. The Ryder Cup captain was on a Texas highway in the Hill Country west of Austin, Texas, when he got a call from his wife.

Lamar Haynes, Payne's lifelong friend from the golf team at SMU, had just left his mother's house in Shreveport, Louisiana. He was preparing to travel to Houston to meet Payne for dinner. His mother had died days earlier, and he wanted to talk to his friend about how to deal with the loss of a parent. Payne had promised him they would have a margarita.

Hal Sutton was at lunch with his father, also in Shreveport. Tom Lehman and Davis Love III were checking on golf course design projects of their own. Lehman was in the Rocky Mountains outside Denver, out of range of cell service. Love was in Tennessee. Lee Janzen, the foil who had beaten Payne twice in the U.S. Open, was on the third tee at Bay Hill in Orlando for a charity event. Mark O'Meara was not far away from Janzen. He was in his car with his wife, driving to the Stewart house to be with Tracey on the worst day of her life. Dick Coop, Payne's longtime psychologist and advocate of a pre-shot routine to improve concentration, had just arrived in Louisville, Kentucky, to speak to a gathering of golf professionals. Chuck Cook, Payne's longtime golf instructor, was at a club in a town called Spicewood, Texas. He was giving a lesson while his cell phone received a hundred unanswered calls. Peter Jacobsen, who had confronted Payne in the men's room after the 1989 PGA Championship at Kemper Lakes, was on a treadmill at his home in Oswego, Oregon, where the television was tuned to the news. He stopped the machine and called Mike Cowan, his former caddie, who was now working for Tiger Woods and who was in a hotel room in Houston when everyone learned that Payne was on the derelict airplane represented by a green icon on the radar screen at the NORAD Cheyenne Mountain Complex.

"Mike," Jacobsen said when Cowan answered. "Did you hear?"

Cowan: "I heard."

Jacobsen asked if Mike Hicks was on the Learjet, too.

Cowan: "Mike's standing right next to me."

Jon Brendle left in a panicked rush, wearing a T-shirt and shorts. He sprinted to the house next to his, let himself in through a side door, and found Tracey in her office. She was on the phone. She was talking to the FAA. She had known since a friend called from Chicago that her husband's flight was in some kind of peril. She had been watching the news. She had been praying. Tracey saw Brendle, stared at him blankly, and said the only thing that she could think to say: "They're going to run out of fuel." She was numb. Phones rang all around her. She stepped outside, sat down, and cried. Her home began to fill with friends.

Brendle left the Stewart house, picked up Aaron and Chelsea, and told them there was a problem with the airplane, that their father and his friends and the pilots were asleep. Aaron wanted to call Payne. Brendle handed the boy his telephone. The call went to voice mail.

"Hi!" Aaron heard his father's voice say. "You've reached Payne Stewart's phone. He's not with it right now, but if you leave a message, I'll tell him you called!"

Brendle heard Aaron talking.

When the Stewart house came into view, the street was lined on both sides with cars.

Captain Chris Hamilton finished his mission at 10:12 a.m. and returned to Florida. Two F-16s from the Oklahoma National Guard—call sign TULSA13—later intercepted N47BA as news channels broadcast speculative interviews with aviation experts and the public debated whether the Learjet should be shot down if it threatened a city like Omaha or Sioux Falls. NORAD and the FAA determined that the Learjet had about an hour of fuel left. If the estimate held, the engines would starve over a remote portion of northeastern South Dakota. Four CF-18s from the Royal Canadian Air Force were prepared to scramble, should the Learjet cross the international boundary. The Learjet had been flying itself for almost three hours.

The pilots from Oklahoma flew with the Learjet until 11:50 a.m. Two fighters from the North Dakota Air National Guard, under the call sign NODAK32, relieved them so they could refuel. At 12:10 p.m., as the pilots from Oklahoma rejoined the mission, the first engine on N47BA wound down. The autopilot disengaged. The stick-shaker warning deployed, and the yoke between the pilots' legs began clattering noisily—a safety function designed to alert operators of an imminent aerodynamic stall. There was a gentle bank to the east, a dip of the right wing, a slight lean. The nose of the white derelict airplane with gold-and-gray trim pitched toward a cattle pasture in the rain-dampened prairie, eight miles down.

"The target is descending," one of the pilots from North Dakota reported. "He is doing multiple aileron rolls. Looks like he's out of control."

A pilot from Oklahoma described a "descending spiral" at fourteen thousand feet, as if N47BA were rotating around an invisible axis.

"It's soon to impact the ground," he said at 12:12 p.m.

A group of pheasant hunters from South Dakota and Texas walked slowly through harvested corn on the sixty-five-degree afternoon, their German wirehaired pointers trotting alongside. They heard a great noise. It was the roar of the F-16s, banking. There came a glint or a flash or a streak. The hunters were too far away to see it vividly. Was it lightning?

It was about this time when, in Florida, a son heard his father's voice and begged him to wake up.

CHAPTER NINETEEN

Four troopers with the South Dakota Highway Patrol followed the final moments of the last flight of Payne Stewart from outside their headquarters in Aberdeen, not far from the border with North Dakota. One of them looked through binoculars and thought he saw military jets and a parachute. He was mistaken about the parachute. That was the Learjet in full fall. Kevin Bakke, a captain, ordered the other three troopers to get in their patrol cars and speed toward Mina, a small farming community of 750 residents and a recreational lake west of Aberdeen, where the tumbling Learjet would collide with the ground. They got there in fifteen minutes, shortly before the parade of other vehicles on the same mission. They did not see the impact. They found a jagged crater, eight feet deep, forty feet long by twenty-one feet wide, surrounded by what looked like confetti from a ticker-tape parade. They could make out vestiges of the oblong fuel tanks, poking from the mud like two white eggs. They saw a tire.

Law officers surrounded the crater with yellow tape that wobbled in the breeze. There was no fire because there had been no fuel; the debris field looked like something a strong tornado would impart after a direct hit on a small house. First responders who sped to the site in fire trucks and ambulances searched the hole for survivors. They knew they would have no success. Soon helicopters thumped overhead. The deputies and troopers asked witnesses what they had seen. They said they had seen an airplane come straight down from the sky like a shooting star.

In Houston, hushed reporters stood around televisions at Champions Golf Club and listened to the confirmation. Ana Leaird and the rest of the PGA Tour staff on-site took their seats for an emergency meeting convened by Henry Hughes, a PGA Tour executive in charge of the Tour Championship. They needed to prepare for circumstances that had no precedent. They canceled the pro-am outing scheduled for Tuesday. They dedicated additional desk room and telephone lines in the media tent. They created room for satellite news trucks to park. After the meeting, as she walked back to the media tent, Leaird saw an empty space in the player parking lot. *Reserved for Payne Stewart* read a placard tied to a green steel fence. Most of the players hadn't arrived, and it wasn't unusual to see an empty space on a Monday, but Leaird paused to stare at it. Her colleague, a media official named Lee Patterson, reminded her that their long and sad day had just begun.

"This is what we do," Patterson said.

Big network news trucks lumbered in. The tour briefly considered canceling the tournament but decided against it. Steve Pate played nine holes to clear his mind. Other contestants who came early to practice found it too hard to concentrate and left. Later that evening, Melanie Hauser put her hands on the keyboard and started her first story about the death of Payne Stewart. She wrote about how long she had known Payne, going back to a college tournament he had won in Austin. She wrote about the U.S. Open and the Ryder Cup. She wrote about the donation Payne made in 1987 after he broke his first slump at Bay Hill. She remembered the last time she'd seen Payne. He was on the balcony at The Country Club. He had grinned at her below.

Hauser made herself type.

"Our paths crossed constantly for twenty-two years," she wrote. "I saw him lose Byron Nelsons and Houston Opens and U.S. Opens. I watched him win a PGA and took him to task for what we'll call a little immature behavior. I saw him walk hand-in-hand with Tracey across a field when he gave away one of those Nelsons. I marveled at the changes I saw over the years and the man who dug deeper than he ever thought he could to win that second Open."

She concluded, "It won't be an easy week on anyone. Golf, which seemed so important Monday morning, is suddenly nothing more than a job that must be done."

Tributes to Payne came from all corners, sentimental and forgiving, the way people, even rivals, tend to remember the dead. The golf writer John Feinstein told readers of *USA Today* that Payne "always wanted to get better, even when most people would have thought there was no need." Feinstein remembered the 1998 U.S. Open at Olympic. "He was gracious and patient. He even kept his sense of humor." The longtime journalist concluded, "Stewart didn't always get things right, but he never once claimed he was never wrong. He admitted his mistakes, learned from them and kept on growing. Right up until the day he died."

European players, many of them preparing for the World Golf Championships tournament in Spain, remembered Payne as a fiery and zealous competitor who loved his country, his friends, his wife, his children, his parents, his sisters, his profession, his pranks, his cocktails, his cigars, his parties, his boats, his cars, his faith. There was Colin Montgomerie, reflecting on the concession in the Ryder Cup. It meant even more now, carried more significance, he said. Montgomerie realized how fond he'd grown of Payne during and after the Ryder Cup, and his death, unattended, far from the people he loved and who loved him, struck Montgomerie like a slap. He felt cheated of the chance to say a proper goodbye.

"Above all," Montgomerie told reporters trolling for reaction to the tragedy, "I respected his approach to the game, and never more than at Brookline. In those extraordinary circumstances, it takes a big man to stand up and be counted. Payne Stewart certainly was that."

"Nothing would be enough to express that we have lost a great person," said José María Olazábal. "A great player. A great sportsman."

And this, from Seve Ballesteros, whom Payne always called by his full name, Severiano: *"Nos sentimos como el hielo." We feel like ice.*

Most of the twenty-nine players in the Tour Championship elected to come to Champions on the day after Payne's death. Patterson told them in the locker room to be ready to talk about Payne. Many of them wanted to. They wanted to chuckle about the jokes, picture the plus fours and flat caps, remember the shots that won majors, tell the stories that mattered at this strange time. Tim Finchem, the PGA Tour commissioner, spoke to the mass of reporters at great length. He compared Payne to Walter Hagen, the stylish showman from Rochester, New York, who wore ties and tailored shirts in competition, who took an Austro-Daimler limousine to tournaments in the golden age. Finchem said Tom Lehman would lead a brief ceremony Thursday morning on the first tee, after which the contestants would play twenty-seven holes. He announced that play would be suspended Friday so players could travel to Orlando for the memorial service. The tournament would resume with twenty-seven holes Saturday and the customary eighteen on Sunday.

"We concluded that this set of options was the most appropriate given all the factors involved," Finchem said.

David Duval, Davis Love III, Hal Sutton, and Tiger Woods did press conferences. They struggled to fit the tournament into some kind of sensible perspective, like trying to equate two things that had nothing to do with each other. Duval said he hadn't talked to many players about Payne's death. "We don't know what to say to each other," he admitted. Woods said he looked at a pro-am pairing sheet and noticed the blank space behind his name where the next group was supposed to play. Payne was that missing name. "An empty feeling," Woods said. He said golf seemed insignificant. Love described his first instinct on Monday when he learned in Tennessee that Payne was dead: to go home and see his family. It was personal and haunting and heavy for Love. His father, Davis Love Jr., a teaching professional, had been killed in an airplane crash in 1988. Love said the Tour Championship had lost the importance it had had before October 25. He also said it needed to be played.

"Right now, this is the place for us," Love said.

It was complicated for Sutton, too. He thought a lot about the nights at the Ryder Cup, when he went through a touching and unexpected reappraisal of Payne. Sutton talked about his inviting Payne to his farm in Louisiana to ride a horse. He talked about their conversations concerning future Ryder Cups, when they might be captains. He talked about how their careers had bloomed again as they had reached their forties. "He'd say, 'Let's win one for the old guys,'" Sutton said with a sad smile.

Now one of the old guys was no longer there to win one. One of the shot-makers, the Missouri showman with the pullback motion and the tempo of a ballet danzatore, gone. The men who'd played on the PGA Tour for those two decades with Payne felt that absence more acutely than the younger ones like Woods or Mickelson or Justin Leonard did or could. The week of the 1999 Tour Championship was supposed to represent the crowning of a worthy champion, the conclusion of another season of golf, the last chapter of the '90s, and the prologue to 2000. Now it was a farewell. It was an epilogue. Sutton, Lehman, O'Meara, Payne, and even Paul Azinger, younger but an old soul like Leonard, stood for a way of playing golf that had begun to look quaint and old-fashioned now that Mickelson and Woods lorded over the game with their ferocity and abandon and brutality. Payne had mentioned at Pinehurst that he didn't know how many more chances he would get. Sutton thought about that, too. There were so many hills in golf. Countless hills. Most of them were on courses. But one of them was time itself. Sitting there in the press tent at Champions, as he considered and answered hard questions about Payne, Sutton wondered if he might be approaching the other side of the hill of time. He might even be there.

"As tragic as this is, I think it makes us all evaluate what we are going through in our lives," he said.

No one at the tournament in Houston speculated publicly about what might have happened. Few facts were available. A team of experts with the NTSB began its investigation in earnest that morning in South Dakota and Orlando. The investigators in Florida researched the careers of the pilots and the maintenance and repair records involving the Learjet. The ones on the ground near Mina tried to find pieces that might tell them what went wrong.

Those in the aviation community—pilots, mechanics, scientists, consultants who specialized in reconstructing aircraft disasters— assumed the Learjet had sustained catastrophic depressurization shortly into its flight. The accounts from the military pilots, who had described condensation or frost on the inside of the windows, seemed to suggest that N47BA lost its capacity to maintain its cabin with safe, oxygen-rich levels as it climbed. The pilots and passengers, the logic went, had lost consciousness and died from hypoxia before the Learjet left the airspace of Florida.

The lack of a clear explanation left an awkward pall over Champions. Reporters there asked the players about their flying habits, whether they had fractional ownership of jets, how they felt about air travel now that Payne had perished under such mysterious circumstances. It was an uneasy conversation. No players wanted to talk about flying. The reporters pressed on. Sutton revealed that he had just purchased his own jet and hired his own pilot. He wanted to know the airplane he relied on and the person who was operating it. Love had spoken the day before to the pilots who flew for him. He had asked them to explain the architecture of the airplane, to reassure him that air travel was, by nature, designed with redundant systems to be safe in the event of a problem. More questions came. Finchem announced that the tour had arranged for a small fleet of business jets to take players Friday to Orlando for the memorial service, and flights would be organized for players in Mississippi, where the regular PGA Tour tournament was being played that week, and for the older golfers at the senior-tour event in California. A reporter asked the commissioner if he'd considered retaining larger passenger airliners instead.

Everyone wanted to know where the players were when they learned about the flight of N47BA. The men told their stories. It seemed odd to them that the media were so interested in specifics like that. It seemed intrusive and irrelevant. The wall-to-wall media coverage of the flight on Monday, all the theories and speculation about what was happening eight miles in the air, struck some of the players as too much. It took them to a place that made them consider unsettling scenarios. It could've been them in that airplane with the frosted windows, being intercepted by military pilots eight miles above their distraught sons and daughters and wives.

"I was just like anybody else watching it," a frustrated Sutton said. "I am not sure everybody deserves to know every little detail of what is going on in somebody's life. I have not talked to Tracey or anybody else, but I hope she didn't have to sit there and watch that and hear everything they talked about. That was her husband and her children's daddy in that airplane. If I can caution any of you about anything, it is not the obligation to point out every detail of everything that goes on with everybody. It is not your responsibility. That was a tragic moment. I just know that if that would have been my situation, I wouldn't have wanted to have to deal with everything that was on TV."

Sutton excused himself. He was done talking. It was time to mourn alone, not with an audience. He also had to get ready to play a golf tournament.

He left the tent. The parking space for Payne no longer was empty. It was a shrine now, a spontaneous altar for the dead. Someone had placed sprays of flowers along the green metal fence. Carnations. Lilies. Among the other ephemera, an orange piece of poster board lay on the asphalt. *We will never forget you*, it said in black ink. There was a picture of Payne attached with red ribbon to a bouquet of roses. Someone had left a poem.

More than a thousand miles to the north, investigators with the NTSB removed fragments of the Learjet from the ground and hauled them to be reassembled in an airport hangar in Aberdeen. Payne's class ring from SMU eventually was found. So was his wedding band, the face of his Rolex watch, and a gold pendant he had worn since his engagement to Tracey. There was scant proof in the damp crater of a thirty-pound golf bag. The Mizuno irons, the Titleist driver, the SeeMore putter: splinters of metal, bent and sheared, barely recognizable now as the implements of a man famous the world over for the way he could use them.

Nearby, twenty-one news trucks hummed. Journalists learned that NTSB officials had found the cockpit voice recorder, fourteen feet in the mud. It was unlikely to reveal useful information. It recorded sound from only the final thirty minutes of the flight. But it was evidence, at least, from a crash site that bore few clues. The NTSB team in Florida reported that a valve involved in the Learjet's cabin-pressurization system had been replaced two days before the flight. Investigators in South Dakota searched for other important hardware that might tell them whether certain systems had failed. They were especially interested in the valve that controlled flow from the onboard bottle of pressurized oxygen. Conditions were unfavorable for such a discovery. There was so little left to discover. It was tedious labor, essentially an archeological dig: men and women on their hands and knees, combing wet soil with their fingers, marking locations with tiny red flags, fumbling in their clumsy hazmat suits, breathing through masks. On the Wednesday evening broadcasts, network correspondents reported from outside the yellow tape that authorities were concerned that the fate of N47BA could remain a mystery subject only to deduction and cause-and-effect theory. One government source told a wire service reporter, "I don't know if we'll ever be able to tell what happened from what we dug out of that hole."

Tom Lehman rose early Thursday morning and rehearsed the message he hoped to convey. He had turned forty in March, and he felt the weight and toil of every one of those years as he prepared to deliver his eulogy for Payne. He had thought about the way Payne seemed to be searching, seemed to be yearning to fill a hole in his life before it was too late, and how the 1999 season felt like a reward for his work, how Payne had seemed, to him, anointed to win the U.S. Open at Pinehurst. Lehman chose a passage from a book with instructions for Christian funerals. (He liked this line best: "In such a time, there is but One who can bring light out of darkness.") Lehman knew he was right for this moment. He was strong in his faith. He believed Payne was, too. The temperature hung in the low sixties when Lehman arrived at Champions and saw white chairs arranged in neat rows around the first tee. A flag was at half-staff. Fog clung to the turf. Lehman left footprints in the dew on his walk to his seat.

The ceremony began at 7:45. A member of the Hamilton Bagpipe Band blew the opening bars of "Going Home," a devastating hymn about longing and return, as he marched through the fog from the fairway to the tee, all eyes locked on his steps, his kilt, his pipes. Melanie Hauser and other reporters estimated a thousand people were there, including the players in the field, many of their spouses, volunteers, tour officials, golf illuminati who'd traveled to Houston on sudden notice, and spectators who'd never met Payne but wanted to bear witness. Ben Crenshaw, Payne's Ryder Cup captain, sat with Jackie Burke Jr., the founder of Champions, a former Marine in World War II, tough and rugged and outwardly unsentimental. When the bagpiper appeared through the fog, Burke leaned into Crenshaw and whispered over the notes, "I think the spirit of God is with us."

The music stopped. The tour commissioner spoke first. Finchem called Payne "a great champion, a tenacious competitor, and a real showman." He allowed that Payne "represented the best in golf." Lehman read the passage from the book about funerals. He said, "We will not forget Payne Stewart." He insisted that Payne would want those gathered, including himself, to "get our priorities right, bury the hatchet, [and] don't hold grudges," with no elaboration. Lehman swallowed. He looked at the people in the white chairs. "Payne was a very emotional guy," he told them. "He loved to laugh, and he wasn't ashamed to cry. I'm not going to be ashamed of my tears this morning, and neither should you."

He added, "When he died on Monday, a big part of us died, too." He asked for a moment of silence.

The bagpiper wheeled and walked away, keying "Amazing Grace." He retraced his footprints in the dew, in a fog that the sun was now burning dry. *There goes our friend Payne, and he's not coming back*, thought Henry Hughes, the PGA Tour official in charge of the championship. Eleven hundred miles to the east, in the dales and hollows of the North Carolina sandhills, resort staff made plans to lower the US flag in the morning at Pinehurst. One of the interns, an accomplished bagpiper who hailed from St Andrews, Scotland, was asked to walk the length of the last hole of No. 2, up the hill and along the bend to the right, playing traditional Great Highland music as he retraced the steps the champion had taken in June. The grounds crew decided to pin a tiny black ribbon to the flag at the eighteenth. It would be just like the ones the players were wearing in Houston. Then there would be one more job to do at Pinehurst. The hole would be set in the place where it had been on that Sunday in June when Payne Stewart crouched over a putt to win for the last time in his life.

Two groups went off in the Tour Championship before Bob Estes reported to play his twenty-seven holes. Estes, thirty-three, had completed one of his strongest seasons since joining the tour out of the University of Texas, winning more than a million dollars and finishing high in the Masters and the PGA Championship. He had gotten to know Payne well. Estes also worked with Chuck Cook, Payne's teacher, and Estes and Payne often had played practice rounds together, frequently at the majors. Estes dressed that Thursday morning in black pants and a black shirt, with black shoes. He started on the tenth tee, where Brad Townsend, a reporter for the *Dallas Morning News*, happened to be standing.

"This one's for Payne," he told Townsend in a low voice.

Estes teed his ball, pulled his putter from his bag, and, without another word, tapped it gently through the grass. The ball dribbled sixteen feet. Estes made a double-bogey six on the hole. He completed the long round at one under par—a triumph, given the first shot, which he struck to represent the length of the putt Payne had made to win at Pinehurst. Some players thought it was a questionable decision, a waste of a precious shot in such a big tournament, but to Estes, the sacrifice felt right for the situation, like pausing on the side of the road to let a cortege pass. It was a gesture of respect. Payne deserved that stroke.

"I admire him for that," said Davis Love III.

No one could recall a more muted day of championship golf. It looked like a Tour Championship: bleachers, leaderboards, television towers behind roped-off greens, grill smoke floating from refreshment stands, caddies and contestants moving through the grounds to the rhythmic clack of irons colliding. But it felt like a wake. Players had to will themselves to compete. Volunteers stood with their hands folded, shifting on their feet. Spectators wondered how to act. They hesitated to applaud good shots with the enthusiasm they might usually show. They felt inclined to root for the men struggling the most.

Love, who wore a hat with Payne's initials written under the bill, finished the long day with the lead: seven under par through a round and a half. Tiger Woods was a stroke behind at six under, ahead of three players at minus five and three others at minus four. The matter of playing a golf tournament wasn't easy. It was a day of struggle, full of internal conflict, one of those rare occasions when playing seemed like a necessary duty. Love kept reminding himself that Payne would want him to concentrate on good swings and solid putts. He had a four-footer for birdie on one hole in his round, a simple putt straight up the hill. Then a little Cessna clattered across the sky, pulling a banner that read, *We will remember you, Payne.* Love made the mistake of looking at it. He had to back away from the putt again and again. "You shouldn't be out there playing golf with tears in your eyes," he later said. Lehman shot even par. Sutton was minus two. The shot-makers made their shots, and the Cessna disappeared.

"I must've thought at least two or three dozen times about Payne," said Nick Price.

"I almost feel like I lost a family member," said Hal Sutton.

"I can't think of any day I've seen on tour like this," said Jeff Sluman.

"Everyone's mind wandered," Melanie Hauser wrote in her account of the saddest day of golf she had ever witnessed and ever would. "Everyone felt empty. Everyone felt the pain, especially when the plane circled the course."

Hauser filed her report and left the tent, where the tournament programs had been distributed bearing a new back cover. Gone were the words about Sunday never being the same. Now there was this: "Payne Stewart: 1957–1999." Hauser walked past the space in the players' lot where no courtesy car was parked. There were more roses. More notes. Hauser had decided to remain in Houston instead of going to Orlando for the service, so she wasn't there Thursday evening and Friday morning when the players, escorted to the airport by police, boarded the fleet of chartered business jets and flew to Florida in silence.

CHAPTER TWENTY

Ana Leaird, the tour media official at Champions, sat next to Steve Pate on the last plane to leave Houston. Pate never spoke. Leaird's mind drifted: to the crowds around the televisions on Monday morning, to the lilies in the parking lot, to the arduous day of golf on that suffocating Thursday, to the bagpiper, the footprints, the fog. When she felt the descent and bank that meant the pilots were preparing to land, she looked through one of the cabin windows and saw a procession of jets ahead. There was the one that Nick Price used. It was right behind the plane that Jack Nicklaus owned, which was lined up behind Greg Norman's, all of them aimed at the runway in a line like cars exiting an interstate. *The entire golf world is landing in Orlando,* Leaird thought. All aircraft arrived without incident.

Three thousand people took their places at the First Baptist Church of Orlando. They included a hundred professional golfers—Lehman, O'Meara, Sutton, the others in their forties—and Payne's mother, Bee, and his two sisters from Springfield, Lora and Susan. They passed an arrangement in the foyer, pausing to consider Payne's trophies from the U.S. Open and the PGA Championship, family pictures, a pair of plus fours, and a framed message from Aaron and Chelsea that read, "We love you, Dad. We will miss you." They listened for ninety minutes as stories were told from an altar ringed by yellow roses and a gold chalice and photographs of the showman in his finest moments: smiling broadly with his family, hoisting trophies. They heard a recording of Vince Gill singing a song he wrote for Payne. Chuck Cook told a funny story involving champagne. Paul Azinger put on a black flat cap and rolled up his suit trousers, revealing argyle socks like the ones Payne wore, and opened with a memory: Payne had once bought a fancy bass boat, Azinger remembered, and had started its outboard marine engine in the garage. "An outboard engine cannot run without water," Azinger said wryly. "And it exploded." The church shook with laughter. "And then he made the mistake of telling me. And I told everybody." More laughs, louder now.

Azinger needed that levity. He knew it was about to get tough. He'd been thinking a lot about the words he would use now, and more broadly about his message. He'd been thinking about how he'd met Payne on the putting green in Mississippi in 1982. He'd been remembering how cocky he was, so full of himself that he seemed to vibrate. Azinger also had been remembering those occasions after his cancer diagnosis when Payne drove to Bradenton from Orlando to spend a day with him in a fishing boat, not so much to cheer him through phony optimism but just to be a friend, a presence. Azinger knew now that Payne had helped him. And he knew that he had helped Payne, too. He appreciated that more than he ever had. It saddened him that it had taken a death to get him to this point. But he also felt fortunate. He felt chosen, in an unfathomable way, to express to this gathering at First Baptist that the life of Payne Stewart had become a story of realization and salvation, of recognition and change. It had purpose. It had meaning. This, Azinger had decided, would be his testimony. He would accentuate the man Payne had become. That was the man who had perished Monday morning as the world watched and wondered and waited. That was the man they were mourning now. Azinger removed the flat cap. He unrolled the suit trousers. He sighed.

"To try to accept the magnitude of this tragedy is the most difficult thing that I've ever had to do," Azinger began. He read from the Bible. He said Payne wore the "crown of righteousness." He said, "He was the life of every party and loved to cook." He said, "Payne Stewart loved life." He said he and Payne had played five holes in a practice round the week before at Disney, where Payne had begun his career in professional golf, where dreams actually did come true. He said they'd talked about the Ryder Cup. He said Payne had told him that he hoped to be the captain in 2003. Azinger said Payne had told him that he and Hal Sutton would be his cocaptains. "I'm so thankful for those words," he said.

Azinger sniffed. "Payne was a vicious competitor," he said. "He only played to win. This was all he ever knew. But not long ago, we started to see something new, something totally different. We started to see a man that was interested in people. He was as interested in people as he was in golf. Payne became gracious in victory and gracious in defeat, and only God can do that, because only God can change hearts." He concluded with this: "Goodbye, Payne." He barely could utter the words.

Then Tracey rose from the front row, where she had been sitting with her children, all of them in black. She walked to the altar with her brother. "When I met Payne, I thought he was the most beautiful man I had ever seen in my life," she said. "After eighteen years of marriage, he was still the most beautiful man I had ever seen. Not because of the way he looked on the outside anymore but because of what he was on the inside." She said there was now a party under way in heaven. No one could believe her strength. Tracey and her children led the three thousand people from the church. Lehman, O'Meara, Sutton, and the hundred other professional golfers stood on both sides of the aisle. Tracey thought of them as her honor guard.

In South Dakota, the Bethlehem Lutheran Church in Aberdeen held a service that drew three hundred. The nineteen investigators with the NTSB now conducted most of their work at the airport hangar, seventeen miles from the crash site, where flatbed trucks had delivered from the crater what remained of N47BA and its contents. An aerodynamic analysis in Washington had determined that the Learjet struck the ground at about six hundred miles an hour.

The NTSB investigator in charge in South Dakota was a former air force pilot named Robert Benzon, who'd flown Douglas C-47 Skytrain military transport planes in Vietnam. Benzon had worked a number of high-profile crashes for the NTSB, most of them involving commercial aircraft, among them Pan Am Flight 103 in Lockerbie, Scotland, and Continental Flight 1713, a DC-9 passenger jet that crashed in Denver shortly after takeoff in a snowstorm in 1987. Benzon typically didn't investigate incidents involving small business jets, but he happened to be on call Monday when the FAA alerted his office of an aircraft not responding. And that aircraft happened to be carrying a famous athlete.

Benzon and his colleagues had spent five days at the crater, combing it for clues. They'd purchased and borrowed metal detectors in Aberdeen. They'd found pieces of the pilots' oxygen masks and wondered if they'd been activated. They'd found fragments of the cooler, the one carrying snacks. One of the early questions about the demise of N47BA involved its contents, about whether the cooler was holding dry ice, a solid form of carbon dioxide. The investigators already had answered that question: no. Benzon was convinced now that depressurization had caused the incapacitation of the pilots. There was no other plausible explanation—for the silence on the radio, for the missed turn toward Dallas, for the condensation on the windows. There also was no way to prove it. Benzon and the other investigators had located, examined, photographed, and cataloged thousands of pieces of N47BA. The investigators placed the pieces on the waxed floor of the hangar in Aberdeen. Many were smaller than a man's hand. They placed the tiniest ones on tables. Most were beyond recognition. When they stood back and considered the assemblage, the members of the NTSB team, all of them experienced veterans of gathering facts from the tragic mélange of an aircraft disaster, knew what they were looking at: a riddle that would never reveal its whole truth.

Benzon soon ordered the team to pack up. It was time to return to Washington. He had a report to write. He wished he knew more than what he could write in it.

The chartered jets carrying the players returned to Houston after the service at First Baptist Church. The uneventful hours in the air had given everyone another opportunity to reflect. For some, the image of

Tracey Stewart and her children in their black funeral clothes felt like a blunt reminder to spend less time at their clubs at home and more time in their living rooms. Others kept hearing the words of Azinger. They thought about the idea that it's never too late to change. They thought about balance. They also began to prepare for the remainder of the Tour Championship. They faced another long round of twenty-seven holes on Saturday. The forecast called for rain.

Many in the field came to the golf course the next day with black ribbons attached to their hats and black WWJD bands around their wrists. It was a bright and sunny morning at Champions, temperatures in the seventies, a hiccup of wind from the south—conditions ripe for scoring, the kind that would've inspired Payne to think of posting a round in the midsixties. The atmosphere felt lighter, the mood more buoyant, than it had on that confusing Thursday after the bagpiper walked into the fog. The ABC television broadcast opened with images of Payne over soaring music. The announcers noted that the players looked determined. "They'll be fine out there today," Curtis Strange told Mike Tirico at the start of the coverage. "But how can you go out there and not think about Payne Stewart?"

"The business will go on of golf," Tirico said. "Life goes on. So will we."

It did. At the conclusion of a day interrupted by weather delays, Tiger Woods held the lead at minus thirteen. Chris Perry trailed him by three. Love, Sutton, and Lehman were on the front page of the leaderboard, but they were likely too far behind to challenge the young star from Stanford who had been playing the best golf of 1999. A onetime winner on the PGA Tour, the thirty-eight-year-old Perry said the death of Payne had forced him to confront the nomadic nature of his life in professional golf.

"What I mean by that is priorities," Perry said. He added, "I have three children."

Woods had no children yet. What he did have was a chance to win his seventh tournament of 1999.

"Today was a lot easier to go through than it was yesterday," said Woods, who had sat with Sutton at the service in Orlando. "My mind was a lot more at ease today than it was any time during this week, because it was nice to finally put an end to it and have some kind of resolve and move on."

The last nod to Payne Stewart came in the form of cardboard boxes arranged in the locker room before the final round at Champions. Earlier in the week, Tom Lehman had contacted the clothier that made Payne's signature plus fours. He'd requested twenty-nine pairs in cream, and they were waiting for the players on a gloomy Sunday morning, the last Sunday of the final tournament of the 1999 season. Most of the players elected to wear them. Stuart Appleby did not. He'd gone to Payne's house Thursday night to ask Tracey if he could choose a pair from her husband's closet. She thought it was a lovely gesture. Appleby and Ian Baker-Finch, a fellow Australian, found a pair in red, yellow, green, and blue plaid: Stewart tartan. They fit.

Love put on his cream plus fours and regarded himself in a mirror. Love had been ambivalent about them at first, but as he gave it more thought, it seemed like the right way to say farewell to Payne in the last round of the last tournament. He looked around. Justin Leonard was wearing them. Ernie Els was wearing them. Tom Lehman was, too. Phil Mickelson, Chris Perry. Sutton never hesitated to wear his. Love glimpsed Appleby: the angular frame, the narrow face, the blond hair, the tartan. He looked like Payne. He even, Love realized, walked like him.

Love stepped outside to putt. He saw Lehman.

"This just feels right," Love told him.

"The memorials may be done. But the tributes are not," Tirico said to open the television broadcast.

Woods wore black pants instead. ("You don't have to wear knickers in order to honor and feel resolve for someone," he would explain later. "I don't need to show it outwardly, the pain that I feel inside. And for how much I hold Payne Stewart in honor.") Black pants, black shoes, red shirt: the all-business Sunday uniform of a twenty-three-year-old who, like the man memorialized that week, had a destiny. Woods shot 69 and won the Tour Championship by four, smashing the ball farther and more crisply than a showman from Hickory Hills in Missouri thought possible, putting like Payne wished he could've at Augusta, hitting greens with precision like he had when he was at his best form at Pebble Beach and Hilton Head. Woods drove his ball an average of 290 yards for the week. His longest drive went 329. It was the fourteenth title of Woods's career. It felt monumental. It felt historic. "He's found everything," Love said. "I told the guys the first couple of years he was here, he was not even close to how good he can get. I think we are starting to see that." No one had won seven times in a season since Johnny Miller had won eight times in 1974. No one swung a golf club like Tiger Woods. Not Bobby Jones. Not Ben Hogan. Not Jack Nicklaus. Not Payne Stewart. The Tour Championship was a coronation.

"He is going to be good for a long, long time," Love said. "We are all going to have to get used to it."

"There is no individual who is more dominant in his sport," Mike Tirico told his television audience.

He added, "The legend grows."

Late in the day, the players changed from their cream plus fours and walked to their courtesy cars, grateful for the end of a tumultuous week, soon to leave for the airport, many of them, including Woods, preparing to fly to Spain for the WGC–American Express, the last official full-field tournament of the millennium. Some of the men were going home. All of them longed to be home. They imagined being on an airplane that was flying itself. They wondered about the last thought to cross Payne's mind. Was it Tracey? Aaron and Chelsea? Was it the smooth ascent or the forever visibility? Did Payne look out the window and see how high he was flying? They thought about those last sixty seconds, when gravity was pulling the Learjet straight down. It was getting darker and quieter and lonelier on that Sunday that would never be the same. The old shot-makers and young stars supplanting them passed the media tent, where Melanie Hauser and the other reporters were attempting to chronicle a week like no other. The players passed the flowers and the notes and the poems in one of thirty spots in the parking lot of Champions Golf Club, nine months after the rain fell at Pebble, four after the dales trembled at Pinehurst, one since the walls broke in Brookline, six days since N47BA took to the sky. Trunks slammed. Engines warmed. Night fell. In due time, each space was vacant save for one.

Parking lot, Champions Golf Club, Houston,
Texas, October 25–31, 1999

EPILOGUE

Practice range, Champions Golf Club, Houston, Texas,
October 31, 1999

One week after the Tour Championship, Woods beat Miguel Ángel Jiménez, the wily Ryder Cupper, on the first playoff hole at the World Golf Championship tournament in Spain, where Payne had planned to finish the 1999 season. It was Woods's eighth win of 1999 and his fourth consecutive, going all the way back to the WGC Invitational in August. Lehman and Sutton were a shot behind after three rounds. Sutton fell into nineteenth place with a 78. Lehman shot 80 for a tie for twenty-fifth.

The mementos left in the parking lot at Champions were gathered and gone by the time the players returned to the States.

The 2000 golf season will forever be remembered for the staggering dominance of Woods. He won nine times—twice at Pebble Beach, where the U.S. Open that summer had no defending champion present. On the Wednesday of that national championship in California, Paul Azinger, the de facto eulogist, conducted a brief service on the peninsula in remembrance of Payne, who predictably was a sentimental story all week long. "If golf is an art, Payne Stewart was the color," Azinger told those gathered, including Tracey, who said, "Payne refused to allow failure to rob his hope." Twenty players and Mike Hicks assembled on the famous eighteenth fairway and swatted golf balls into Carmel Cove in tribute: a twenty-one shot salute. The next day, Woods shot a first-round 65. He raced to his first U.S. Open by fifteen shots, a record margin, spectacular, stunning, dispiriting to his peers. The great Jack Nicklaus missed the cut. It was his final U.S. Open. He was fifty-nine and fading. The transition now was complete. The torch, passed. Woods averaged 298 yards in driving distance in 2000, second-longest on the PGA Tour. In 2018, a 298-yard average ranked eighty-third.

The aging shot-makers had to find new ways to compete in the nascent twenty-first century. None of them would ever win another major championship, but Sutton would claim three more titles, including the 2000 Players Championship, where he held off Woods ("Be the right club today!" Sutton begged on the last hole—and it was). Azinger won the Sony Open that winter in Hawaii. Tom Lehman won the Phoenix Open. They were finished with winning on the regular tour after that. O'Meara never won again.

By the conclusion of the 2018 season and in the entire history of tournament golf, only thirty-six players had won majors after they turned forty—a span of time that dates to the first British Open in 1860. Only four of those men had won a major since 2000, including Phil Mickelson's scintillating charge at Muirfield in the final round in 2013, when he was forty-three. Payne remains the last player in his forties to win a U.S. Open.

Mickelson tied for second on five more occasions in the national championship, the last time in 2015. We'll never know what might have happened in 2017. He skipped that U.S. Open to attend the high school graduation of his daughter Amanda, whose impending birth was one of the many story lines in 1999 at Pinehurst. Brooks Koepka, as chiseled and lean as a slot receiver in the Southeastern Conference, an athlete through and through, won that U.S. Open at Erin Hills with, among other attributes, sheer strength. He averaged 323.5 yards on the measured driving holes, which didn't include the eighteenth, where, in the final round, Koepka sent his tee shot 379.3 yards *with a three-metal*. He won the U.S. Open again in 2018. He averaged a modest 318.3 yards in driving distance at Shinnecock Hills, where Payne had first played himself into contention at a U.S. Open in 1986. Thirty-six contestants left Shinnecock in 2018 with an average driving distance in excess of three football fields.

"This is the new age of golf," Steve Stricker observed after he tied for sixteenth at Erin Hills the old-fashioned way: 275-yard drives, sound iron play, a trusty putter, guile, feel, and luck. Stricker finished fifth in the 1998 and 1999 U.S. Opens, where Payne had resurrected his career against the emergence of Mickelson and Woods. "These guys play a different game," Stricker said.

Hal Sutton got his chance to captain a Ryder Cup team in 2004. The US team lost, as it had in 2002 (the matches were postponed a year after the terrorist attacks of September 11), and as it would in 2006, when Lehman was the captain. Paul Azinger was appointed captain for 2008 matches in Louisville, Kentucky; the U.S. won. But the European team took the next three cups. Sergio García, an effervescent rookie who so enamored Ben Crenshaw in 1999, was a captain's pick for the 2018 matches in Paris, where he made his ninth Ryder Cup appearance. Europe won, and García went 3-1-0, passing Nick Faldo to become the leading point winner in the history of Team Europe. Woods also was a captain's pick for the matches in Paris. It had been five years since he had won a tournament. In September, in his last start before the Ryder Cup, he had won the Tour Championship by two at East Lake, the ancestral golf home of Bobby Jones. It was his eightieth title on the PGA Tour. Woods was 15,608 days old—the exact age of Payne when he died. Some called Woods's victory the greatest comeback in the history of the sport. Footnote: Team Europe led the United States by a margin of 10–6 after two days in Paris. There would be no miracles on that singles Sunday. Both Woods and Mickelson lost their singles matches. Now they wonder, as Payne had, when they will be elevated to captain of the team.

Woods won his fifth Masters title in 2019, his fifteenth major championship and first in eleven years. He finished a stroke ahead of Koepka, the long-driving Dustin Johnson, and twenty-five-year-old Xander Schauffele, who hails from La Jolla, California, where Woods, with a fractured leg, beat Rocco Mediate in the 2008 U.S. Open at Torrey Pines. The 2019 iteration of Woods didn't try to hit the ball as far as Johnson or Koepka did, or as far as the younger version of himself had in the early 2000s, even though the course was seven hundred yards longer than the one he had conquered in 1997. He produced measured, prudent golf for those four days in April at Augusta National, his restraint as notable as Payne's in 1999. He manipulated his shots to the right and to the left, drawing off the fairway bunker on the par-five second, fading into the slope at the seventeenth, his control and guile on Sunday rendering challengers as frail as an azalea petal. Woods had a two-shot lead when he flared his drive on the seventy-second hole—that final rising hill to climb in the old Georgia fruit orchard where he had stormed into fame all those years before. He knew a bogey would win. A bogey is what he made. Golf had a new greatest comeback now. The lore of the game grew richer still. Spectators chanted his name as Woods marched through an alley of humanity, hands outstretched, coveting only a touch. He embraced his children, just as his father had taken him in his arms on that day in 1997, when all of golf seemed to shudder and shift.

A month later, Koepka shot 63 in the first round of the PGA Championship on the Black Course at Bethpage State Park. He completed the next day with a 65, beating Woods, who missed the cut, by an astounding seventeen shots.

Koepka led by seven after three rounds. The players and the course seemed to bend to his might. Then he entered the back nine on Sunday, when he mismanaged four consecutive holes and Dustin Johnson, playing the foil and pounding away in a pairing ahead of Koepka, crept near on the enormous leaderboards on Long Island.

But not quite near enough. Keopka won his fourth major by two. Ian O'Connor, a journalist for ESPN, concluded that what he'd seen at Bethpage was simply another iteration of postmodern golf, whose form and function rose from the emergence in the late 1990s of Tiger Woods.

"This is all Tiger's fault, of course, because he inspired a generation of golfers who grew up watching him," O'Connor wrote, betraying neither awe nor spite. "Woods helped make golf a viable option for Brooks and other versatile young athletes who lived in the gym and preferred to look more like NFL strong safeties." It was as if O'Connor were drafting an account of the evolution of the automobile, of how the Volkswagen Beetle led organically to the Porsche 918. The title above his story: "Brooks Koepka is the monster Tiger created." What, you have to ask, will Koepka create?

I write these words in May 2019: The two biggest national championships in American golf will return this season to where Payne made his last stand. On the twentieth anniversary of his finest season—that round number, that platinum year—the 2019 U.S. Open will go to Pebble Beach, the U.S. Amateur to the dales of Pinehurst No. 2. The 1999 U.S. Open would be a natural and deserving storyline, I'm certain, just as Payne would be in October, when people who remember will wonder: *Has it really been twenty years?*

Robert Benzon and his team of NTSB investigators completed a 1,542-page docket on the flight of N47BA. They concluded that the probable cause of the accident was "incapacitation of the flight crew members as a result of their failure to receive supplemental oxygen following a loss of cabin pressure for undetermined reasons." Benzon felt strongly that the two pilots had tried to correct the problem on the airplane before putting on their oxygen masks—an act that might have saved the lives of the six aboard. The emergency checklist they likely consulted (no one knows, and no one ever will, if they had) would have instructed them to don the masks, but not until the pilots had executed a number of other different maneuvers, allowing the time of useful consciousness to expire, which is what led Benzon to his theory. But he could deal only with facts supported by the evidence he found in the dirt in South Dakota. The NTSB report documented the history of the flight, the experience of the two pilots, the contents of the Learjet, the maintenance records of the aircraft, and interviews with SunJet Aviation employees, air traffic controllers, and the military pilots who flew alongside N47BA on October 25. The report was published in November 2000. The NTSB analyzed the first officer's radio transmissions and concluded that she never wore an oxygen mask. The board concluded that the emergency checklist aboard pressurized aircraft such as the Learjet 35 needed to include a "clear and explicit" directive to pilots to don oxygen masks "as a first and immediate action" at the onset of the cabin altitude warning. The board found that a crucial valve regulating oxygen bottles on Learjet 35s could inaccurately be interpreted as on—or off—by pilots. The NTSB also suggested that the maintenance logbook for N47BA failed to rise to expected professional standards.

The board submitted eleven recommendations to the Federal Aviation Agency. As a result, operators and pilots of certain types of aircraft today undergo more thorough training in awareness of hypoxia. Unannounced inspections of aircraft maintenance records occur more frequently. The emergency checklist for pilots in a depressurization emergency instructs them to put on their masks before doing anything else. In other words, flying now in an airplane like the Learjet 35 is safer because of what likely happened aboard N47BA in 1999. No one died that October afternoon in vain.

The Stewart and Fraley families sued Learjet in Orange County, Florida. Their lawyers argued that the company used an inadequate valve adapter in its cabin-pressurization system and that its failure resulted in the deaths of six people. The families sought $200 million in damages, based on lost earnings. The trial lasted a month in the summer of 2005. A jury of six found Learjet bore no responsibility for the accident. "We did this to honor the people who perished on this airplane," Gregory McNeill, one of the families' lawyers, said after the verdict. "When [federal investigators] could not find a cause of the crash, we decided we could not leave this terrible tragedy unsolved." But unsolved is what this terrible tragedy remains.

The PGA Tour established a Payne Stewart Award in 2000 to honor a player with exceptional "charity, character, and sportsmanship." Its winners include Ben Crenshaw (2001), Hal Sutton (2007), Davis Love (2008), Tom Lehman (2010), and Peter Jacobsen (2013). The Missouri Sports Hall of Fame in Springfield commissioned a statue of Payne, unveiled in 2000. Pinehurst introduced its own famous bronze likeness of the Missouri showman, created by sculptor Zenos Frudakis, on a misty morning in 2001. Tracey, Aaron, and Chelsea attended the dedication, as did Mike Hicks and Dick Coop. They had dinner the night before at the Pine Crest Inn, one of Payne's favorite places in Pinehurst, an institution in the village that serves good food and better drinks, and where diners can admire Payne's flowing signature on a wall. "Tracey, she was still so shaken," Frudakis would say many years later. "I was next to her, but I didn't want to bother her. I felt like I would be trespassing on her emotions." The statue, which captures Payne at the fist-pumping and leg-kicking moment he won his second U.S. Open, has become one of the most photographed artifacts in golf at a resort that still, on most Sundays of the year, cuts the hole on No. 2's eighteenth green in the place it was on that Sunday of valor. In Payne's hometown, the Springfield-Greene County Park Board renamed one of its courses for Payne and his father. Then, in 2017, the founder of a golf resort near Branson, Missouri, announced that Tiger Woods would be the architect of record for the newest addition to Big Cedar Lodge: a golf course to be called Payne's Valley. A museum dedicated to Payne and his career is also planned. The World Golf Hall of Fame inducted Payne in 2001.

John Cornish, the general chairman of the 1999 Ryder Cup matches, received Payne's letter of gratitude shortly before his death. It was the only such letter he received from a member of either team. "I was really touched by it," said Cornish, who added that he wonders if he might be the recipient of the last letter Payne ever signed. The letter is kept in the archives in one of the yellow clapboard buildings at The Country Club in Brookline, a pitch shot from the eighteenth green, where Payne shook the hand of Colin Montgomerie in the final act of the 1999 Ryder Cup.

Everyone kept something that would remind him or her of the life and times and last stand of Payne Stewart. Chuck Cook, his long-time teacher and friend, kept the note Ben Crenshaw left on the green during the practice round at the 1999 Ryder Cup. Tracey Stewart, who never remarried, kept her husband's shirt from his singles match at the Ryder Cup, among so many other mementos of their years to-gether. It hangs in a cedar closet in her home in Orlando. Many of the players on that team kept the picture of Payne in his pepper pajamas the night they celebrated their many miracles on singles Sunday. Charlie Adams and Lamar Haynes, Payne's teammates at SMU and his closest friends, kept their own photographs. Except for stories, that's all they have. Mike Hicks, still a caddie on the PGA Tour, kept a pair of plus fours Payne wore at the 1998 U.S. Open, where the last stand had begun.

Jon Hoffman keeps the cattle away from his pasture where N47BA fell to earth. A second-generation stock and grain farmer on thou-sands of acres of grassy South Dakota prairie, Hoffman built a fence around the large engraved rock that marks the place on his property where Payne and the other five occupants, long dead, collided with the ground. The rock, unearthed by the impact of the Learjet, came from the crater Benzon and his colleagues mined for clues. The wives of those who had died had it inscribed with a verse from the Bible and the names of all who perished. Hoffman used to get a lot of visitors who were curious to see the rock, but not so many all these years later. Still, if people do inquire, Hoffman takes them out to the pasture beyond the railroad tracks, down the gravel road that once was choked with ambulances, police cars, fire engines, and news trucks. They'll stand in silence in the heavy presence of the rock, imagining again what it must have been like on that brilliant October afternoon in the Upper Midwest.

"They all remember what they were doing that day," Hoffman, an enduringly patient witness to the tragedy who still discusses that day in low tones, said by telephone in January 2019. "People lost their lives there. They are basically buried there. That is a gravesite. I felt like it was their burial site. That's why I didn't want any cattle on the top of it." That's why he erected the fence that's still there today. Hoffman wanted to harness and protect the spirits of those six.

Nowadays, when members gather for a round of golf at Hickory Hills Country Club in Springfield, they bring well-engineered titanium drivers bearing movable weights or adjustable hosels designed to influence flight or trajectory, designed to make golf easier to play. They use balls manufactured for distance *and* spin, not one or the other like it used to be when Payne learned the pullback motion. Their putters look like laboratory instruments. They might carry as many as four hybrids in their bags. They peer through laser range finders that tell them exactly how far it is to trees and bunkers that players used to have to calculate with steps or imagination or experience. On weekends, when players at Hickory Hills watch golf on television, they listen as broadcasters describe a player on the PGA Tour by reciting his spin rate, swing speed, ball speed, launch angle, strokes gained in six categories, FedEx Cup points amassed, and even how many pounds he can squat in the gym. None of those variables mattered as data points in 1999. Most of them hadn't even been invented as data points at that time. Those broadcasters employ an electronic tracer to follow the flight of a golf shot. They use a digital grid to map the flow of a green. High-definition, ultra-slow-motion cameras capture and analyze grips, takeaways, pivots, swing widths, shaft leans, wrist cocks, hand positions, belt-buckle positions, movements of the hips, movements of the feet, angles of the knees, angles of the elbows, and the split second of indisputable truth when club meets ball. Those concepts mattered, of course, in 1999. But the older players of that era didn't get, or need, to see them with a fancy camera. They needed to feel them in their fingertips and their feet. They needed to see them in their minds' eyes, as did the shot-maker from Missouri who has a flat marker in a small cemetery near a busy road in Orlando, where, on a damp spring morning in 2018, a tattered American flag flutters on a stick and Jon Brendle, Payne's friend and next-door neighbor in 1999, stares again at the gray metal marker at his feet.

In Loving Memory of William Payne Stewart: The Champion of Our Hearts reads the marker, surrounded by stiff St. Augustine grass, engraved with a silhouette of the figure in plus fours and a flat cap leaning on his club, his legs crossed, his last stand complete, forever awaiting his turn to play.

The End

Private cemetery, Orlando, Florida

REPORTING AND SOURCES

Of the many sources used for this project, none was more important than the National Transportation Safety Board's report about the events of October 25, 1999. My finding the report—completely by happenstance one Saturday night in November 2016—led to the idea of this book. Its conclusions had never been reported in a significant level of detail, so I had a place from which to start and work backward. Included in the language of the 1,542-page document was the manifest for the so-called accident flight, which mentioned a "golf bag weighing about thirty pounds." The bag was the only item of cargo mentioned in the report.

I remember the confusion of that day twenty years ago. I was a reporter for the *St. Louis Post-Dispatch,* a newspaper that occasionally covered news as far away as Springfield, in southwest Missouri, where Payne Stewart was born and spent his boyhood. All of us in the South County Bureau stood around a television and wondered how and when the ghost flight would end. It was one of those uncertain days that seemed as if anything might happen. Was anyone alive in that Learjet? Had the airplane been hijacked? Would it crash into a city? Would a fighter jet shoot it down? I found, during the course of my reporting, that people remember where they were on October 25, 1999, sometimes at a granular level of specificity: the name of the restaurant, the time of their reservation, who was at their table, even what they were wearing or what they were drinking. They remember the helplessness they felt. I did and do, too. And for some reason, as I was reading the NTSB report on that Saturday night in 2016, I kept thinking about the golf bag in the cargo hold of the Learjet. I began to see it as a vessel for a story; it was, after all, right there from the 1998 U.S. Open to the day Stewart died. That vessel carried a lot more than fourteen golf clubs.

I decided early in my reporting that I would tell a contemporaneous story in real time. I wanted you to feel like you were on the ground with Stewart, watching and hearing and even feeling events as they happened. That bound me to some self-imposed and steadfast rules. Almost exclusively, I used quotation marks only for words spoken at that particular moment, often in a conversation of some kind. Some of those conversations came from interviews, either with an individual reporter or in a press-conference setting. Everything in quotation marks is documented in the notes below, so you can know exactly where I got a verbatim extract.

That story needed a frame. Many of you might've known about, or even watched, the 1998 U.S. Open, the 1999 Pebble Beach Pro-Am, 1999 U.S. Open, the 1999 Ryder Cup, and news broadcasts on the day Stewart died. You might have been aware of the themes of return, redemption, and resurgence that many people ascribed to that season through Stewart's words and deeds. But the season was so much more. It coincided with advancements in golf equipment—perhaps a dull and tedious subject on its own, but crucial to understanding the tour in 1999 and beyond, which is to say the last stand of relevance for Stewart and his peers. The season hinted at an evolution in the way tournament golfers would play golf—perhaps the most significant change in the professional game since Ben Hogan showed his peers in the middle of the century what real practice looked like.

I conducted personal interviews in the following places: Austin, Texas, where Ben Crenshaw, Julie Crenshaw, Chuck Cook, and Scotty Sayers shared their thoughts on the season and, especially from Captain Crenshaw, the 1999 Ryder Cup; Bradenton, Florida, where Paul Azinger spent an April morning with me at Bradenton Country Club; Brookline, Massachusetts, where Frederick Waterman, the historian for The Country Club, took me on a grand tour of the grounds and golf course and arranged for me to spend the night in one of the club's guest bedrooms; Branson, Missouri, where, during the PGA Tour Champions event there, many players who factored into this story answered my questions about 1998 and '99; Chicago, Illinois, where I walked the holes of Kemper Lakes Golf Club as Stewart and Mike Reid had in 1989; Columbus, Texas, where Hal Sutton invited me to his golf and gun club one February afternoon to hear his memories; Dallas, Texas, the hometown of Lamar Haynes and Charlie

Adams, Stewart's teammates at Southern Methodist University and life-long friends, who graciously provided me with more time and material than I can properly thank them for; Houston, Texas, where Tom Lehman and Colin Montgomerie granted me long, thoughtful, and insightful inter-views; Orlando, Florida, where I met for an entire afternoon with Jon Brendle, a fount of perspective for this book and a former PGA Tour rules official who lived next door to Stewart; Pinehurst, North Carolina, where I interviewed volunteers and grounds staff from the 1999 U.S. Open; Spice-wood, Texas, where two business jet pilots, Billy Meyer and Josh White, helped me understand what happened in the airspace on October 25; and Springfield, Missouri, where Stewart's delightful sisters, Lora Thomas and Susan Daniel, spent four hours of a spring morning narrating for me a tour of their hometown from their childhood home to Hickory Hills Country Club. I did the many other interviews by telephone. Some of the mate-rial for the section about the Ryder Cup at The Country Club came from e-mails from club members who were present for the matches.

With the exception of the third and fourth chapters, which deal with Stewart's youth, this story is built entirely with primary sources: firsthand accounts of the events described in interviews and from newspaper articles, magazine stories, broadcast segments, audio recordings, and interview tran-scripts. I'm a former journalist myself and now teach journalism at the Uni-versity of Texas at Austin, but even if I weren't and didn't, I would be remiss to not recognize the role of the news media in this story. Although there is no formal bibliography here, I did extract a number of details and passages from a small collection of books. All of them are noted below in the chapter notes.

Finally, a confession: I had a long talk with myself over the usage of "British Open" instead of "Open Championship." I chose the former for its familiarity to an American audience. I ask for forgiveness among the purists who read this story about a man, a year, an era, a generation, and a thirty-pound golf bag. You—all of you—have my gratitude.

Chapter One

Transcriptions of post-round interviews, moderated by the United States Golf Association and archived by ASAP Sports (www.asapsports.com), provided the dialogue for the scenes from the 1998 U.S. Open. I also used personal interviews with Chuck Cook and Mike Hicks, whose substantial participation in this project has my enduring gratitude, as well as passages from *Payne Stewart,* a biography of Stewart cowritten by his wife, Tracey Stewart, published in 2000 by Broadman & Holman Publishers of Nashville, Tennessee. The description of the final round of the 1993 U.S. Open came from a number of newspaper accounts, notably one written by Jaime Diaz for the *New York Times.* The description of the second round came from newspaper accounts, including STEWART HALFWAY HOME, BUT PUTTS GETTING SLIPPERY, by Clifton Brown, published June 20, 1998, in the *New York Times,* and magazine accounts such as "Holding On: An Impossible Pin Made Making the Cut That Much Harder," by Gary Van Sickle, published June 29, 1998, in *Sports Illustrated* magazine and "Payne Killer: For the Second Time in Six Years, Lee Janzen Put a Hurt on Payne Stewart to Win the U.S. Open," by John Garrity, also published June 29 of that year, also in *Sports Illustrated.* The description of Colin Montgomerie in the second round at Olympic came from *The Majors* (p. 294) by John Feinstein, published in 1999 by Little, Brown and Company of Boston, New York, and London. Interviews with Paul Azinger, Lee Janzen, Tom Lehman, and Hal Sutton helped me see the big picture from that U.S. Open. So did my time—telephone calls, text messages, e-mails, and personal visits—with Lamar Haynes, who was so incredibly helpful to me that I doubt it is possible to properly thank him. But I have tried.

Chapter Two

Chuck Cook and Mike Hicks were critical to the reporting of this chapter, too. They remembered important moments with incredible texture and detail. The quote from Stewart about the sand-filled divot in the final round came from "Looking Back on the 1998 U.S. Open," by Jim McCabe, published June 10, 2012, in *Golfweek.* I reported the scenes from the third and fourth rounds of the 1998 U.S. Open from interviews with Cook, Hicks, and Tom Meeks, as well as accounts in newspapers and magazines, importantly "Not the Foggiest Notion: To Win the Open, Two Young Players Must Do Some Clear Thinking," by Jaime Diaz, published June 29, 1998, in *Sports Illustrated;* "Olympic Showed Stewart Still Had It," by Bob Harig, published May 22, 2012, on ESPN.com; "Looking Back on the 1998 U.S. Open" (McCabe, 2012); and "Payne, the 1998 U.S. Open, and the Divot," by Lee Pace, published April 30, 2014, in *Pinehurst Heritage*. Dialogue for these scenes came from the ASAP Sports transcripts from interviews with Stewart and Lee Janzen dated June 20 and 21, 1998; passages in *Payne Stewart* (pp. 229–239); and video archived at www.usga.org, the website of the United States Golf Association.

Chapter Three

Reporting for the part of this chapter about the aftermath of the 1998 U.S. Open at Olympic came from *Payne Stewart* and from personal interviews with Chuck Cook, Mike Hicks, and Justin Leonard. The observation from Johnny Miller came from a video filmed for *Golf.com*, dated April 13, 2013, at Pebble Beach. Reporting for the passages about Springfield, Missouri, was conducted during a weeklong trip to the area in April 2018, including that tour of the city with Stewart's sisters, Lora Thomas and Susan Daniel, on April 16. Details about Hickory Hills Country Club came from a personal visit to the club, an interview with Cathy Reynolds, and from *The Architects of Golf*, by Geoffrey R. Cornish and Ronald E. Whitten, published in 1993 by HarperCollins and one of the well-worn reference books on my shelf of beloved golf books. The aphorism from Sam Reynolds, the head professional at Hickory Hills, came from *I Remember Payne Stewart* (p. 13), compiled by Michael Arkush and published in 2000 by Cumberland House of Nashville, Tennessee. The anecdote about the PING Anser putter, including how it was conceived and named, came from *Karsten's Way*, a book about the PING founder Karsten Solheim written by Tracy Sumner and published in 2000 by the Solheim Foundation. The detail involving Bill Stewart's conversation with Payne's golf coach in high school came from *Golf in the Ozarks* (p. 53), by Monte McNew, published in 2006 by Arcadia. (I should also mention here that, as a Missouri native—I grew up in a south suburb of Kansas City called Grandview and spent the summers of my youth at a cabin on Mile Marker Thirteen of the Lake of the Ozarks—I was pleased to write about my home state from a position of sound authority. I've always wanted to write a few words about Missouri, and this book afforded me that chance.)

Chapter Four

Details about Stewart's years at Southern Methodist University were reported from records kept at the ever-helpful SMU department of athletics in Dallas, Texas; personal interviews with Charlie Adams, Mark Hanrahan, and Lamar Haynes, his SMU teammates; a tour of SMU with Adams and Haynes on July 20, 2018; and a telephone interview with Chip Stewart, the son of head coach Earl Stewart and, in his years at the University of Texas at Austin, one of the fine Longhorns to play under George Hannon. Answers to Stewart's "athlete questionnaires" came from photocopies of the original documents supplied by SMU, where I spent an afternoon in 2018, examining its archives. The dialogue between Stewart and his father came from *Payne Stewart* (p. 46). The quote from the 1979 Southwest Conference Championship came from STEWART WINS SWC GOLF TITLE TO GAIN COLONIAL INVITATION, by Eddie Sefko, published April 23, 1979, in the *Dallas Morning News*. The quote from Stewart after his college eligibility had ended and the quote from his college coach from the same time came from notes provided by SMU. The scene from the night before the 1979 Missouri Golf Association Amateur Championship came from personal interviews with Tom O'Toole and Jim Holtgrieve, who recalled Bill Stewart's apology for his son's behavior in the final match; other scenes from that week were reported from interviews with Mark Hanrahan and Jack Garvin, a board member with the Kansas City Golf Association and the Missouri Golf Association, and the de facto historian for both. Passages having to do with the PGA Tournament Bureau in the 1950s were reported from *The History of the PGA Tour*, published 1989 by Doubleday and written by Al Barkow. Details about the Stewart's two years on the Asian Golf Circuit came from personal interviews with Terry Anton, passages from *Payne Stewart*, and helpful e-mail exchanges with Ong Cheow Eng, the director of communications for the Asian Tour in Sentosa, Singapore. Insights about Stewart's relationship with Tracey Ferguson came from Anton, who played the Asian Golf Circuit with Stewart and witnessed many of the early encounters in Asia between Ferguson and Stewart in 1980 and '81. The dialogue from the Australian Open (p. 68), Ferguson's visit to Springfield (p. 70), and Q-School (p. 72) came from *Payne Stewart*.

Chapter Five

The quote from the drive between Monday qualifiers came from *Payne Stewart* (p. 78). The quote from the second round of the Magnolia Classic came from the MAGNOLIA TIED AT HALFWAY MARK, by Chuck Abadie, published April 10, 1982, in the *Hattiesburg American.* The quote about the tour's needing "more blond-haired, blue-eyed guys" came from *Payne Stewart* (p. 80). The quote from the final round of the Magnolia came from FAST-STARTING STEWART EARNS MAGNOLIA TITLE, by Jerry Potter, published April 12, 1982, in the *Clarion-Ledger* of Jackson, Mississippi. The quotes about the "navy-blue suit" and "attitude" came from *Payne Stewart* (pp. 81–83). The quotes from the final round of the Quad Cities Open came from BIRDS SING STEWART'S QCO MARCH, by Gordon Nelson, published July 19, 1982, in the *Dispatch* of Moline, Illinois. The quote from the Colonial came from *Payne Stewart* (p. 92). The conversation between Tracey Stewart and Paul Celano came from interviews with Celano corroborated in *I Remember Payne Stewart* (p. 70). The suggestion from Harvie Ward that Stewart treat golf "like a job" came from *I Remember Payne Stewart* (p. 71). The quote from the 1986 U.S. Open came from NOT EVEN THE KNICKERS COULD SAVE STEWART FROM SIXTH PLACE, by Bob Fowler of the *Orlando Sentinel,* published June 16, 1986. The criticism from Jack Nicklaus after the 1987 Ryder Cup was noted in "Dialogue with Payne Stewart: A Past U.S. Open Champion Reflects on His Wins, His Losses—and Himself," from an interview conducted by Guy Yocum and published in the March 1999 edition of *Golf Digest* magazine. The quote from Tracey Stewart about quitting came from *Payne Stewart* (p. 103). Details about Stewart's donation of his first-place earnings from the 1987 Bay Hill Classic came from STEWART PROVING HE'S NOT JUST A TALKER—HE'S A DOER, by George White of the *Orlando Sentinel,* published April 17, 1988. The praise from Fred Couples, Lee Trevino, and Mark Wiebe was part of a story published May 18, 1987, in *Sports Illustrated* called "One From the Heart," by fellow Hachette author Rick Reilly. The "Rolls-Royce" quote attributed to Harvie Ward came from *I Remember Payne Stewart* (p. 71). The quote from Dick Coop came from *Payne Stewart* (p. 116). The quote from Stewart about his exercise routine came from STEWART GETTING TIRED OF SEEING STORIES

AND PAYNE AND MISERY, by Greg Stoda, published March 5, 1989, in the *Dallas Times Herald*. Details about the Wilson Whale driver, which Stewart used in the 1989 MCI, came from a fascinating history of the club on the Louisville Golf website.

Chapter Six

The quote from PGA president Mickey Powell came from KEMPER LAKES GETS '89 PGA CHAMPIONSHIP, by Bob Verdi, published June 8, 1985, in the *Chicago Tribune*. The observation from Larry Mize after his practice round at the 1989 PGA Championship came from a notebook item in PREGNANT PAUSE IN CALCAVECCHIA'S PLANS, published on August 7, 1989, in the *Chicago Tribune* and written by Reid Hanley. The quote from Arnold Palmer's post-round interview after his opening 68 came from PALMER'S PLAY PUTS MAGIC IN MIND, published on August 11, 1989, in the *Tampa Tribune*. The quote from Stewart involving Jerry Pate came from *Payne Stewart* (p. 123). The scene depicting the immediate aftermath of the '89 PGA Championship came from personal interviews with Paul Azinger, Peter Jacobsen, and Mike Reid; a personal visit to Kemper Lakes Golf Club in June 2018; video footage from the championship on PGA.com; *The Payne Stewart Story*, by Larry Guest, published in 2000 by Stark Books; and the following newspaper and magazine accounts: RADAR IS JAMMED DURING APPROACH; STEWART WINS PGA, by Brian Hewitt of the *Los Angeles Times*, published August 14, 1989; STEWART CHARGES TO WIN P.G.A., by Gordon White of the *New York Times*, published August 14, 1989; REID'S CLASS AFTER LOSS EARNED RESPECT, by Richard Mudry, a columnist for the *Tampa Tribune*, published August 15, 1989; and "Putting on the Style," by E. M. Swift and published August 21, 1989, in *Sports Illustrated*. The note about Stewart's interview in December with the *Springfield News-Leader* came from PAYNE-FUL ATTITUDE FOR THE '90S: STEWART LOOKS TO MAKE MARK IN NEW DECADE, published December 17, 1989. The post-round quotes from the 1990 MCI Heritage came from STEWART WINS 3-WAY PLAYOFF, by Ron Green, published April 16, 1990, in the *Orlando Sentinel*. Passages from the 1990 PGA Championship pre-tournament press conferences came from WHO'S AFRAID OF CONTROVERSY? NOT STEWART, by Gordon White, published in the *Orlando Sun-Sentinel* on August 9, 1990, and SHOAL CREEK SPARKS PGA

TO CHANGE SITE POLICY, by Ed Shearer of the Associated Press, published in the *Anniston Star* on August 9, 1990. Other details about the controversy at Shoal Creek were reported from interviews and accounts including RACISM ISSUE SHAKES WORLD OF GOLF, by Jaime Diaz of the *New York Times,* published on July 29, 1990, and HALL THOMPSON, WHO STIRRED GOLF CONTROVERSY, DIES AT 87, by Bill Pennington, also of the *Times,* published October 28, 2010. Details about the final round of the championship came from STEWART HAS TOUGH FINAL DAY, by Tim Rosaforte of the *Palm Beach Post,* published August 13, 1990, and A WEEK THAT'S WORTH FORGETTING (AND FAST), by Scott Korzenowski of the (Fort Myers, Florida) *News-Press,* published August 13, 1990.

Chapter Seven

Scenes from the 1991 U.S. Open at Hazeltine were reported from video footage of the championship and from media accounts. The quote about the USGA's getting "what it wanted" came from SCORES SOAR AS WINDS KICK IN, by Jon Roe of the Minneapolis *Star Tribune,* published June 16, 1991. The quote about "good breaks" appeared in STEWART A SURVIVOR, by Galyn Wilkins, published June 18, 1991, in the *Fort Worth Star-Telegram.* The Dave Anderson column, BEWARE THE AILING GOLFER, was published June 18, 1991, in the *New York Times.* The Rick Reilly story in *Sports Illustrated* was published June 24 of that year. That same account included the statement from Stewart that "I'm as good as I thought I would be." The admonition from Perry Leslie, beginning with "America doesn't want to hear how good you think you are," came from *I Remember Payne Stewart* (p. 53). Stewart's statement about Jack Nicklaus as a Ryder Cup captain's pick came from PAYNE SAYS JACK'S STARE ISN'T ENOUGH FOR RYDER CUP SPOT, an Associated Press report published August 1, 1991, in the Fort Myers *News-Press.* His clarification came from PGA CHAMPIONSHIP MAY BE LOSING MARQUEE NAMES, a report by Tim Rosaforte published August 7, 1991, in the *Palm Beach Post.* The quote from Fred Couples at the PGA came from COUPLES CAUTIONS BIG HITTERS, by Dan Dunkin, published August 8, 1991, in the *Indianapolis Star.* The quote from Jack Nicklaus about John Daly came from OVER DRIVE: JOHN DALY SHOCKS WORLD WITH PGA WIN, by John Garrity, published August 19, 1991, in *Sports Illustrated.*

The quote from Kenny Knox about Daly came from LONG COURSE WORKS TO DALY'S ADVANTAGE, published August 12, 1991, in the *Palm Beach Post*. The quotes from Stewart about his post–U.S. Open slump came from WAIT A MINUTE, "MR. POUTMAN," by Jayne Custred, published June 18, 1992, in the *Houston Chronicle*. The quote from the 1993 Memorial came from AZINGER'S "MIRACLE" SHOT FROM BUNKER WINS BY ONE, by Jaime Diaz, published in the *New York Times* on June 7, 1993. The passage from Paul Azinger's press conference after the 1993 PGA Championship came from AZINGER TAKES MAJOR STEP WITH PGA TITLE, by Larry Guest, published August 16, 1993, in the *Orlando Sentinel*. The conversation aboard the business jet between Stewart and Azinger after the Skins Game is from *Zinger*, by Paul Azinger and Ken Abraham (pp. 52–63), published in 1995 by HarperCollins (New York). It was corroborated in my interview with Azinger at Bradenton Country Club. The observation that "I was staring my mortality down" also came from my interview with Azinger. The description of the Spalding commercial came from the commercial itself, available on YouTube. The quote from the 1994 Masters came from SOUR STEWART GIVES GAME A REST, by Melanie Hauser, published April 9, 1994, in the *Houston Post*. The admonition from Tracey Stewart came from *Payne Stewart* (p. 191). The quote from the 1995 Houston Open came from the same book (p. 197). The scene from the 1996 Players Championship involving the reporter from Houston came from *I Remember Payne Stewart* (pp. 166–167), and the same book provided the scene with the autograph seeker at the Masters (pp. 124–125). The detail about how Tiger Woods prepared for the 1997 Masters came from his book *The 1997 Masters: My Story*, published in 2017 by Grand Central Publishing, and cowritten with Lorne Rubenstein (p. 49).

Chapter Eight

Scenes from Stewart's visit to Austin before the 1999 Bob Hope Chrysler Classic came from one of my many personal interviews with Chuck Cook. Details about the history of the PGA Tour at Pebble Beach came from *Pebble Beach Golf Links: The Official History*, by Neal Hotelling, published in 1999 by Sleeping Bear Press. The scene on the seawall from the 1992 U.S. Open media day came from interviews with Cook and from *The Payne*

Stewart Story (pp. 125–126). The dialogue between Stewart and Mike Hicks before the 1999 Pebble Beach National Pro-Am came from *Payne Stewart* (p. 255). The note about Bobby Jones came from *The Grand Slam: Bobby Jones, America, and the Story of Golf,* published in 2004 by Hyperion (New York), in which author Mark Frost cites Jones's observation about losing. The quote from Clint Eastwood came from "What a Payne: For the Third Time in the Last Four Years, Weather Short-Circuited the Pebble Beach Pro-Am, and Only One Player, Payne Stewart, Had No Cause to Complain," by Alan Shipnuck of *Sports Illustrated,* published February 15, 1999. The weather description came from the Associated Press in a story published February 7, 1999, in the *Herald & Review* of Decatur, Illinois; the same story provided the quote from David Duval. The quote from Stewart about the rain in the final round came from one of my many personal interviews with Peter Jacobsen. The announcement from tournament director Arvin Ginn came from STEWART GETS THE DAY OFF, BUT HE STILL TAKES FIRST PLACE AT PEBBLE BEACH, by Clifton Brown, published February 8, 1991, in the *New York Times.* The exchange between Stewart and Tom Meeks on the practice range at Isleworth came from an interview with Meeks and Stewart's longtime friend Lamar Haynes, who was not there but corroborated Meeks's account through his memory of a conversation with Stewart. Transcripts from the post-round interviews provided all other quoted material from the tournament unless otherwise stipulated.

Chapter Nine

The quote from Mark O'Meara after he won the 1998 Masters came from A MAJOR PUTT FOR A MAJOR TITLE; O'MEARA SINKS A 20-FOOTER ON NO. 18 TO WIN IN AUGUSTA, by Clifton Brown, published April 13, 1998, in the *New York Times.* O'Meara's observation after his practice round at the 1999 Masters came from ROUGH IS ONE CHANGE AT AUGUSTA, by Vartan Kupelian, published April 4, 1999, in the *Detroit News.* Brandel Chamblee's description of his Zoom golf club came from CHAMBLEE LANDS IN NEW PLACE, by Joe Biddle, published April 9, 1999, in the (Nashville) *Tennessean.* The quotes from Tom Lehman and José María Olazábal after the final round came from "Basque in Glory with the Cold-Blooded Skill of a Surgeon," by Jack McCallum, published in *Sports Illustrated* on April 19, 1999. The dialogue between reporters and Stewart at the MCI Classic came from transcripts of post-round interviews archived by ASAP Sports. The quote from Glen Day, the winner, came from BRAND NEW DAY AT MCI CLASSIC, an Associated Press report published April 19, 1999, in the *Capital* of Annapolis, Maryland. The AP preview of the U.S. Open was published June 13, 1999, in the *News Journal* of Wilmington, Delaware. The passage from the *Montgomery Advertiser* was published in a summary of wire reports published June 16, 1999. The line from the Del Lemon column in the *Austin American-Statesman* was published June 12, 1999. The quotes from Rees Jones came from COURSE TO GIVE OPEN CHALLENGERS A TEST, an Associated Press report published June 12, 1999, in the *Journal Gazette* of Matoon, Illinois.

Chapter Ten

The quote from Johnny Revolta before the 1936 PGA Championship at Pinehurst came from page 149 of *The Life & Times of Donald Ross*, by Chris Buie, published in 2016 by Classics of Golf (Stratford, Connecticut). The language from the tournament program came from the same book (p. 180). The observation from Donald J. Ross came from *Golf Has Never Failed Me: The Lost Commentaries of Legendary Golf Architect Donald Ross*, published in 1996 by Sleeping Bear Press (Chelsea, Minnesota). The "slaughter of the ancients" quote came from "1962 U.S. Amateur: Harris Leads Changing of the Guard," by Ron Driscoll, published April 1, 2014, on the USGA website. The quote from Corey Pavin came from a Gannett News Service account under the headline A KINDER, GENTLER OPEN COURSE? in the June 15, 1999, edition of the *Democrat and Chronicle* in Rochester, New York. The data about golf equipment in 1999 came from the *Darrell Survey: Golf Equipment Almanac 2000*, published in 2000 by the Darrell Survey Company. The conversation between Stewart and Tom Meeks during a practice round at Pinehurst came from two sources: an interview with Meeks and a supporting account in "My Shot: Tom Meeks," by Guy Yocum, published July 7, 2007, on GolfDigest.com. The quote from Curtis Strange in *Sports Illustrated* magazine was published February 19, 1996. Much of the other reporting about that championship came from personal interviews with Chuck Cook, Mike Hicks, journalists, and USGA officials who were there, and the following players: Paul Azinger, Ben Crenshaw, Tom Lehman,

Davis Love III, and Hal Sutton. All remaining quotes from players in the 1999 U.S. Open came from interview transcripts at ASAP Sports. Observational details about the Pinehurst Resort and the No. 2 course came from a two-day visit I made to the property in October 2018. Alex Podlogar, the media relations manager at the Pinehurst Resort & Country Club, has my eternal gratitude for simply making stuff happen and getting things done.

Chapter Eleven

Unless otherwise noted here, dialogue from the first, second, and third rounds of the U.S. Open came from interview transcripts at ASAP Sports. The quote from Donald J. Ross about the first hole came from the course tour on the Pinehurst website (www.pinehurst.com). The quote from Jack Nicklaus after the first round came from NICKLAUS FEELS AGE WITH FIRST-ROUND 78, a wire service report published June 18, 1999, in the *Des Moines Register*. The thought from Mike Hicks during the second round came from a personal interview. The quote from Stewart about the pin positions in the second round came from PINNED AT PINEHURST, by Jimmy Burch of the *Fort Worth Star-Telegram*, published June 19, 1999. The encounter involving Stewart and journalist Melanie Hauser was reported from a personal interview with Hauser. The column by Bill Lyon was published June 20, 1999. Stewart's answer about whether he would've left a U.S. Open for the birth of his child came from BABY TALK, a notes feature in the *Palm Beach Post*, also published June 20, 1999. The admonition from Mike Hicks to Stewart on the eighteenth fairway of the third round came from an interview with the caddie. The quote about the difficulty of Pinehurst No. 2 from Tom Lehman came from LEHMAN'S SATURDAY IS ANYTHING BUT SPECIAL, by Jon Roe of the *Minneapolis Star Tribune*, published June 20, 1999. The quote from Lee Janzen after the third round came from NEW STAT NEEDED: GREENS STAYED-ON IN REGULATION, by Paul Kenyon of the Knight-Ridder News Service, published June 20, 1999, in the *Clarion-Ledger* of Jackson, Mississippi. The quote from David Duval came from ALONE UNDER PAR, STEWART IS ALONE ON THE LEADER BOARD, by Clifton Brown, published June 20, 1999, in the *New York Times*. The quote from Stewart about "opportunity" came from "Payne Stewart's Other Big Putt and Fist Pump," a video published on the YouTube channel of the Pinehurst Resort. All other quotes from the third round came from interview transcripts at the ASAP Sports website. Other physical details came from my visit to Pinehurst described in the notes for chapter 10.

Chapter Twelve

Reporting for this chapter came from interviews with Chuck Cook, Mike Hicks, reporters who covered the U.S. Open at Pinehurst, and a number of volunteers at the championship, as well as from my visit to Pinehurst. The quote from the *New York Times* about Bobby Jones and the Grand Slam of 1930 came from "Setting a New Standard: Bobby Jones and the 1930 Grand Slam," by Damon Hack, published August 19, 2011, on Golf.com. I found on YouTube the NBC broadcast of the final round and a *Golf Channel Classics* special about the championship. The Johnny Miller quote came from that NBC broadcast. The quotation from the Dan Jenkins story about the 1960 U.S. Open came from *Jenkins at the Majors: Sixty Years of the World's Best Golf Writing, from Hogan to Tiger* (p. 38), published in 2009 by Doubleday. The quotation from Herbert Warren Wind came from the classic *Following Through: Herbert Warren Wind on Golf,* published in 1985 by Ticknor & Fields. The quote from Arnold Palmer after the 1962 U.S. Open came from BRIGHT ROAD OPEN TO ROOKIE CHAMP, by Joe Greenday, published June 18, 1962, in the *Philadelphia Daily News.* The quote from Hicks on the twelfth hole came from *Payne at Pinehurst* (p. 254), by Bill Chastain, published in 2004 by St. Martin's Press. The quote about the gallery noise from Ron Crow, the walking scorer, came from an interview, as did the quote from Payne about needing a minute before signing his scorecard. The thought from Hal Sutton in the locker room after Stewart made the winning putt came from one of my interviews with Sutton. The quote about luck from Colin Montgomerie came from *Payne at Pinehurst* (p. 240). The quote from Bee Stewart came from "Payne Relief: A Clutch Finishing Putt and a New, Improved Personality Helped Payne Stewart Reverse Last Year's Narrow Loss at the U.S. Open and Win a Scintillating Showdown at Pinehurst," by John Garrity, published June 28, 1999, in *Sports Illustrated.* Commentary from the NBC broadcast of the final round in 1999 came from a variety of online sources, including "1999 U.S. Open Final Round 17th Hole," on the Pinehurst YouTube channel. All dialogue from the post-round press conferences came from transcripts of the interviews available at ASAP Sports. The quote about making the Ryder Cup team came from "Securing the Ryder Cup Spot," an un-bylined note from ESPN dated Monday, June 21. The quote about peace from Stewart came from "Payne Relief," by John Garrity of *Sports Illustrated*. The scene at the home of Mike Hicks was reconstructed through interviews with Hicks and from "Remembering the Final Round in 1999," by Peter McCleery, published June 18, 2014, in *Golf Digest*.

Chapter Thirteen

Much of the reporting for this chapter came from interviews with Ben Crenshaw, Julie Crenshaw, Mike Hicks, Justin Leonard, Davis Love III, Tom Lehman, Mark O'Meara, Steve Pate, Bill Rogers, and Hal Sutton. I also spoke with reporters who were at the PGA Championship and the press conference announcing the captain's picks for the Ryder Cup. The Frank Luksa column in the *Dallas Morning News*, mentioned early in the chapter, was published June 21, 1999, under the headline THIS TIME AROUND, STEWART CLOSES DOOR AT U.S. OPEN. The story by Jaime Diaz in *Sports Illustrated*, "Peace Be with Him: Payne Stewart Schooled His Juniors with His Mastery of the Inner Game," was published June 28, 1999. The column by Christine Brennan, "Making Par Perfect Strategy for Stewart," was published June 21, 1999. The story in *Sports Illustrated* by John Garrity, "Payne Relief: A Clutch Finishing Par and a New, Improved Personality Helped Payne Stewart Reverse Last Year's Narrow Loss at the U.S. Open and Win a Scintillating Showdown at Pinehurst," was published June 28, 1999. The quote from Dick Coop about pressure came from "Peace Be with Him," by Diaz. The quotes from John Philp, the greenkeeper at the Carnoustie Golf Links, came from MAN WHO MADE BEAUTIFUL MONSTER, by David Davies, published July 14, 1999, in the *Guardian*. The quote from Stewart about maturing came from STEWART: TOUGHER, THE BETTER, by Christine Brennan of *USA Today*, published via syndication July 14, 1999, in the *Cincinnati Enquirer*, where I found it. The observations from Stewart and Mark O'Meara after the first round of the British Open at Carnoustie came from "Carnoustie Beats Up Stewart, O'Meara," by Brian Creighton of Reuters, published July 15, 1999, on ESPN.com. The quote from Stewart about the length of the rough came from "Stewart Wants Knee-High

Weeds Out for 2000 Event," a notebook item in the July 18, 1999, edition of *Florida Today*. The statement by Jean Van de Velde after the third round came from "Go Down Swinging," a Golf Channel documentary about the 1999 British Open that premiered July 9, 2018. Other pieces of the ABC broadcast came from "Golf Channel's 'Go Down Swinging' Recounts the Infamous 1999 Open," by Martin Kaufmann, published July 8, 2018, on the *Golfweek* digital edition.

Chapter Fourteen

The long quote from David Duval about compensation for the Ryder Cup came from "Resolved: Ryder Cuppers to Play for Pride, Not Pay," by Gary Reinmuth, published August 11, 1999, in the *Chicago Tribune*, as did the quote from Mark O'Meara about the meeting to address the controversy over Ryder Cup pay. The quote from Duval about "not being used" came from TO PAY OR NOT TO PAY . . . by Bob Harig, published August 5, 1999, in the *St. Petersburg* (Florida) *Times*. The quote from Tiger Woods about the issue also came from Harig's column. The quote from Sergio García after the final round of the PGA came from "A New Twist," by Alan Shipnuck, published August 23, 1999, in *Sports Illustrated*. So did the quotes from Mark O'Meara and Tiger Woods. The observations from Crenshaw about García in the final round of the PGA Championship and about the marvels of the modern game came from PGA DRAMA POINTS TO MANY SHOWDOWNS, by Michael Wilbon of the *Washington Post*, published August 17, 1999, in (where I found it) the *Austin American-Statesman*. (The quote from Crenshaw about "routine drives of three hundred yards" also came from the Wilbon column.) The quote from Julie Crenshaw about the captain's picks came from CRENSHAW: RIGHT GRIP ON THIS CLUB, by Bob Ryan, published August 17, 1999, in the *Boston Globe*, as did the quote from Ben Crenshaw about his job as captain. His quotes about Pate and Lehman came from CRASH COURSE IN GRIT, by Bob Duffy, published August 17, 1999, in the *Globe*. The quote from Lehman came from LEHMAN, PATE ARE THE PICKS, by Jim McCabe, published August 17, 1999, in the *Globe*. The observation from Fred Couples about his not being picked for the Ryder Cup team came from a press conference transcript from the WGC NEC Invitational on August 28, 1999, archived at ASAP Sports. The quote from

Crenshaw about his experience at the 1968 U.S. Junior Amateur came from *A Feel for the Game: From Brookline and Back,* by Crenshaw with Melanie Hauser (p. 39), published in 2001 by Doubleday (New York). An interview with Brookline historian Frederick Waterman, published in August 2013 on the Golf Club Atlas website (https://golfclubatlas.com/feature -interview/feature-interview-with-frederick-waterman/), provided much of the historical detail about The Country Club, as did my personal visit to the club in November 2018. The quote from Crenshaw about "feelings" came from A COURSE "DRIPPING WITH HISTORY," an un-bylined report from the Associated Press published August 31, 1999, in the *Springfield* (Missouri) *News-Leader.* The quote from Tiger Woods after the NEC Invitational came from WOODS' STELLAR YEAR ISN'T FINISHED YET, another un-bylined Associated Press report published August 31, 1999, in the *News-Leader.* The quote from Crenshaw came from CRENSHAW IS PLOTTING THE COURSE, by Joe Concannon, published August 31, 1999, in the *Boston Globe.* The question Payne asked Justin Leonard about "getting ready" as the Ryder Cup approached came from my interview with Leonard. The quote from Hal Sutton after the practice round at The Country Club came from A COURSE "DRIPPING WITH HISTORY." The observation from Payne about his role as emotional leader, as well as the quotes from Leonard and Pate about the course, came from CHEMISTRY TEST FOR OLD SCHOOLER, by Bob Ryan, published August 31, 1999, in the *Boston Globe.* Accounts from the 1913 U.S. Open mentioned in this chapter came from *The Greatest Golf Tournament of Them All: The 1913 United States Open Championship Held at the Country Club,* a collection of newspaper stories from that year, published in 1988 by The Country Club. The reflection about the club from Francis Ouimet also came from that publication. The "on paper" quote from Payne came from an un-bylined note published August 5, 1999, in the *St. Petersburg Times.*

Chapter Fifteen

Reporting for this chapter derived from my visit to The Country Club, in November 2018, and interviews with Ben Crenshaw, Julie Crenshaw, Mike Hicks, Justin Leonard, Davis Love III, Tom Lehman, Mark O'Meara, Steve Pate, Bill Rogers, and Hal Sutton, as well as Colin Montgomerie.

Unless noted otherwise, all quoted material in the chapter came from those interviews and from broadcasts of the press conferences at The Country Club archived at the H. J. Lutcher Stark Center for Physical Culture and Sports at the University of Texas at Austin in Austin, Texas. The quote from Seve Ballesteros came from *Famous 5*, a documentary broadcast September 24, 2018, on the Golf Channel. The quote from Hale Irwin about "swagger" came from *Us Against Them: An Oral History of the Ryder Cup* by Robin McMillan (p. 133), published in 2004 by HarperCollins (New York). The observation from Ben Wright came from "Why Ryder Cup Wasn't the Same After War by the Shore 25 Years Ago," by Doug Williams, published September 20, 2016, on ESPN.com. Quoted passages from Stewart, Ben Crenshaw, Mark James, Davis Love III, and Mark O'Meara on Wednesday came from press conferences broadcast on the Golf Channel. I saw the note to Payne from Ben Crenshaw. Chuck Cook showed it to me one afternoon in 2017 over ribs and brisket at the County Line on Lake Austin, where he and I met many times for interviews for this book. The admonition from Payne to Love in the foursome match came from an interview with Love. The conversation between Crenshaw, Sutton, and Maggert came from various media accounts and from one of my personal interviews with Sutton, and it was confirmed by Crenshaw. The quote from Sutton after the Saturday sessions came from EUROPEANS THWART U.S. RALLIES, CARRY 10–6 LEAD TO SINGLES, by Doug Ferguson of the Associated Press, published September 26, 1999, in the *Pittsburgh Post-Gazette*. The partial quote about "boisterous bleachers" came from HECKLERS TAKE AIM AT MONTY, an un-bylined Associated Press article in the same edition of the *Post-Gazette*. The quotes from Paul Lawrie and Sutton about the crowds Saturday came from OLD ROOKIE DELIVERS FOR EUROPE, by Ed Sherman, published September 26, 1999, in the *Chicago Tribune*. The quote from Colin Montgomerie also came from OLD ROOKIE DELIVERS FOR EUROPE. The short scene in the locker room after play ended Saturday came from an interview with Rogers and from *Us Against Them* (pp. 204–205).

Chapter Sixteen

Reporting for this chapter also came from my visit to The Country Club and from interviews with Ben Crenshaw, Julie Crenshaw, Mike Hicks,

Justin Leonard, Davis Love III, Tom Lehman, Mark O'Meara, Colin Montgomerie, Steve Pate, Bill Rogers, and Hal Sutton. I leaned a lot in this chapter on "Inside Golf's Greatest Comeback: Behind the Scenes of the Final 24 Hours at the Battle of Brookline," by Tim Rosaforte and John Hawkins, published September 11, 2010, on GolfDigest.com, for quoted material in the team hotel the night before the singles matches; unless noted otherwise, quotes from that setting came from that exceptional oral history. (Thoughts and impressions from that night, however, came from the thoughtful and patient interviews Crenshaw, Rogers, and the players granted to me, including the quoted thought from Sutton, who is one of the best interviewees in golf, in my experience.) Unless otherwise noted, all quoted material from the singles matches and post-round interviews came from NBC and Golf Channel broadcasts. The exchange between Stewart and Montgomerie after their singles match was recalled during my interview with Montgomerie. The thought from Bill Rogers after Payne conceded his match came from my interview with Rogers. The conversation between Payne and Sutton at the Four Seasons Hotel came from "Inside Golf's Greatest Comeback" and from my interviews with Sutton.

Chapter Seventeen

The October 4 letter from Payne to John Cornish was shared with me by the recipient, as was the story in the epilogue about when it arrived. The quote from Michael Bonallack, the secretary of the Royal and Ancient Golf Club, came from "Abused Europeans Might Skip Future Ryder Cups," an Associated Press report published October 14 on ESPN.com, as did the "John Wayne" quote from Martin Johnson of the *Daily Telegraph*. The quote about "lions" came from "Bad Manners at the 1999 Ryder Cup," by John Hopkins, who covered the matches for the *Times* of London and wrote about the experience years later for *Links* magazine. The column by Thomas Boswell in the *Washington Post*, THE RYDER CUP, A TARNISHED FINISH, was published September 28. The "polite silence" observation from the Dunhill Cup, and the quote from Tom Lehman, came from an Associated Press report published October 8. The exchange between Stewart and Peter Kessler came from "King of the Q&A," by Peter McCleery, published June 11, 2008, at GolfDigest.com. The quote from Stewart at the First

Orlando Foundation dinner came from *Payne Stewart* (p. 285); additional details from that event came from newspaper accounts published October 18 in the *Orlando Sentinel*. The reconstruction of his speech to the Golf Clubmakers Association meeting in Austin came from a video recording of the event provided by Jim Hopkins, an Austin golf professional who was present that night. The quote about playing the Disney came from THERE'S NO PLACE LIKE HOME, published October 21, by Hunki Yun of the *Orlando Sentinel*. The "blunder" accusation in the *Sentinel* came from its October 22 edition in a notes section called "Classic Report." Other details about Stewart's interview with Mark McCumber at the Disney tournament came from "Stewart Keeps Quiet About Chinese Imitation," an Associated Press report published October 22 and found on ESPN.com.

Chapter Eighteen

Much of the reporting for this chapter came from publicly available government documents, including the Aircraft Accident Brief adopted on November 28, 2000, by the National Transportation Safety Board and the Group Chairman's Factual Report issued by the NTSB on January 11, 2000. I should mention here the significant contributions of Robert Benzon and Dave Hirschman. Benzon, the NTSB investigator in charge of the team that investigated the last flight of N47BA, spent a great deal of time with me as I reported and wrote this and the subsequent chapter. He also reviewed certain language involving his work and his team's report. Hirschman, a former colleague of mine at the *Commercial Appeal* in Memphis, Tennessee, now is the pilot editor at large for the Aircraft Owners and Pilots Association. He is an accomplished pilot and extraordinary editor who read all passages of this book involving N47BA. His suggestions improved them tremendously. Vikki Hale, a volunteer with the Houston Golf Association who served at the 1999 Tour Championship, was kind enough to mail a tournament program; without it, I never would have seen the cover or the darkly prophetic words on the back. All dialogue in this chapter between air traffic controllers, the pilots of N47BA, and military pilots came from the factual report and from a broadcast report from NBC News that provided a cockpit recording of United States Air Force captain Chris Hamilton and the air traffic controller in Jacksonville,

Florida. That report is available on YouTube at www.youtube.com/ watch?v=tA-nvkN7Ual. Of the many media accounts used for this chapter, I found most helpful Leigh Montville's riveting story for *Sports Illustrated*, "The Ghost Plane: For Three Endless Hours Last October, the Entire Nation Watched, Horrified but Helpless, as a Runaway Jet Carried Payne Stewart and Five Others to Its Terrible Destination," published April 10, 2000. The description of the pilot in the parking lot at Dallas Love Field came from an interview with Charlie Adams. Conversations from October 25 involving Leader Enterprises and the Stewart home came from *Payne Stewart* (pp. 296–304). All other conversations from that day represented in this chapter came from interviews with the subjects involved.

Chapter Nineteen

The scenes depicting the early reaction at the Tour Championship in Houston came from personal interviews; tournament transcripts; the National Transportation Safety Board reports of the flight; and magazine, newspaper, and television accounts of October 25. The quote from Lee Patterson came from an interview. The language from Melanie Hauser's column, written the night of Payne's death, came from a version of the piece that Hauser e-mailed to me. The John Feinstein column mentioned in this chapter, STEWART: ONE BIG NAME ABLE TO ADMIT HIS FAULTS, was published October 29. Reaction from international players came from HE WAS A GREAT FRIEND OF GOLF AND OF EVERYONE, by David Davies, published October 27 in the *Guardian*. The quote from the unidentified government official at the crash site in Aberdeen came from INVESTIGATORS SIFT THROUGH CRASH DEBRIS, an un-bylined Associated Press published October 29 in the *Dallas Morning News*. The scene from the first tee at Champions before the first round of the tour championship was reconstructed from a video recording of the ceremony broadcast on the Golf Channel, interviews with players and tournament officials who were there, and various newspaper accounts, including SOMBER START IN HOUSTON and TEARFUL TRIBUTE TO STEWART, by Jerry Potter, published October 29 in *USA Today;* the reporting of Melanie Hauser; and the work of Brad Townsend, a reporter for the *Dallas Morning News*. The statements from Nick Price, Hal Sutton, and Jeff Sluman after the first day of the tournament came from the personal notes of former *Sports Illustrated* golf writer Gary Van Sickle, who graciously shared them with me. (My thanks, Gary.) Verbatim language from accounts written by Melanie Hauser came from versions of those accounts supplied by Hauser. The transcripts of player interviews at Champions Golf Club are available through ASAP Sports, and include interviews with Bob Estes, Tim Finchem, Davis Love III, Hal Sutton, and Tiger Woods. Material for this chapter also came from personal interviews with Love, Sutton, Paul Azinger, Tim Finchem, Peter Jacobsen, Lee Janzen, Tom Lehman, Justin Leonard, and Mark O'Meara.

Chapter Twenty

The thought from Ana Leaird came from an interview. The scene from the memorial service came from www.youtube.com/watch?v=NiU_qb1gNvY and from WITH SMILES AND TEARS, STEWART'S FAMILY AND FRIENDS SAY GOODBYE, by Clifton Brown, published October 30 in the *New York Times;* FAMILY, FRIENDS CELEBRATE STEWART'S LIFE, published October 30 in the *Dallas Morning News;* and from *Payne Stewart* (pp. 307–309). Much of the ABC broadcast of the Tour Championship, which allowed me to describe the three days of play, is available on YouTube. My interviews with Paul Azinger, Jon Brendle, Chuck Cook, James Cramer, Ben and Julie Crenshaw, Susan Daniel, Bob Farren of the Pinehurst Resort, Melanie Hauser, Vicki Hale, Lamar Haynes, Mike Hicks, Henry Hughes, Lee Janzen, Ana Leaird, Justin Leonard, Tom Lehman, Davis Love III, Tom Meeks, Mark O'Meara, Tom O'Toole, Steve Pate, Lee Patterson, Hal Sutton, and Lora Thomas also were instrumental in reconstructing the mood and texture of Champions Golf Club and the service for Stewart in Orlando. Finally, a nod to fate: I am quite familiar with the grounds at Champions. I covered the 2003 Tour Championship there as a sports reporter for the *Austin American-Statesman,* and I've had the privilege of playing the Cypress Course with my friend Nick Cristea, a member there. I possess an uncanny and, to be honest with myself, somewhat useless capacity to remember golf courses. But that knack came in quite handy as I wrote the last words of this book. I was, in a sense, there. My final hope is that you, too, felt like you were there—from the first round of the 1998 U.S. Open to the walk through the parking lot of Champions on that Sunday in 1999, when the last stand of William Payne Stewart was beginning to register as one of meaning, significance, and worthy of this effort. Fore, Payne. Dead aim. Play away.

Epilogue

The words of Paul Azinger and Tracey Stewart at the 2000 U.S. Open at Pebble Beach came from "Players Fire Off Tribute to Stewart," a Reuters account published June 15 on ESPN.com. The quote from Steve Stricker after the 2017 U.S. Open came from "U.S. Open 2017: Brooks Koepka Muscles His Way into History," by Dave Kindred, published June 18, 2017, on the *Golf World* website. The language from the Payne Stewart Award criteria came from the PGA Tour web page for the award. The observation from Zenos Frudakis, the sculptor who created the statue at Pinehurst, was in a story published in the January 2019 edition of *Pine Straw* magazine. The observation from Jon Hoffman, one whose property N47BA crashed, came from a personal interview.

ACKNOWLEDGMENTS

I'm grateful for everyone who assured me a long time ago that this was a book worth doing. This special group of friends, old and new, includes Tim Anderson, Bryan Burrough, Jim Hornfischer, Lamar Haynes, Peter Jacobsen, Bill Minutaglio, Kate Winkler Dawson, and Jon Brendle, who cleared his afternoon on a Saturday in May of 2018, opened the passenger door of his charming old Range Rover, and shepherded me around Orlando to show me where Stewart lived and worked and played. Our tour started at a country club. It ended at the cemetery.

Brant Rumble, my editor at Hachette, was a delightful and thorough collaborator who knew just what to say and exactly how to say it. I also thank David Lamb at Hachette and Mauro DiPreta, who read the earliest versions of this book. The drafts I sent them were so much better for the careful and merciless readings from a number of people I trust, notably Scott Hill, a coconspirator of mine at the *Commercial Appeal* in Memphis, a soul hopelessly enamored with golf like I am, and one of the best word editors and most decent men I've known. Zephyr Melton, a former student of mine at the University of Texas at Austin, assisted greatly with research.

I'm grateful for the quiet belief from a lot of meaningful people who have pushed me by example or intent: Dale Alison, Megan and Ron Balsdon, Ralph Barrera, Pat Beach, John Bridges, Mike Butterworth, all the Cocherls of Kansas City, Robert and Kim Cohen, Eileen Flynn DeLa O, Mike Enos, Amanda and Chris Fuqua, Judy Goldberg, Jeff Haney, Lynn McDowell Harmon, Ann Riley Hill, Jay Janner, Jeremy and Kristen Lander, Chris and Cindy Lanter, Kathleen McElroy, Laura and Rob Mellett, Mike O'Connor, Ron Parker, Tony Plohetski, the Robbinses of Lee's Summit (Art, Valie, Courtney, and Kelsey), John and Machele Forinash

Ruddy, Blake and Liz Rooney, Steve Sands, Brian and Joy Standefer, Paul Stekler, David Waters, Ann Weiler, the one and only Jeff Wiltfang, and Jackson, Erin, and Kathy McDowell Robbins, a sister outlaw of staggering importance to her family down here in Austin.

Thank you, for reasons you and only you know, to Ken Fuson. (A deal is a deal, Ken.) Thank you to Lucero, the sound of Memphis, for reasons I and only I know. Thank you, for all the reasons, to Jeff Wright, one of my oldest and truest friends. He once literally gave me the shirt off his back, except it actually was in his closet, and not on his back, and he didn't really give it to me; I rather took it one night while he was gone. (I see that green plaid shirt every morning. I'm wearing it in a picture on my dresser. It's from one of my first head-over-heels dates with the woman who became my wife.)

Her name is Suzy. She deserves her own line here for being the inspiration behind every good thing I've known since the night we met.

That includes our children, Lila and Henry, our brightest lights. I wrote every line of this for them.

I also wish to thank my father, Gary Robbins; my brother, Jeff, and his wife, Sandra; my in-laws, Don and Donna Sharbutt; my *other* in-laws, Monica and Steve (and their great boys) Parsons. And, finally, I want to mention my mother, Mary Frances Robbins; she was a dreamer who raised her two sons to believe they could do crazy-big things like write a book. I roughed out the first paragraph of this story on a late-night flight between the flickering cloud banks of a raging Missouri thunderstorm to what would be the last morning I saw her alive. Mom died May 20, 2018, with her husband and her boys at her bedside. I feel so much peace knowing she knew that I was under way.

INDEX